MW01629773

THE BASICS OF DRAWING

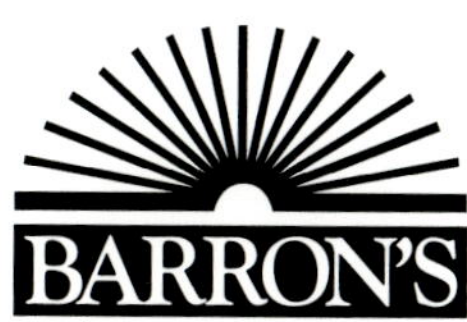

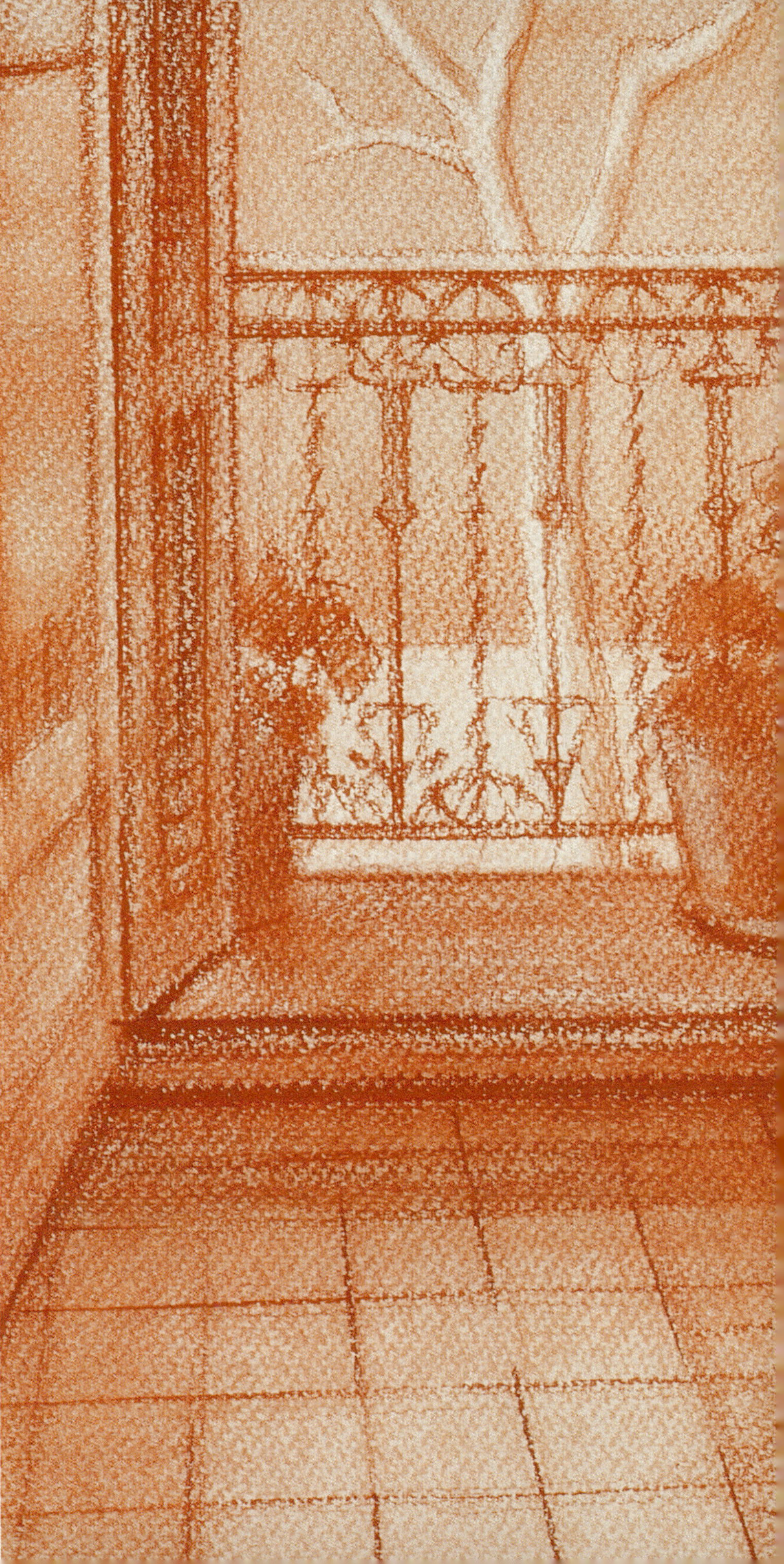

Texts: Gabriel Martín Roig
Exercises: Marta Bru, Carlant, Almudena Carreño, Mercedes
          Gaspar, Gabriel Martín, Esther Olivé de Puig,
          Esther Rodríguez, Óscar Sanchís
Photography: Nos & Soto

Original title of the book in Spanish: *Las Bases del Dibujo*
© Parramón Ediciones, S.A.—World Rights
Published by Parramón Ediciónes, S.A.
Barcelona, Spain

**Translated from the Spanish by Michael Brunelle
and Beatriz Cortabarria**

All inquiries should be addressed to:
Barron's Educational Series, Inc.
250 Wireless Blvd.
Hauppauge, NY 11788
www.barronseduc.com

ISBN-13: 978-0-7641-5862-9
ISBN-10: 0-7641-5862-7

Library of Congress Catalog Card No.: 2004114879

Printed in Spain
9 8 7 6 5 4 3 2 1

CONTENTS

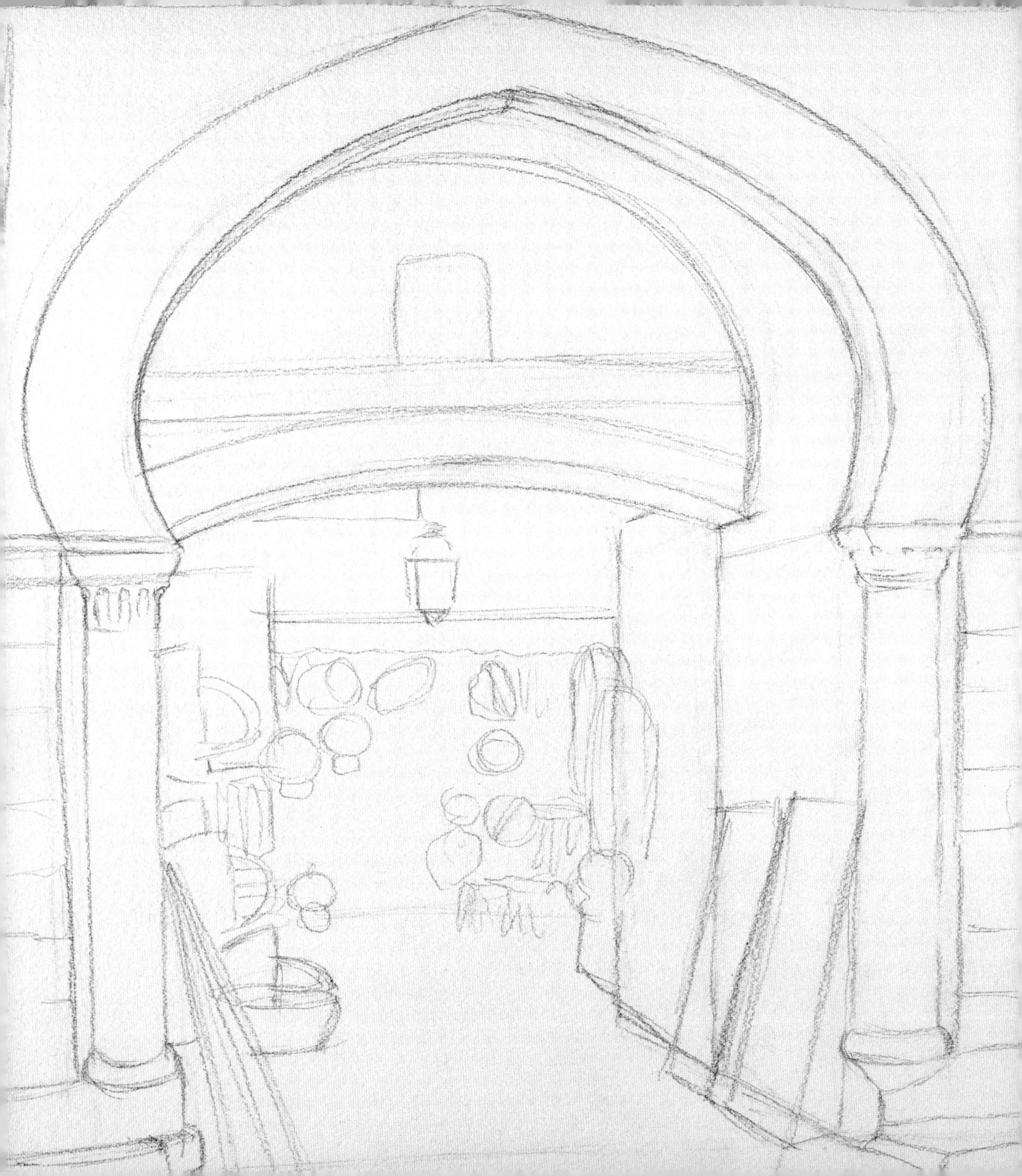

Every person draws for different reasons. Some seek the free and uninhibited expression of their feelings in the act of drawing; others think of it as a tool for detailed study; many consider it a way of ridding themselves of tension, or a sort of therapy. Whatever the reason for drawing, it is always gratifying and fun.

In reality, drawing is much more than that: It is a challenge, a way of seeing the world, an exploration, an analytical view, a way of self-control, a reaffirmation of one's personality, a suffering, a pleasure… Drawing, regardless of technique or personal ability, requires seeing and understanding, choosing and interpreting, in addition to using the imagination. Above all, a person needs to have enthusiasm and the willingness to look at things with a critical eye, to use different media and methods, and to try it all over again when things do not turn out as expected.

Drawing evolves like everything else in life, and teaching methods are modified to relate to a new audience and to encompass the social structure of the time. This book was born as a response to those new needs and to be more in tune with the present. Putting to one side the study of materials, it concentrates on teaching a way of seeing and on showing how to translate what you see into lines on paper. In this sense, it provides innovative methods for teaching how to draw that encourage practice and learning by doing from the beginning, without dwelling on techniques and theoretical principles that are difficult for a beginner to understand. The exercises are accompanied by a series of sections that, in addition to helping you understand, will contribute to the development of technique and of certain effects for each exercise. They act as support for the exercises, with the purpose of helping you understand some of the principles of drawing and solve the problems that may arise during each exercise.

To get started, we encourage you to experiment with different media and to practice the exercises that we propose. As you discover your own style and ideas about drawing, you will want to draw in a more subjective and personal way.

Do not limit yourself to learning only a little bit about isolated techniques. Experiment with your materials and try them yourself, because the possibilities of each medium cannot be fully explained in writing.

GETTING TO KNOW THE MATERIALS. The first step in the development of your drawing abilities is to familiarize yourself and to become confident with the great variety of drawing media. You will discover that each medium has its own particular characteristics. Getting acquainted with them will help you become proficient and create certain effects.

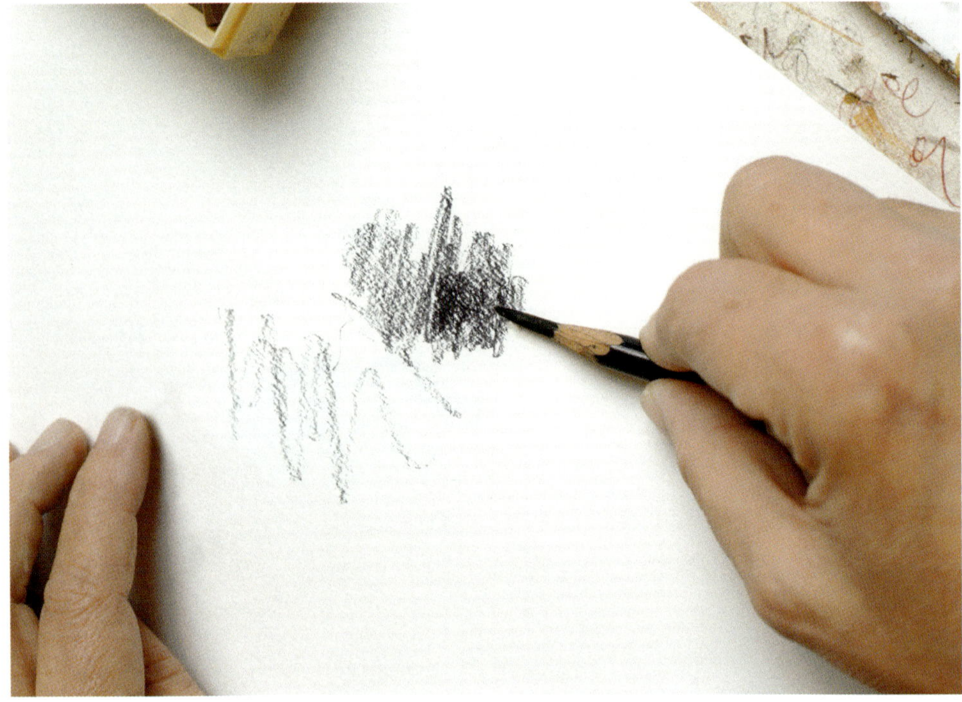

THE GRAPHITE PENCIL.

The graphite pencil is the most common and widely used drawing medium. It is available in many grades of hardness, ranging from very soft or extra soft to very hard or extra hard. Both are equally effective for simple line work and for showing detail, tone, and texture. Pencils respond instantly to the pressure applied to them.

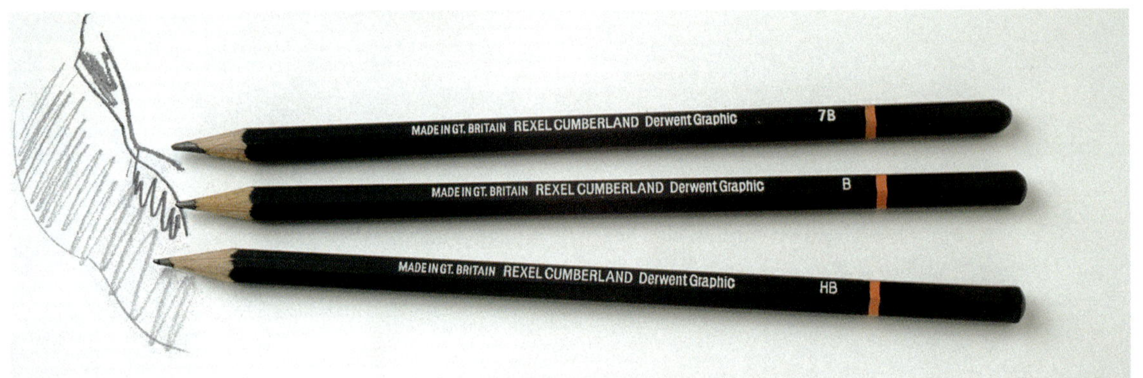

HARD AND SOFT PENCILS.

The line created with a hard pencil is light gray, and does not become darker no matter how many layers are applied to the paper. The tip does not glide smoothly when shading. A soft pencil's lead is thicker than that of a hard one. The line created with a soft pencil is oily and soft; and unlike a hard one, a soft pencil glides easily on the paper when shading.

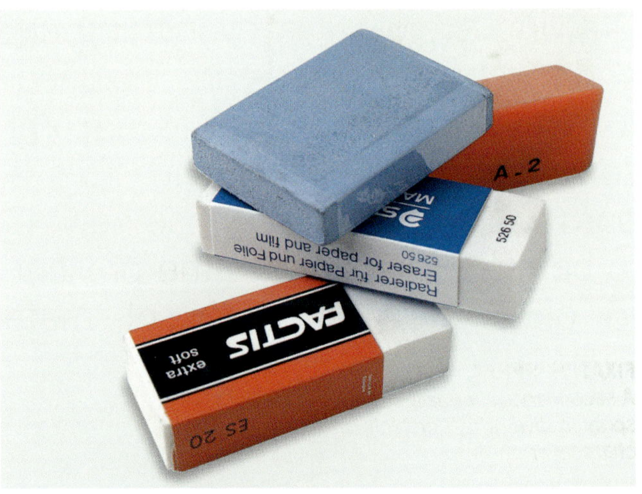

ERASERS.

The eraser is a very important drawing tool because it is not only used to eliminate lines, but is also used for drawing. It is often used during the first phase of the drawing for blocking in and for drawing the basic lines, but is also used during the last phase to create highlights.

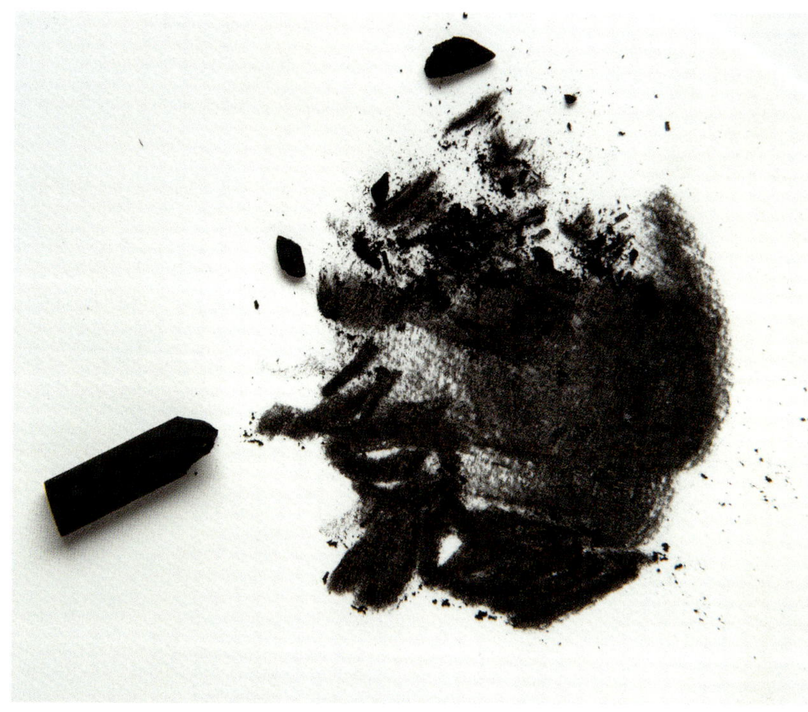

VINE CHARCOAL.

The charcoal stick is a carbonized vine. It can be either thick or thin. When rubbed against paper it leaves a matte gray mark that is not very dark. It is used on large-format drawings. It is very useful for shading effects, gradations, and diffusions. When you need more detailed or defined lines, it is possible to combine charcoal sticks with compressed charcoal pencils.

CHALK.

Chalk shares some of its properties with charcoal in that it is easy to handle and has a similar granulated texture. However, the quality of its line is somewhat greasier and therefore more stable. Brown and sienna chalks impart solidity to forms, black is deep and rich in nuances, and white is ideal for creating highlights. There is also a reddish variety of chalk, called sanguine, which provides great warmth to the drawing.

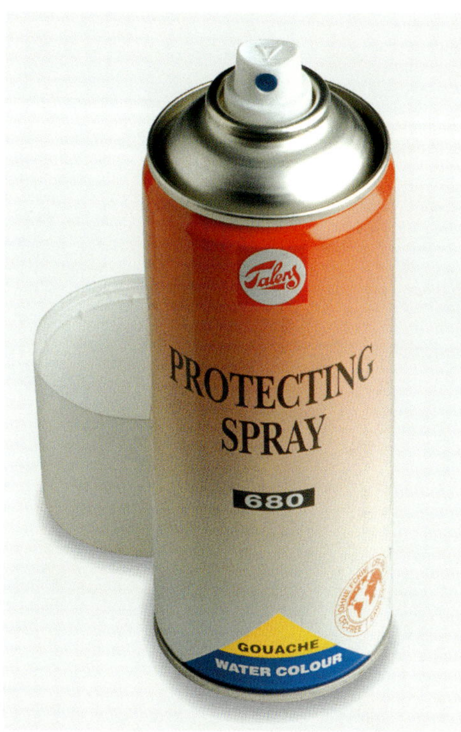

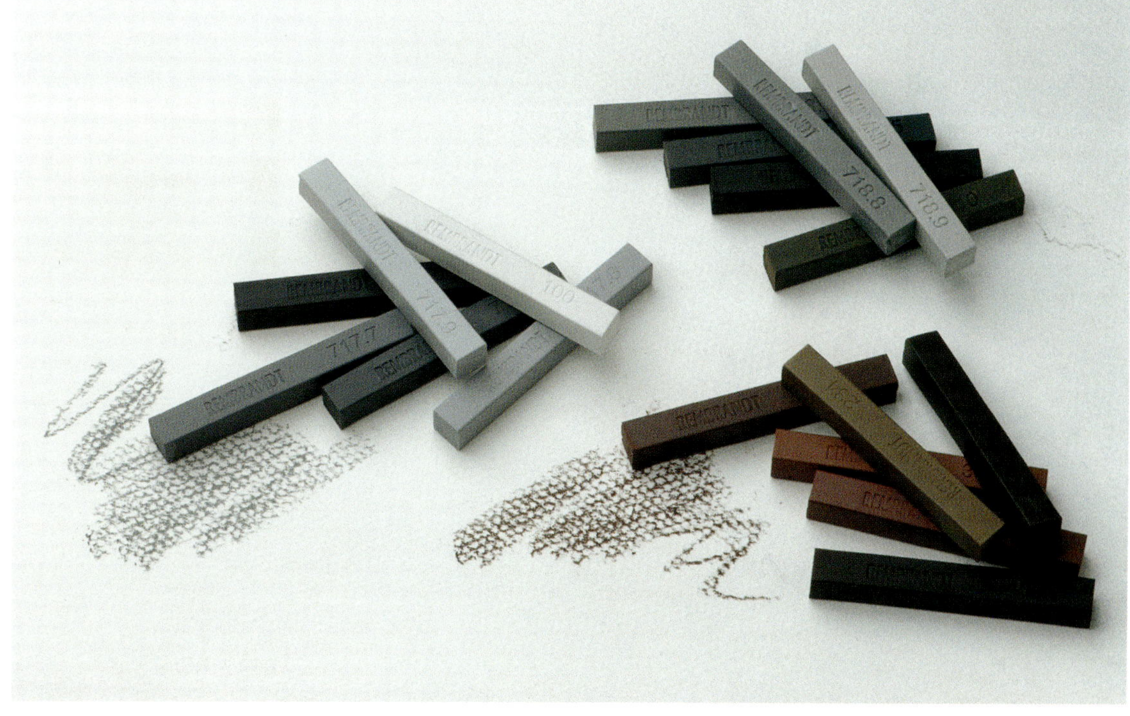

FIXATIVE SPRAY.

A secondary, yet equally necessary material is spray fixative, which protects drawings done with charcoal or chalk.

CHOOSING THE SUPPORT. This factor is as important as the drawing medium itself. The final result of the work, including the intensity of the line as well as the quality of the finish, will vary considerably depending on whether the paper is smooth or textured, heavy or light.

A PAPER FOR EACH DRAWING MEDIUM.

Each medium requires a specific paper. For graphite pencils, we recommend using fine-textured or smooth papers, which allow rich gradations and easy blending. Fine and smooth papers are also good for drawing with oily pencils, crayons, or colored pencils. If you want to draw with charcoal or chalk, it is best to use a medium-grain paper because it retains the pigment particles better and offers greater abrasion. Heavy-grain papers are best reserved for large-format work done with chalk or charcoal. They give the drawing a very granulated texture as well as an energetic and expressive shading. Do not be afraid to draw on watercolor papers, which have very distinctive textures. They add a charming effect to the drawing and are very durable.

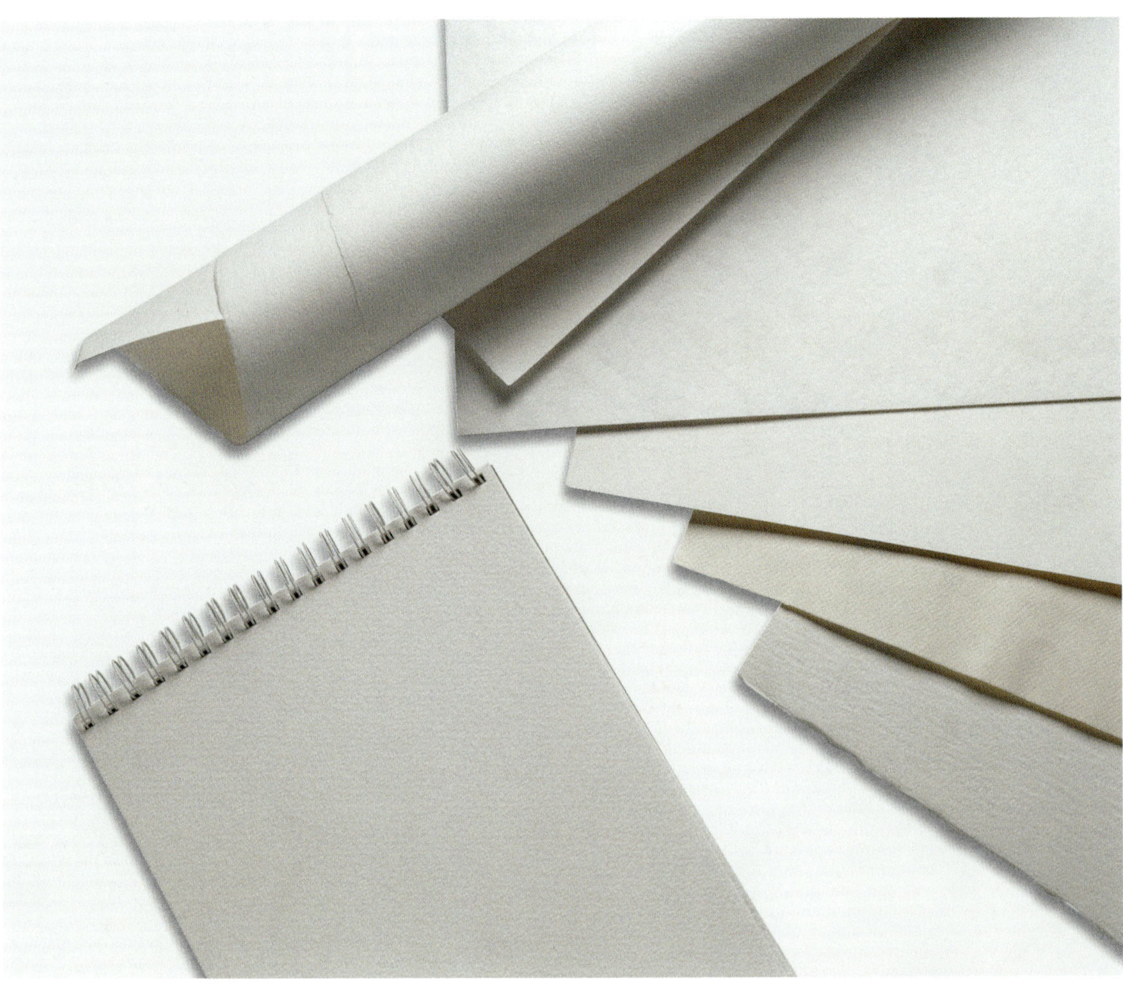

FRONT AND BACK.

Drawing paper has a front and a back. Either side can be used for drawing, although for most drawings the front side, which is less smooth, is used. To confirm this, simply hold the paper near a light. Fold one corner over and notice the difference in texture between sides.

A RIGID SUPPORT.

When drawing, the paper cannot be placed against just any surface. It must be attached to a hard and smooth surface that has no texture which can affect the purity of the lines and colored areas. If you work on a surface that has lines, cracks, texture, or holes, they will leave unwanted marks on the drawing. MDF or plywood boards are best because they have flat, smooth surfaces. Ideally, the board should be larger than the paper attached to it.

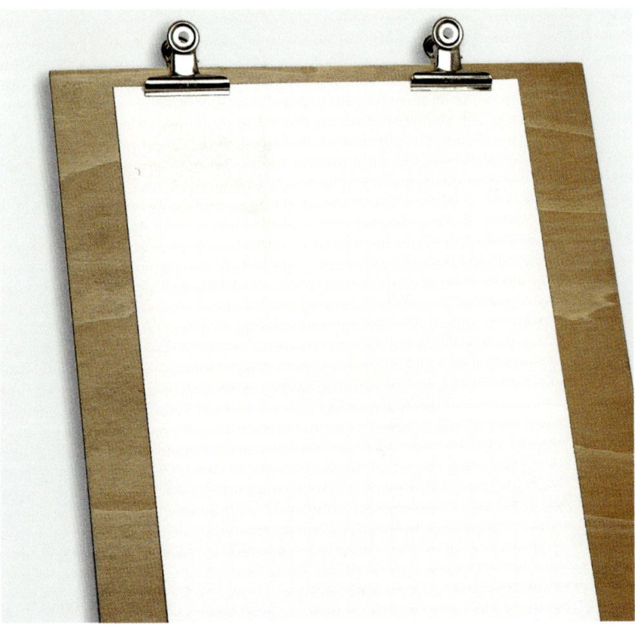

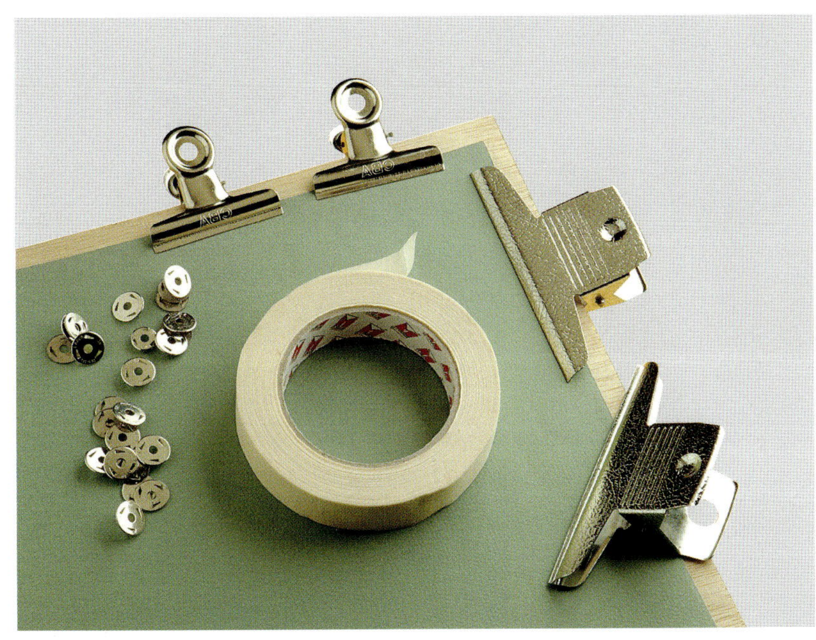

SECURING THE PAPER.
The paper can be secured to a piece of hard cardboard or a wood surface with masking tape, thumbtacks, or clips. This way, the paper will not wrinkle or fly away easily with the wind when working outdoors.

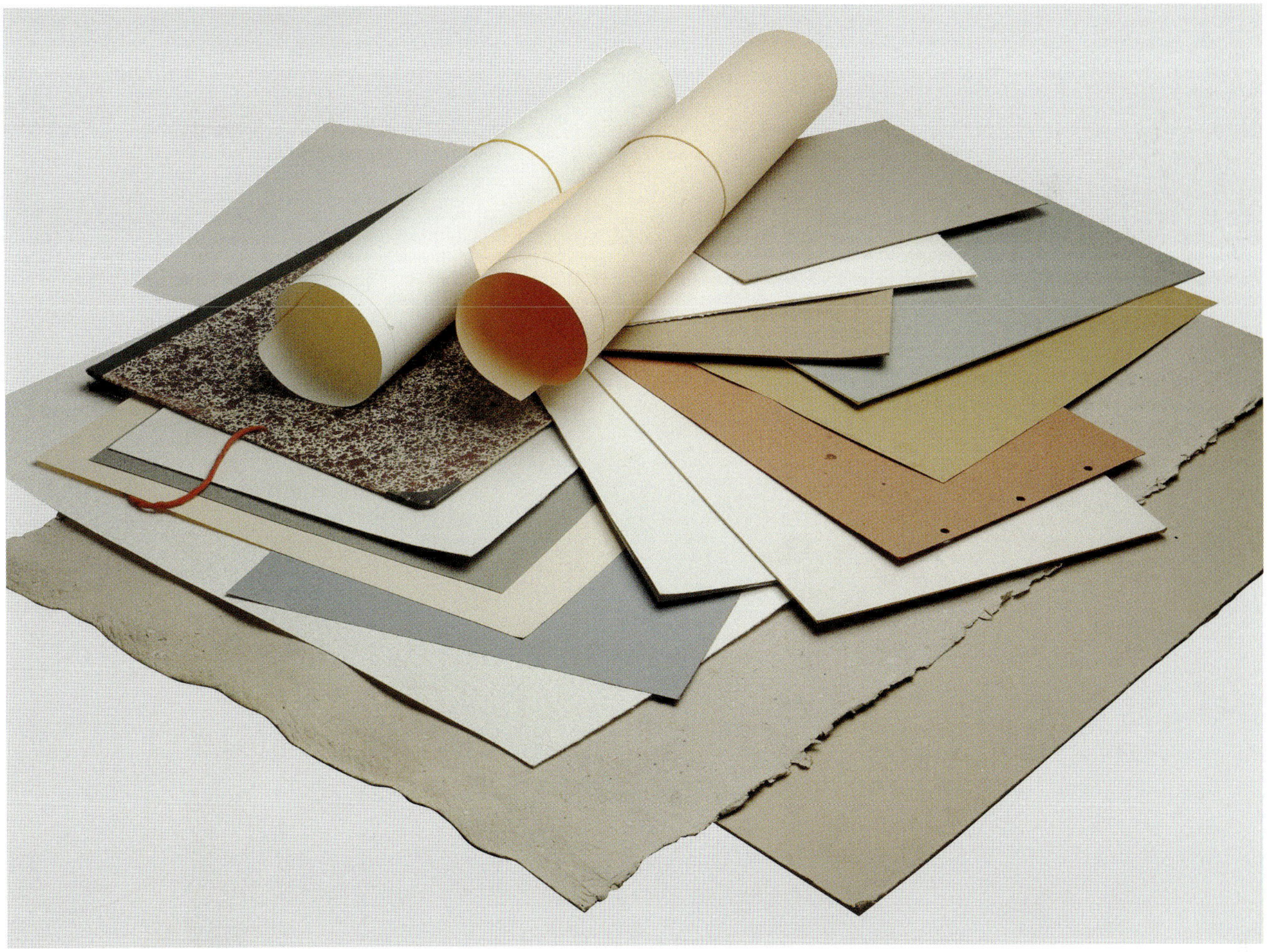

A VARIETY OF PAPERS.
Keep samples of a variety of papers. This way, you will be able to test any medium on them before you begin to draw.

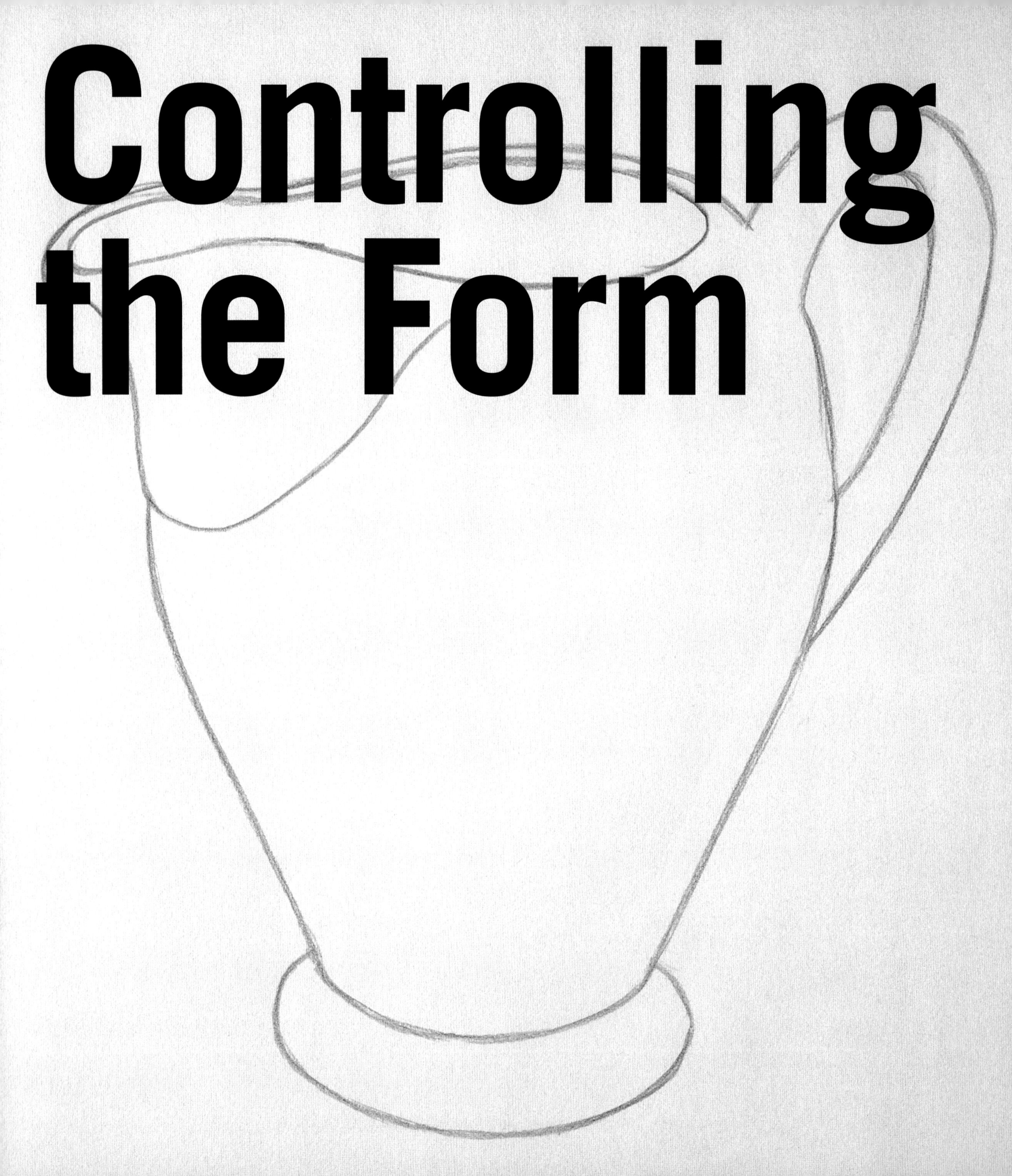

Controlling the Form

The shape of an object used as a model is determined
by its outline. The features that stand out define its
identity. They are the starting point of the sketch or the
diagram that gives it form. This does not mean that the
object is a strict representation of its outline, because
its form is always linked to the design of the internal
framework, imaginary lines, and other underlying
structures. In the same way that you must practice to
teach your hand to draw, you must also train your eye to
see those underlying schemas that help you identify the
distinctive features of each form. This is why the artist is
encouraged to understand before acting, to observe the
structure of what he or she sees before beginning to
draw, to recognize an innate framework upon which
the definitive form of the model could be based.

DIFFERENT WAYS OF BLOCKING IN. For the beginner, controlling the model's form can present some challenges, especially when its shape is symmetrical. Controlling the form is not only a matter of manual dexterity; there is also a method for blocking in symmetrical objects correctly. During the first phase of the learning process, it is important to establish the axes of symmetry and to reduce each shape to a few simple structural sketches that will be easy to memorize and correct if you make a mistake. Let us look at some examples.

1.

AXES OF SYMMETRY. The axes of symmetry are established by drawing a very simple grid that divides the rectangle according to its halves and diagonals. This geometric division helps articulate the surface of the work in accordance with the object that needs to be reproduced. These grid lines are guidelines that help you draw the outline of an object with harmony and proportion. Get accustomed to drawing axes of symmetry before you begin any drawing and you will notice the difference.

2.

GEOMETRIC STRUCTURE. The shape of an object can also be resolved by synthesizing the model using the geometric forms that are contained in it. If you select the correct forms, you will be able to draw a symmetrical object quite accurately, with few mistakes.

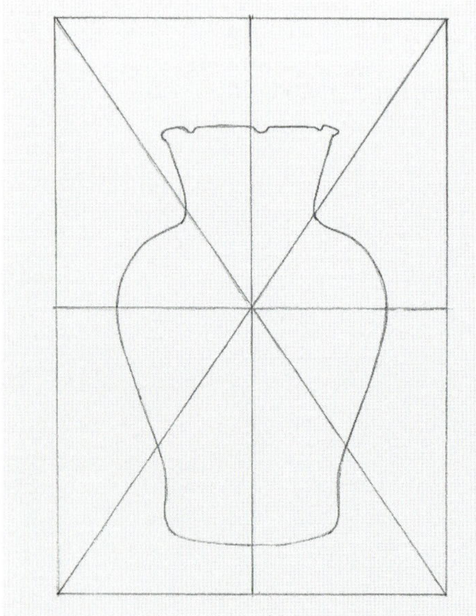

The axes of symmetry make it possible to make a good, well-balanced composition and to draw a symmetrical object with the same outline on each side.

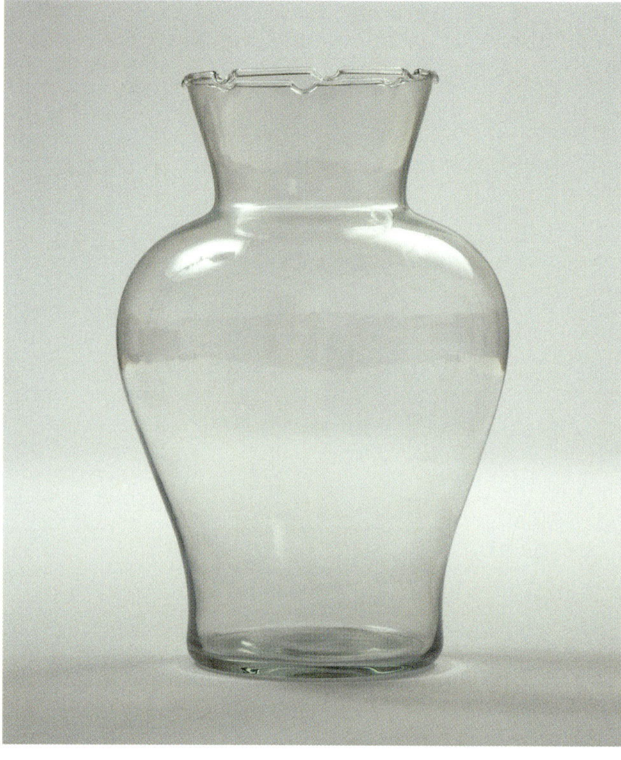

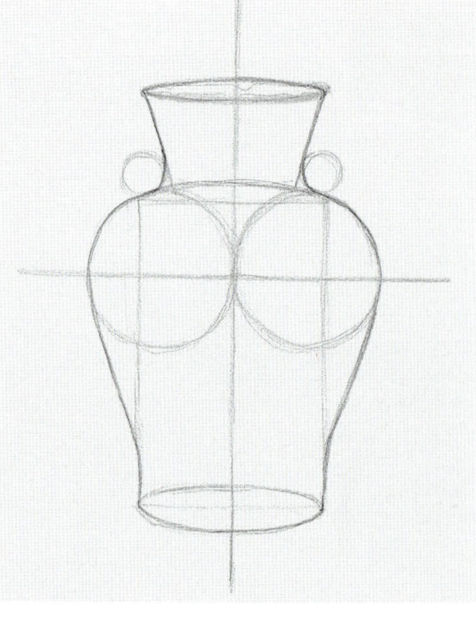

Draw the horizontal and vertical axes of symmetry, followed by a rectangle. Place an inverted trapezoid over it, along with two identical circumferences, one on each side. Draw the final outline based on these shapes.

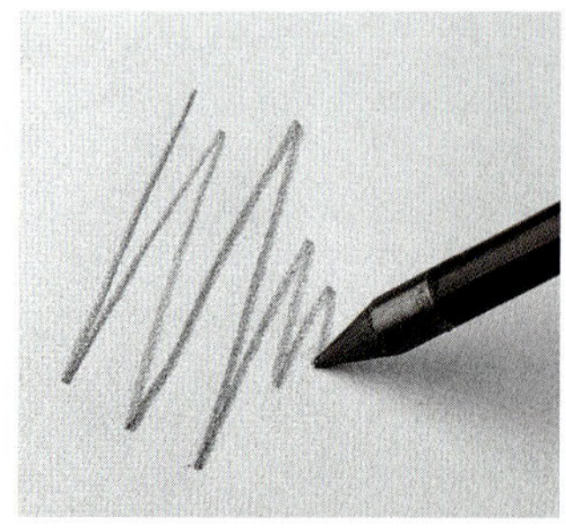

Forget the ruler, the compass, and the square when you draw; every line should be drawn freehand. This way, even when the lines are not completely even, you will become more proficient at it.

3.

SYSTEM OF COORDINATES. Another interesting method for blocking in an object's form is based on controlling the measurement of each one of its parts. To do this, first draw horizontal and vertical lines to define the height and width of the object, identifying each point by its coordinates. Once the measurements have been established, simply draw the outline of the object through the points indicated.

4.

MODULES OR BOXES. Any model, no matter how irregular or complicated it may be, can be bounded by a flat box or geometric shape. This is the technique of blocking in using modules: when an object is drawn, its shape is encased by a square module that should be as high and wide as the model. If you need to be more precise, several square boxes can be combined.

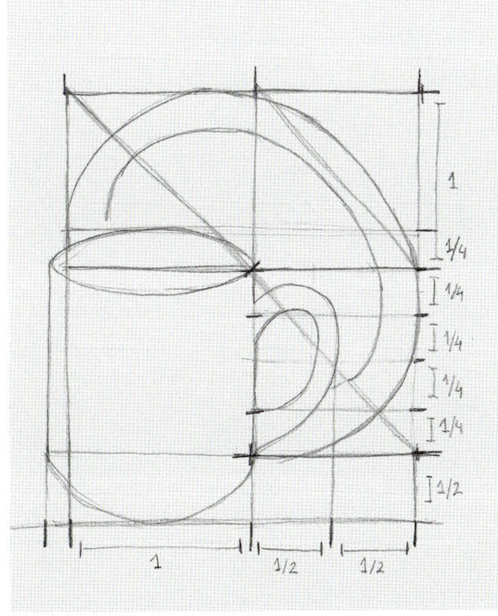

The most important thing is to measure the height and width of each area. From that point you can begin indicating coordinates on these lines, making sure that they take into account the object's size variations. Once the measurements have been established, the outline can be drawn.

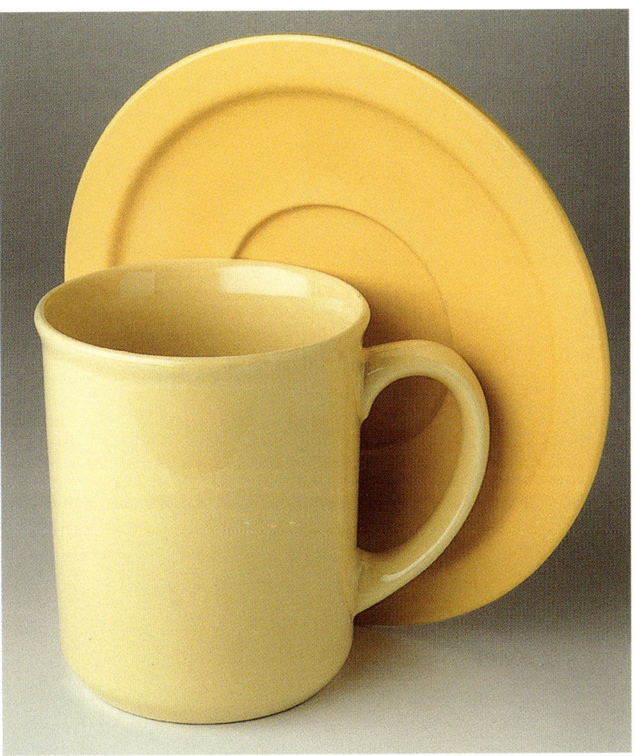

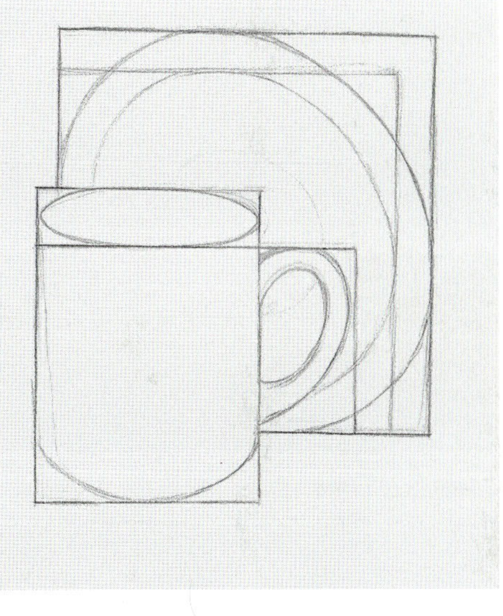

The first box defines the height and width of the cup, and the second one, that of the plate. They can be complemented by other boxes that provide additional information about the model.

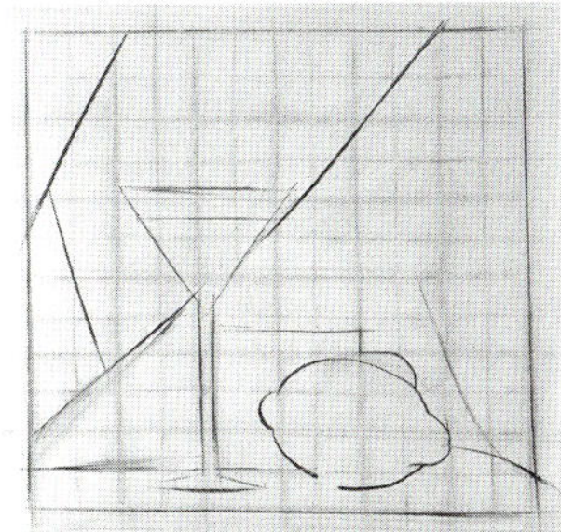

Blocking in using graph paper is not common among beginners. Normally, it should only be used when copying a photograph or a print that is to be reproduced in a size larger than that of the original. The squares facilitate blocking the model.

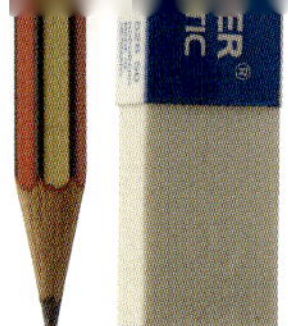

5.

BLOCKING IN SYMMETRICAL OBJECTS. The exercises that follow show the most common method for structuring and blocking in a symmetrical model. At first this may look easy to do: you simply draw one side, then repeat the process on the other side as closely as possible. This task may be more challenging than it appears because it requires great attention and control of the line.

THE SCHEMATIC APPROACH. This consists of blocking in the outline of an object with polygonal lines, drawing a general view of it. This is done by drawing the contour with sketchy strokes, using a series of straight, short lines that gradually define the profile.

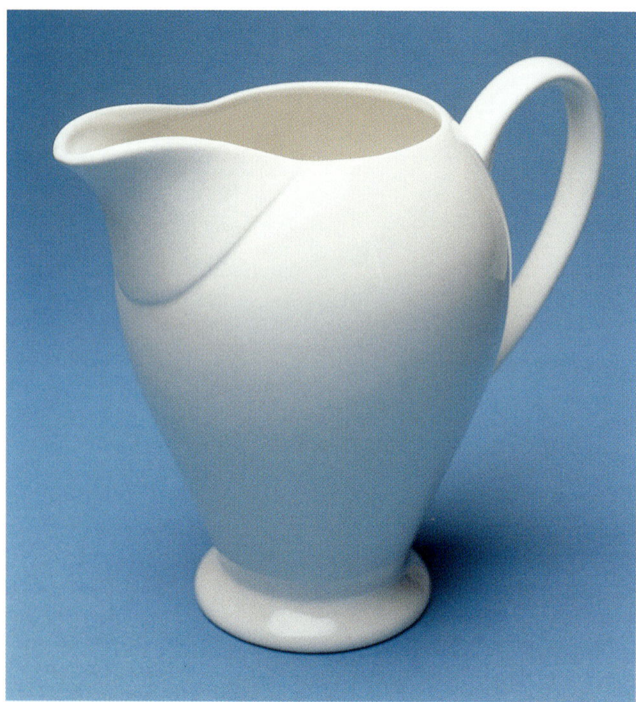

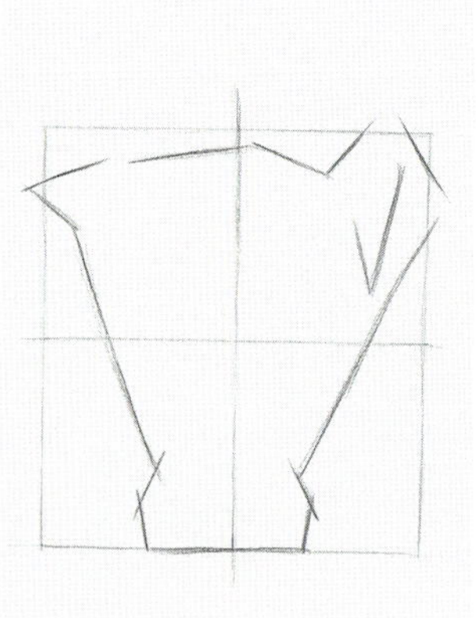

The first lines are a series of straight and short strokes that establish a sketchy outline of the object. This is a visual approximation that will require adjustments and corrections.

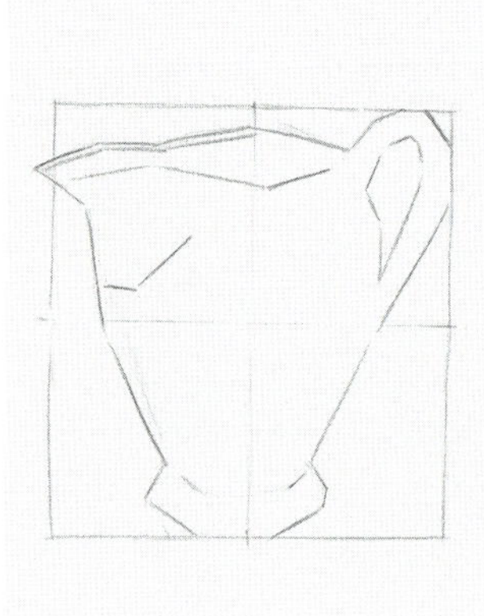

The lines are erased and redrawn, correcting the basic shapes to perfect the drawing.

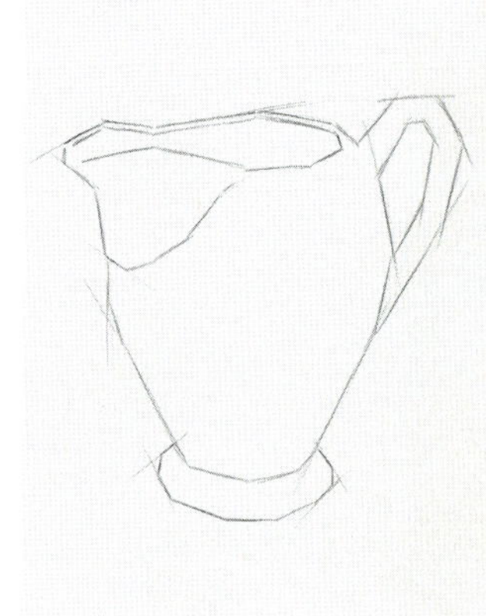

In the end, the straight lines are replaced by rounded lines that are softer and less angular. You must erase the previous step, and to redraw the object with rounded lines, following the traces of the pencil lines.

A square box is always very helpful when drawing an object. By marking each side you will get very useful reference points that can be used to sketch the outline of the model.

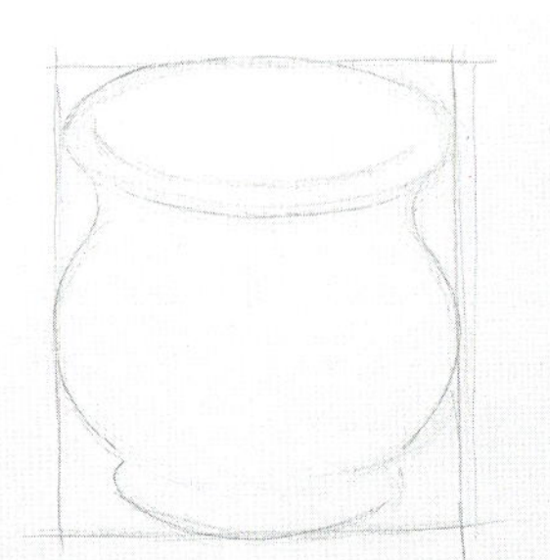

Professional artists develop a sketch of the model using quick, accurate, and loose marks, although much practice is needed to arrive at this point.

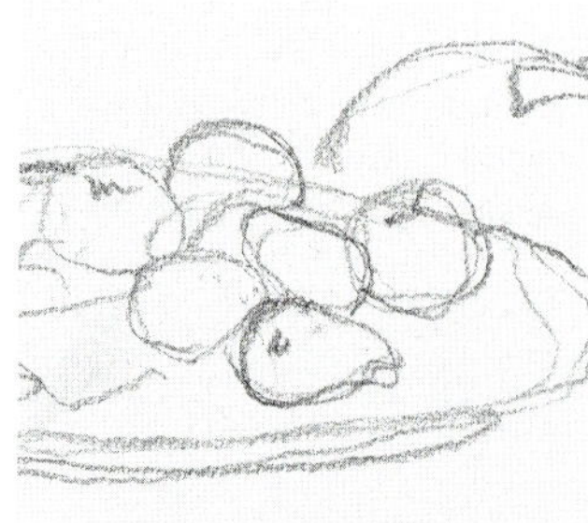

6.

THREE-DIMENSIONAL FORMS. If you analyze the shape of any object you will notice that nearly every object can be fitted inside a geometric shape. Beginning with three-dimensional geometric shapes will make it easier to draw the structure of the model and to represent its volume. To aid in blocking in the objects, the geometric shape creates a transparent, imaginary volumetric background, as if it was a box whose sides make contact with each side of the object being drawn.

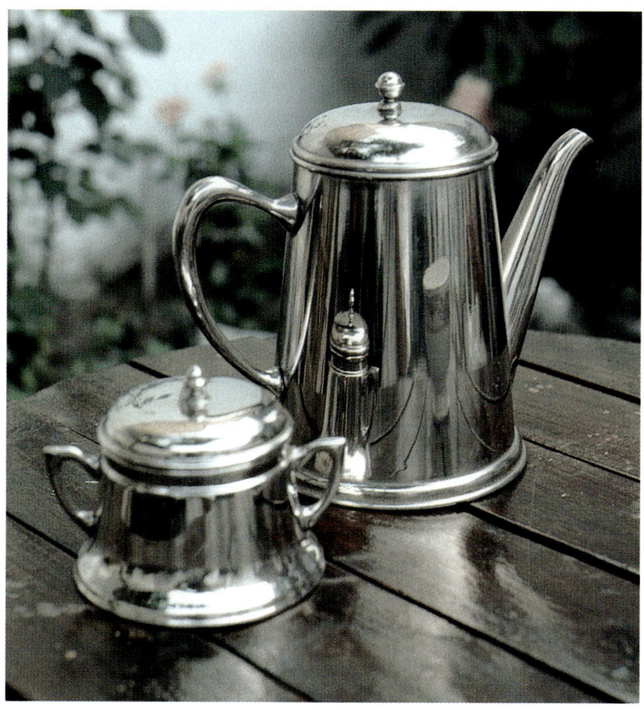

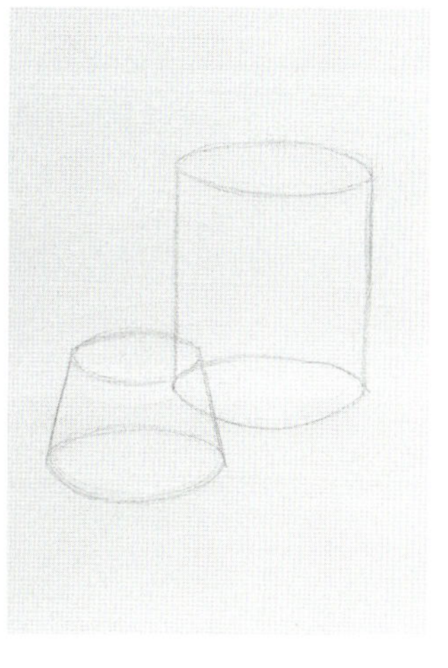

The first step of the drawing is to synthesize every element within two simple geometric forms: a cylinder for the coffeepot and a trapezoid for the sugar bowl.

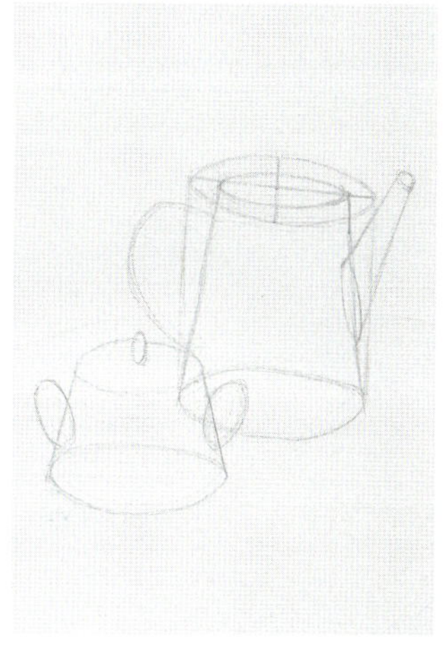

Based on these geometric structures, we begin to draw each form, paying special attention to the contours of the objects. This way, the coffeepot's cylinder becomes a trapezoid. We use ellipses to establish the placement of the handles.

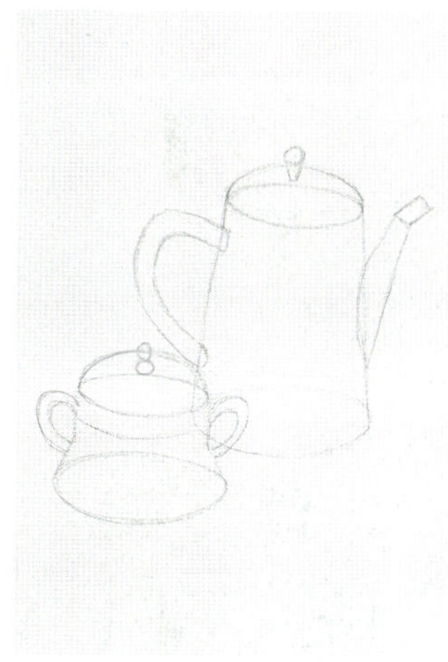

The lids are drawn using half of a sphere. The handles are already in place, as well as the spout of the coffeepot, which was drawn with straight lines. When everything is sketched, the initial geometric box is erased.

If a shape appears in foreshortening, it can be drawn gradually or with transverse sections that will look attached.

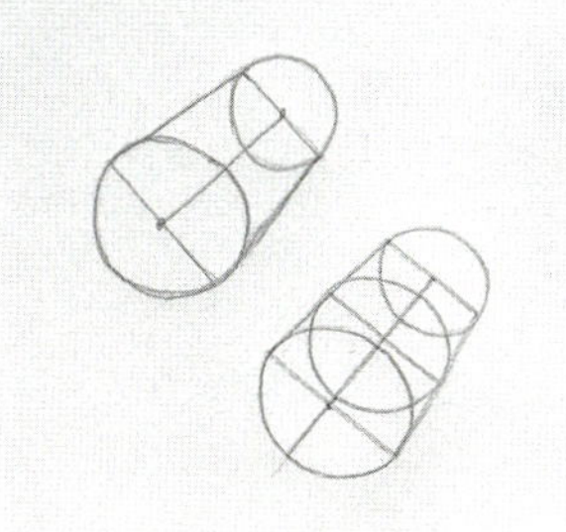

Imagining the objects as if they were transparent is a good tool for understanding their internal structure, creating a clean drawing, and controlling the angles and proportions of the representation.

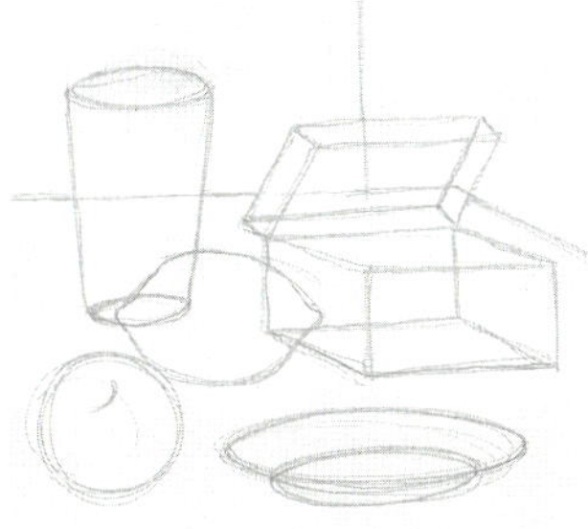

CONTROLLING THE LINE. Becoming proficient at drawing fluid lines, knowing how to hold the pencil correctly, being aware of the variety of lines, and training the hand to perform various motions are essential for successfully defining the outline of any drawing.

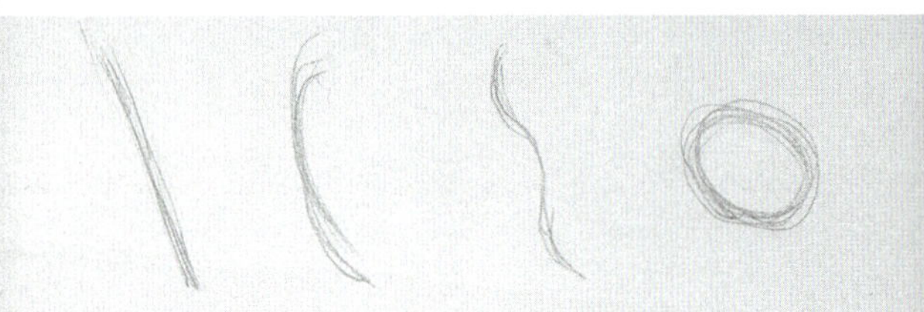

The tentative line is one of the first ones that an amateur artist should learn. It consists of drawing several lines, one over the other, to sketch the form of the model. This line is standard in the first stages of a drawing.

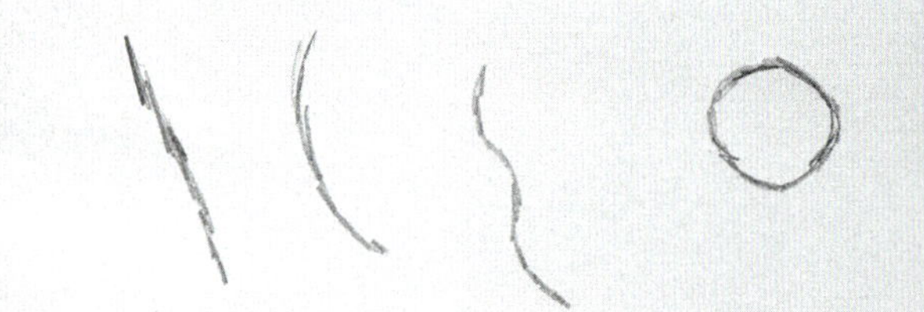

Inexperienced artists tend to draw with inconsistent lines that lack continuity, a practice that should be avoided.

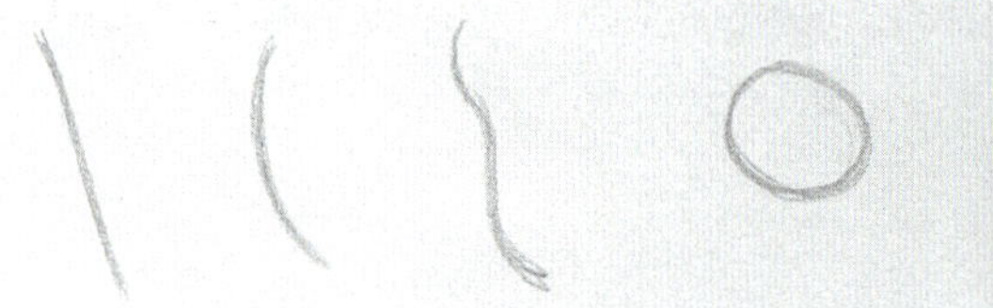

When drawing, you need to be able to control the line. You should aim to draw with decisive, direct, and uniform strokes.

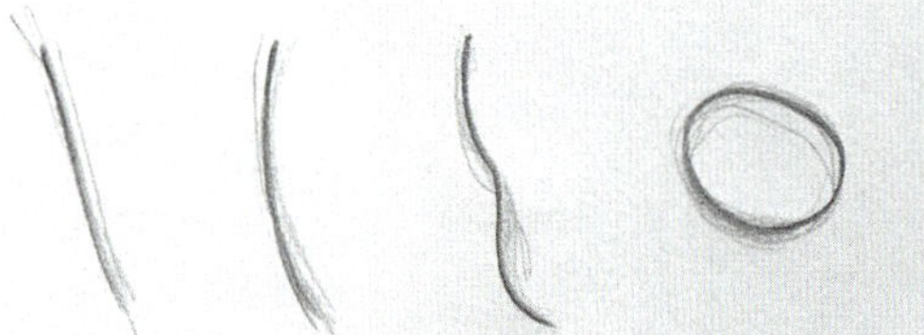

Line control in a drawing is the result of successive tentative marks that leave an imprint on the paper after each stroke. Precision in the form is developed as firmer and darker lines are superimposed over the others.

SOLIDIFYING THE LINE. When the drawing's outline has been completely defined, it is reinforced with a more liberal and firm hand. To do this, it is very important to sketch the preliminary lines very softly so they can be easily corrected.

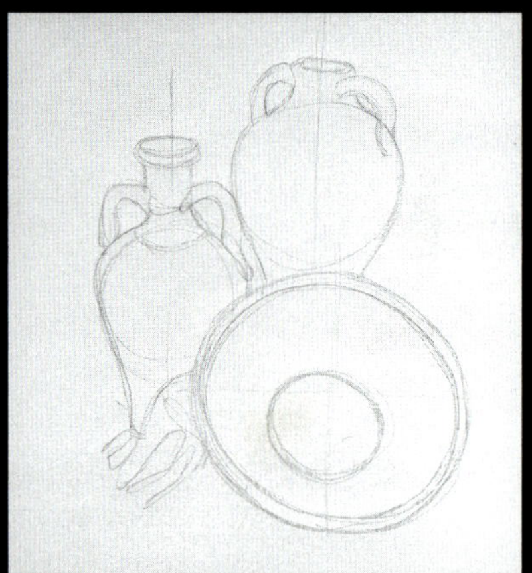
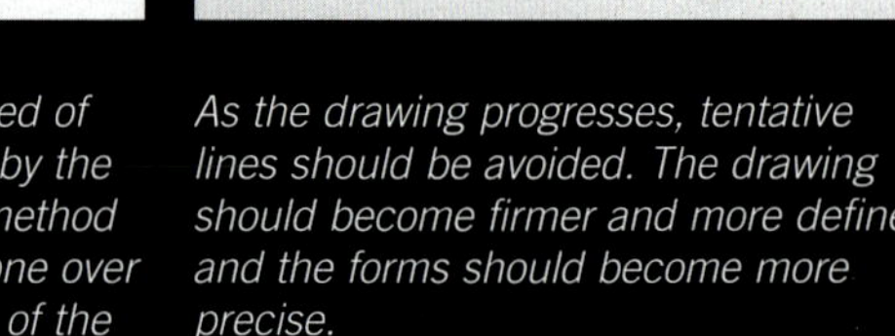
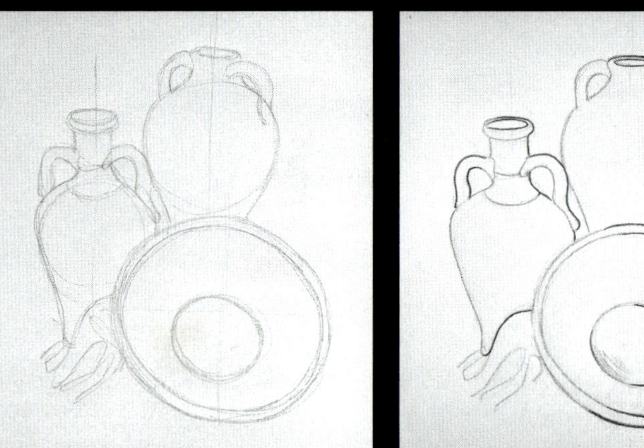

The preliminary layout is composed of quick, loose lines that are drawn by the artist as an approximation. This method allows several lines to be drawn one over the other to describe the outlines of the objects.

As the drawing progresses, tentative lines should be avoided. The drawing should become firmer and more defined and the forms should become more precise.

Finally, reinforce the drawing with new, heavier lines that make it stand out against the background. Lighter lines are reserved for the highlights and for the model's interior details, creating a three-dimensional effect.

CONTROLLING THE LINE. Once the basic structure of the objects has been established, you can begin to outline the form, paying more attention to the stroke. The secret of a professional drawing resides in the movement of the hand in conjunction with the forearm; they often move as a single unit.

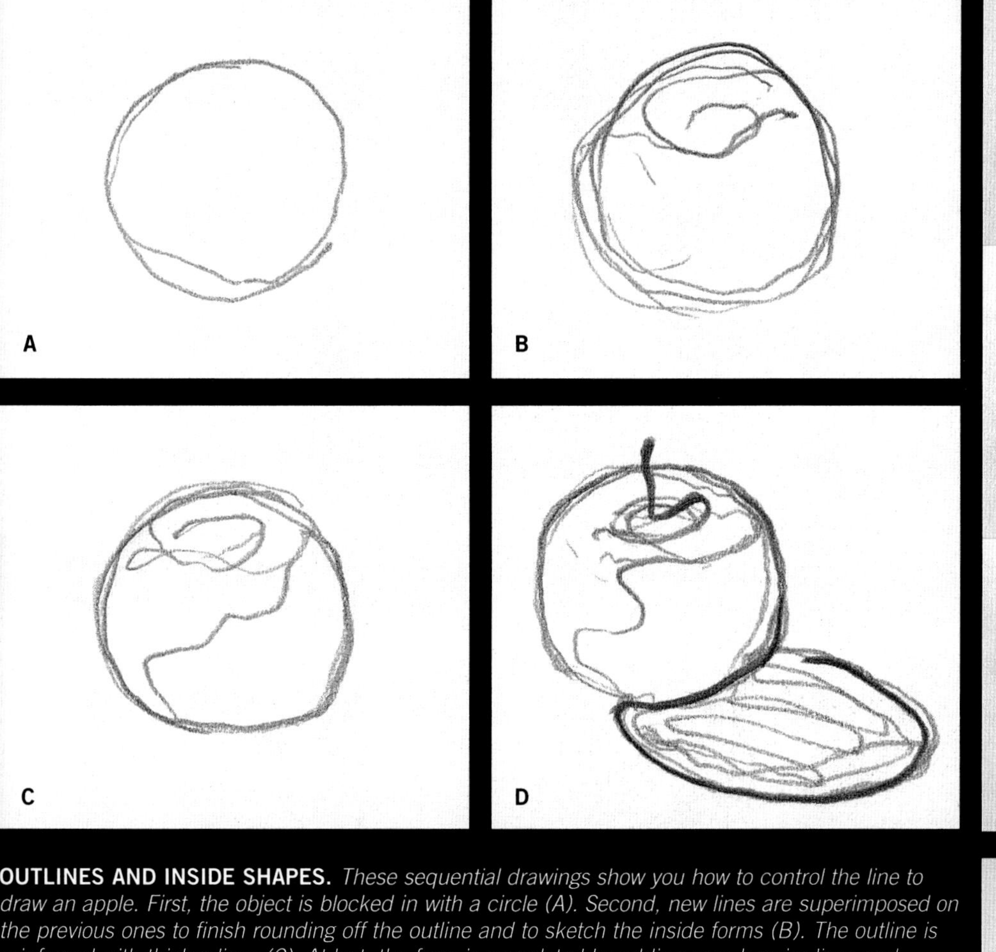

A

B

C

D

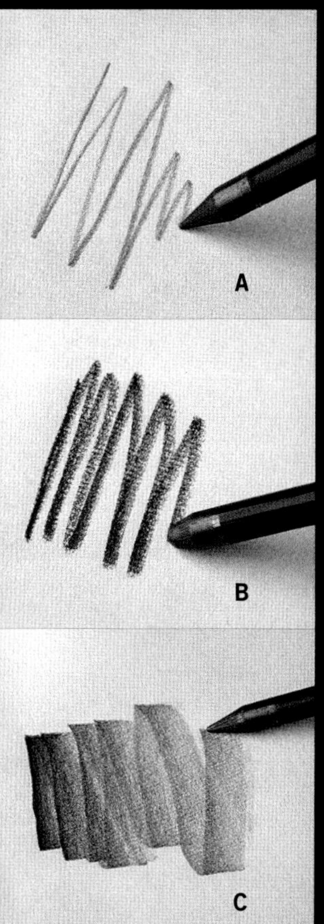

ANGLE OF THE POINT. *The shape of the point and the angle at which the drawing tool is held are important for controlling the quality of the line. The results vary depending on whether the point is sharpened (A), worn (B), or held at a low angle (C).*

OUTLINES AND INSIDE SHAPES. *These sequential drawings show you how to control the line to draw an apple. First, the object is blocked in with a circle (A). Second, new lines are superimposed on the previous ones to finish rounding off the outline and to sketch the inside forms (B). The outline is reinforced with thicker lines (C). At last, the form is completed by adding new, heavier lines and projecting the shadow (D).*

DRAWING ELLIPSES. *Shown here are the most common mistakes made by beginners, who tend to draw the ellipses too short and either too sharp or too rounded, like a sausage. These errors should be avoided.*

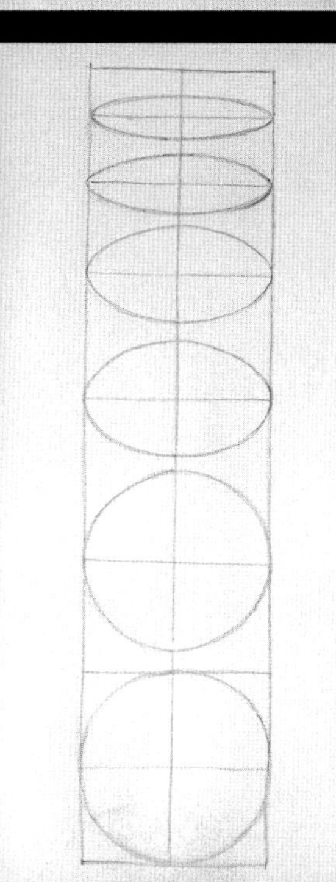

DRAWING ELLIPSES. *Many objects are drawn based on circles seen in perspective. Therefore, learning to draw ellipses is one of the requirements for being an artist. As the circle gradually becomes an ellipse, its four parts will decrease in height until they become rectangles. This exercise is ideal for drawing glasses, vases, and plates.*

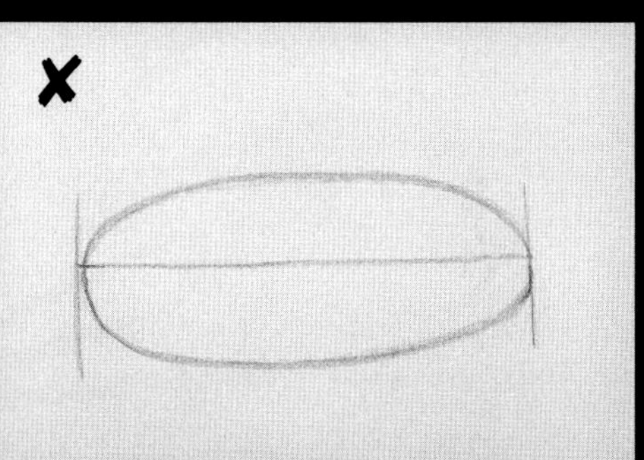

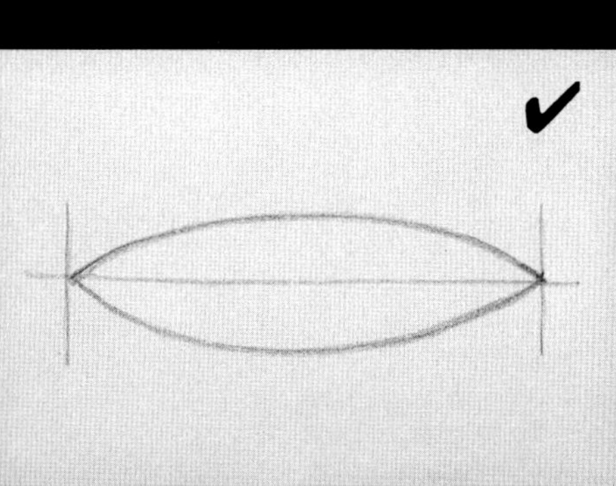

GEOMETRIC APPROACH. You can use several approaches to the model when you begin to plan a drawing; one of them is to interpret the forms with geometric figures that help you control the proportions.

7.1

BUILDING WITH FIGURES. Blocking in should be the most elaborate and intense phase of the process. The entire structure of the drawing depends on it. Blocking in allows you to make sure that it is balanced, that the proportions are correct, and that there are no mistakes in the lines that require greater precision. In this exercise, we will use geometric shapes as if they are pieces in a puzzle.

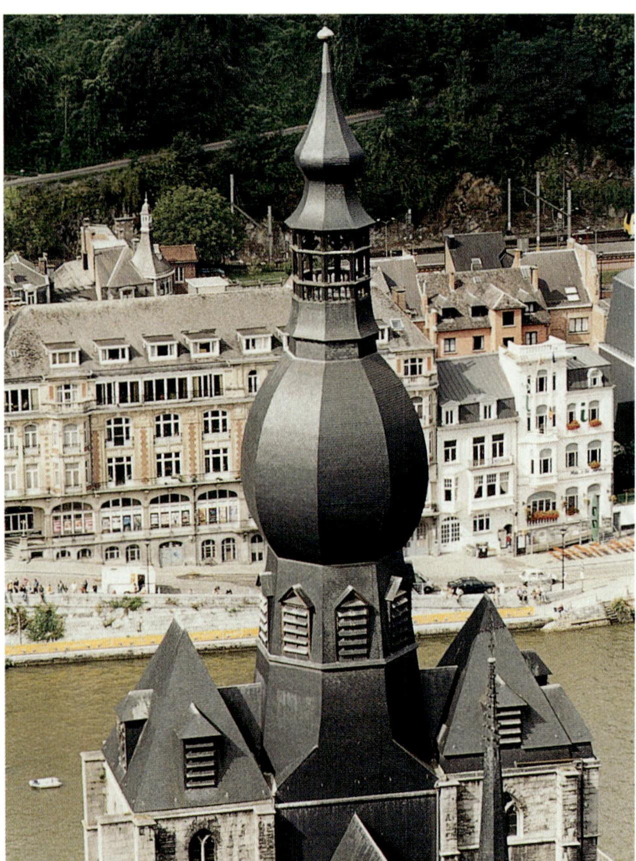

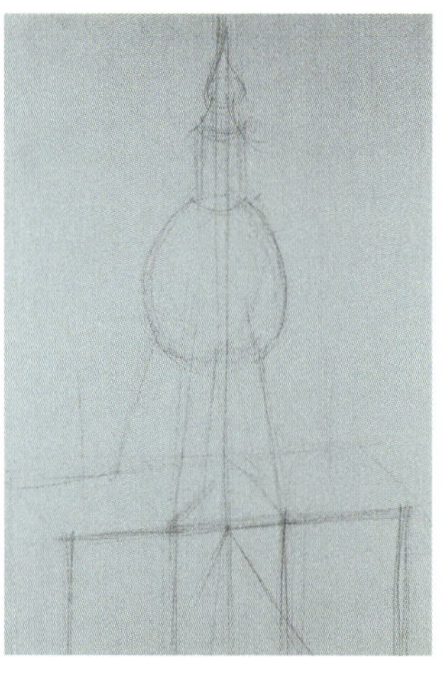

The base of the tower is represented by a rectangular shape. The lower section of the bell tower presents a pyramid-like form topped off by a huge egg. The cone-shaped top of the bell tower is superimposed upon it.

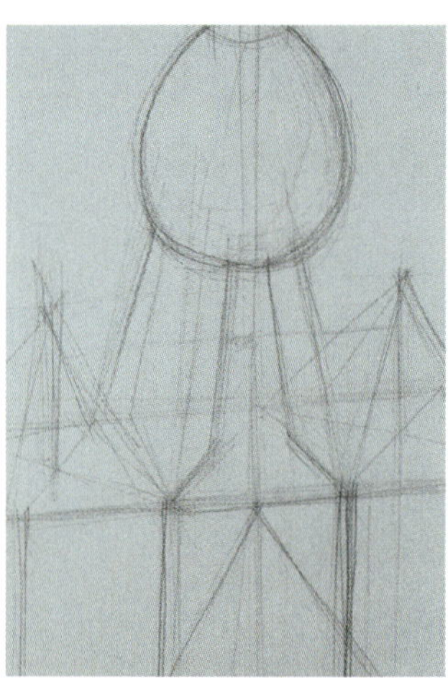

When drawing structures as if they were transparent, you can use horizontal and vertical lines, in addition to axes, to help with the process of comparing reference points with diagonals and tangents.

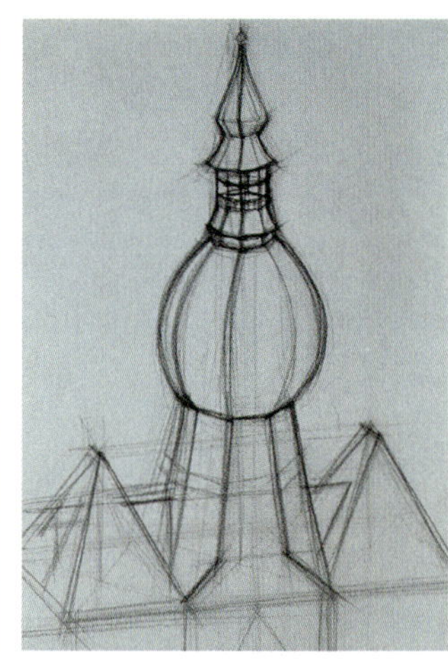

This drawing, completely defined by structural lines, reveals the different geometric shapes that constitute the building's shell. When the artist is completely satisfied with the drawing, the lines are darkened with firmer and more decisive strokes.

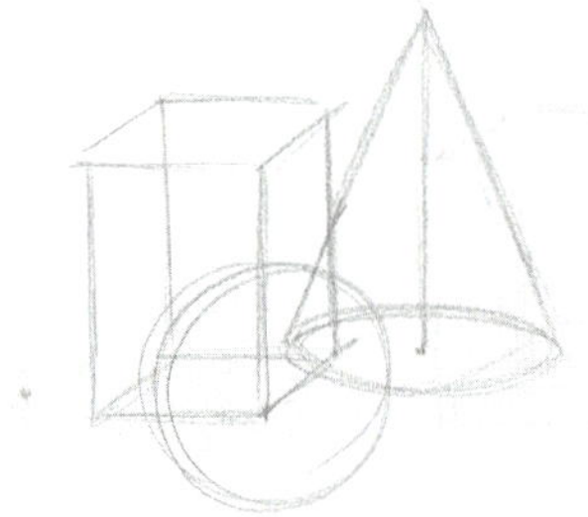

Cézanne proclaimed that "In nature, everything is modeled after three fundamental shapes: the sphere, the cone, and the cylinder. One must learn to paint these three very simple figures, and from there you can do anything you want."

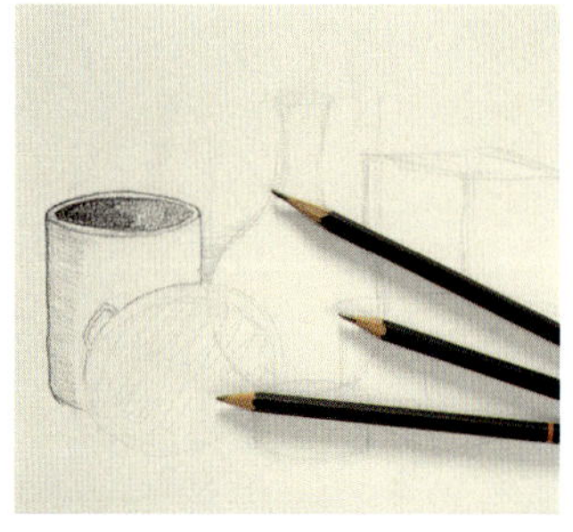

To block in the geometric shapes, we recommend starting the drawing with a pencil that produces light lines, such as an HB, then working with softer pencils as the drawing progresses.

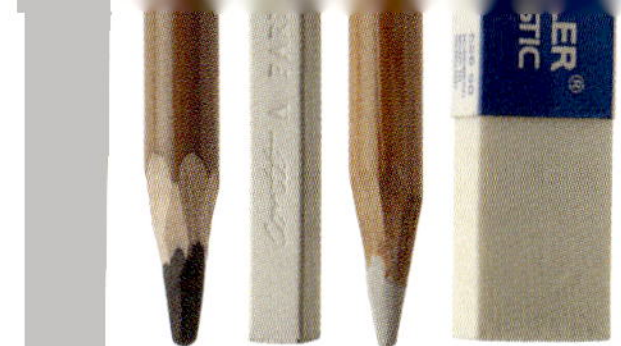

7.2

CONSOLIDATING THE DRAWING AND SHADING. After several geometric shapes have been superimposed to achieve the model's structure, they are connected with lines to define the outside shape. The phase is completed with light shading that provides a sense of volume to the grouping.

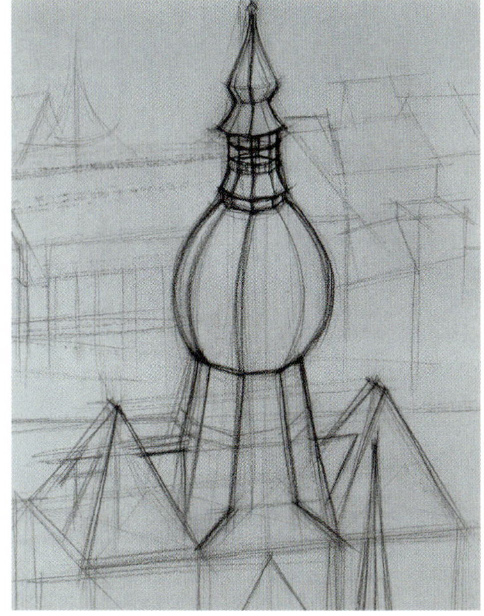

You have drawn the model as if the geometric shapes were transparent, made of glass. Now, redraw the outlines trying to envision the forms as opaque bodies. Only the visible outlines are taken into account; erase the initial structural lines to avoid confusion.

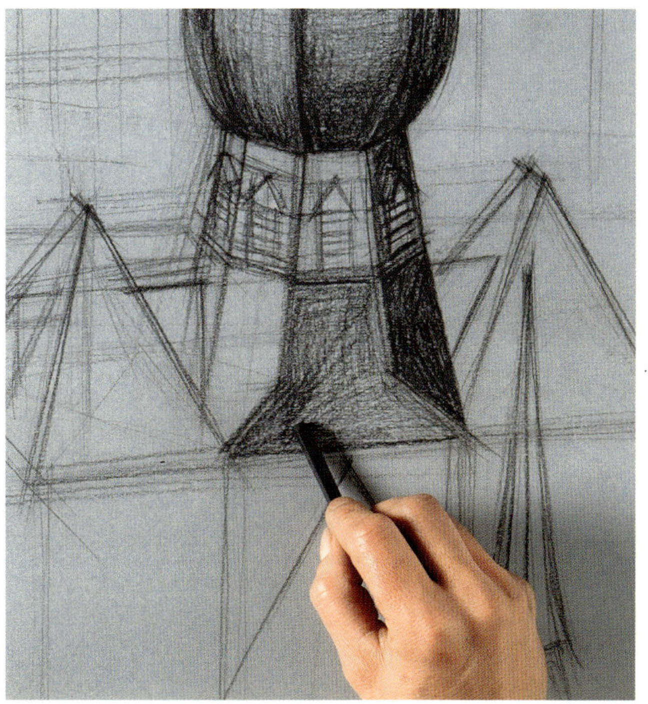

Emphasize the shaded areas to give the geometric shapes a greater feeling of volume. The shaded parts are lightly drawn with the side of a chalk stick.

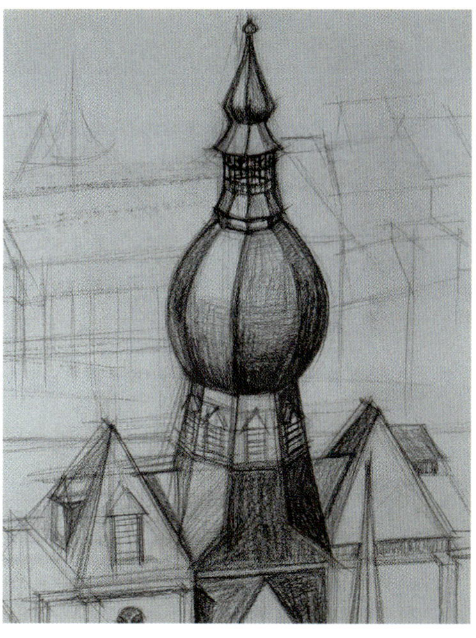

Darken the right side of the bell tower. This tone, very close to black, establishes the main contrast between light and dark, helping to emphasize the tower's profile against the background. It also becomes the point of reference for the darkest tone in the drawing.

To draw an apparently complex object, first draw a rectangular box to contain it; next, based on this, develop the form.

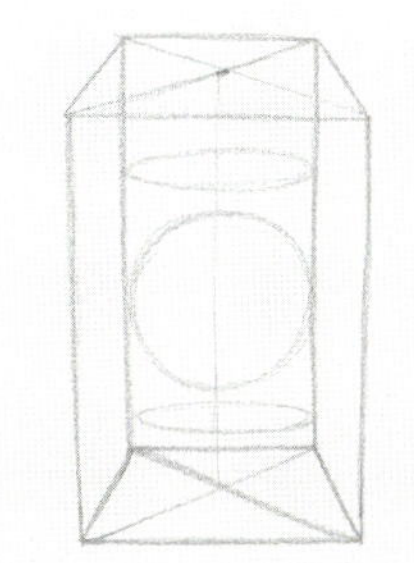

When blocking in objects inside geometric shapes, do not forget to draw the axis of symmetry, a perpendicular line that divides the figure in two and acts as a reference point.

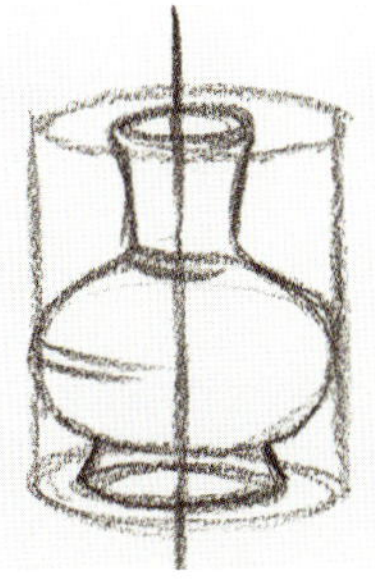

7.3

GEOMETRY, HIGHLIGHTS, AND VOLUME EFFECTS. The last stage consists of shading and modeling the forms. The dark shading and the white chalk highlights will eventually cover any underlying or structural lines that are still visible.

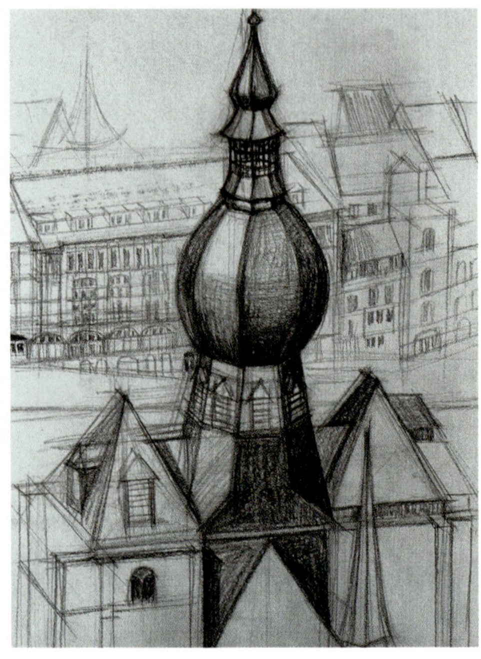

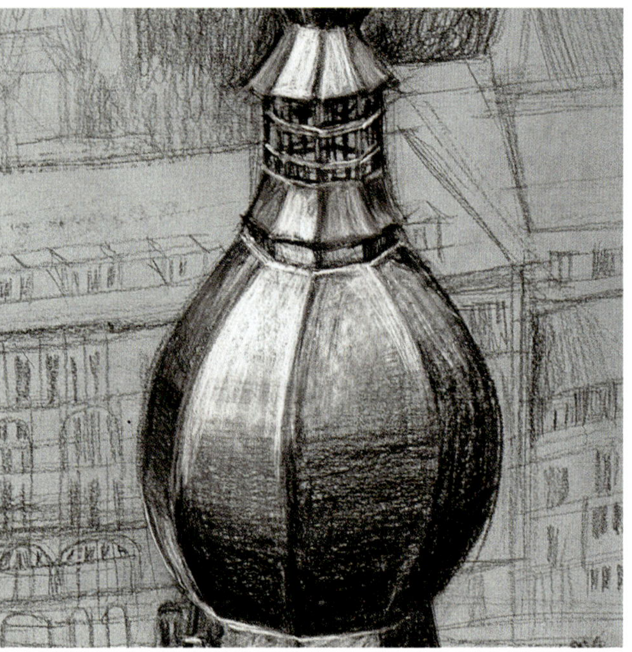

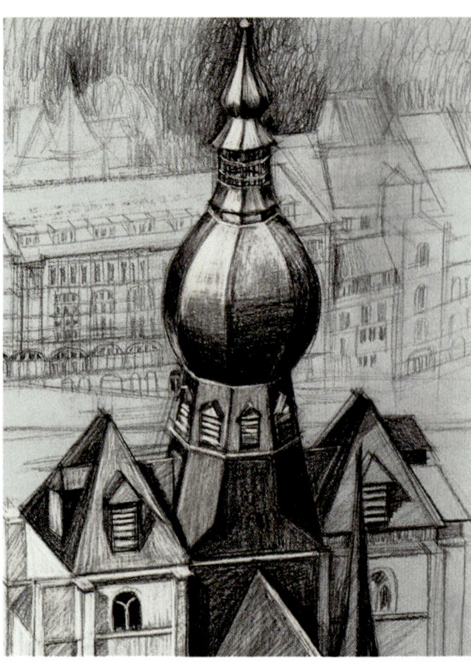

Create the background by sketching the façades of the buildings. The background should be dynamic, without too many details. Draw it without pressing too hard on the chalk; some areas can even be left out.

Emphasize the areas of light with white chalk. Dfferentiation among the various sides of the tower bell is achieved with contrasting tones. This effect is created where two sides that have different amounts of light meet; this way each plane is defined according to its position relative to the source of light.

Finish drawing the building with a variety of light and dark tones. To give your drawing more contrast, add lighter whites and draw new dark areas, superimposing these tones on the previous ones. This causes the foreground to stand out against the light gray background.

Chalk produces much better results when it is used on colored backgrounds.

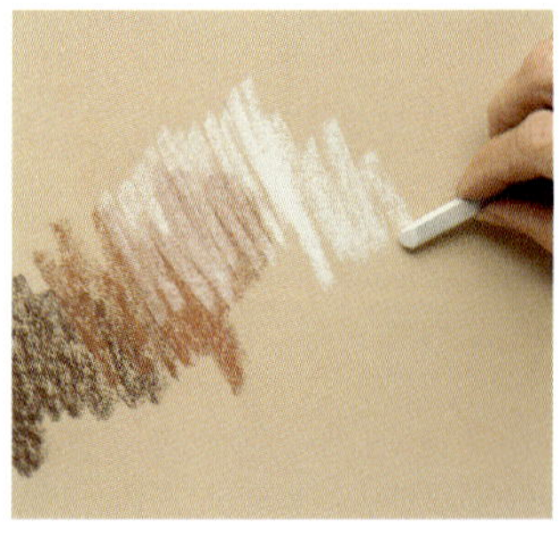

The final phase of the drawing consists of completing the lower part of the building, which is created by combining light lines made with white chalk and shaded areas drawn with black chalk. A very soft new gray layer is applied to the background. It is important to draw the background in a more sketchy manner so you do not take away importance from the foreground. Drawing by Esther Olivé de Puig.

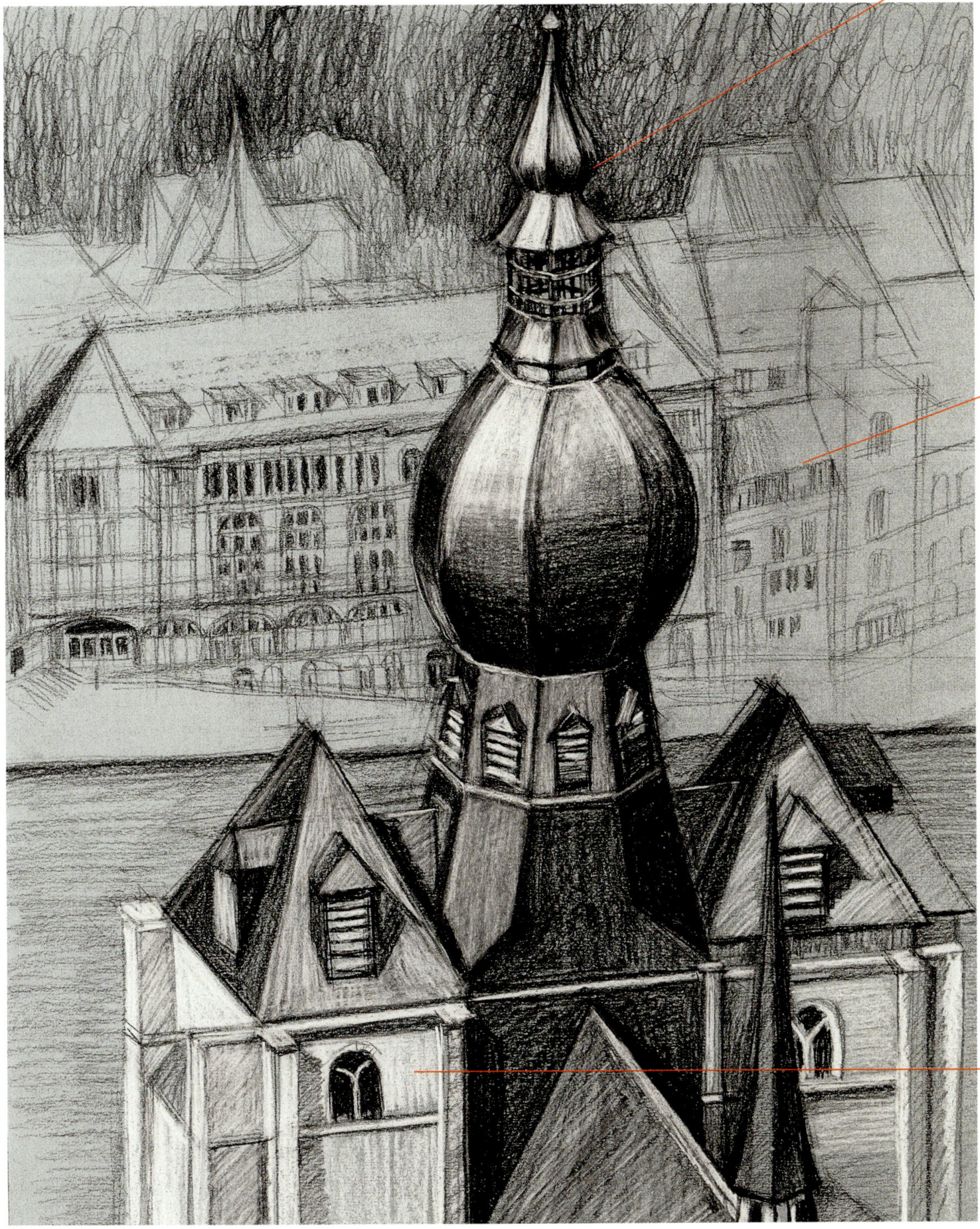

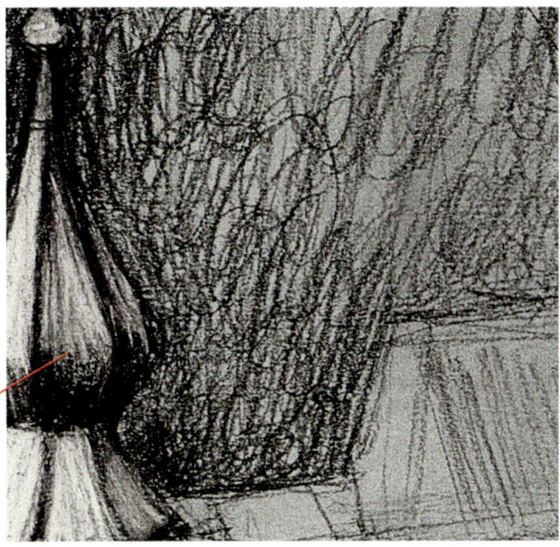

When an object in the foreground is superimposed against a gray background, you can darken it around the outlines to emphasize its profile even more through the effect of contrast.

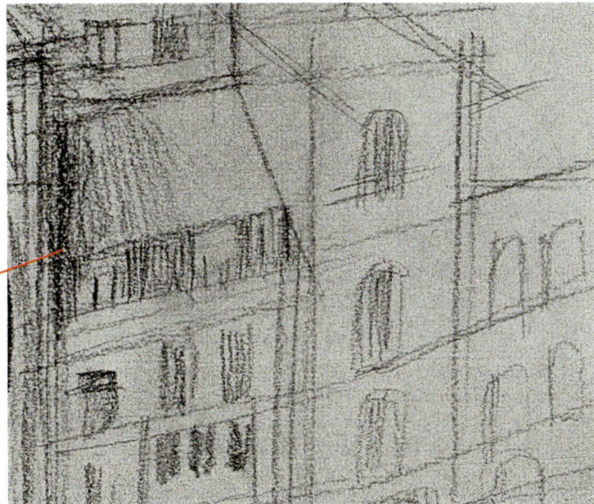

The buildings in the background are drawn to look like sketches. No white chalk lines are used here because the color of the paper provides the intermediate tones.

To differentiate among the various planes that receive similar amounts of light, the artist can resort to the use of lines drawn in different directions. While the walls have vertical lines, the shadows of the pilasters are drawn with diagonals.

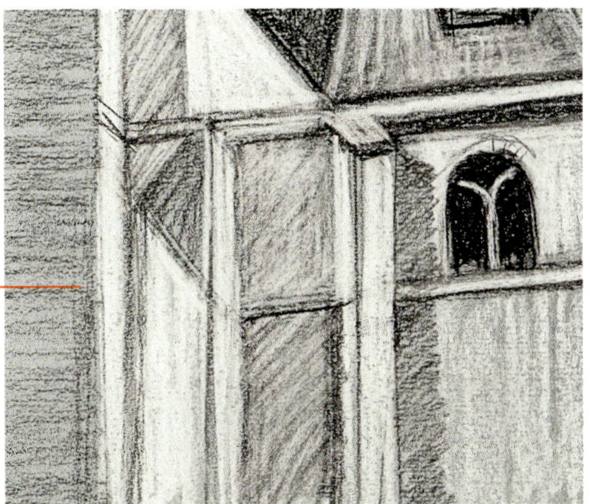

INTERIOR LINES. All objects have interior lines that help block in the drawing or resolve its form much more easily.

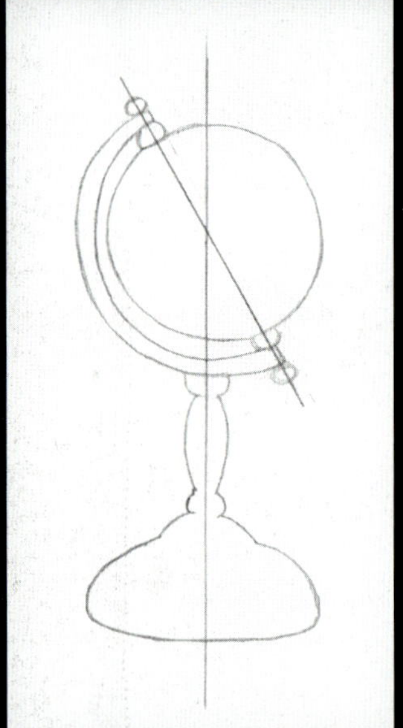

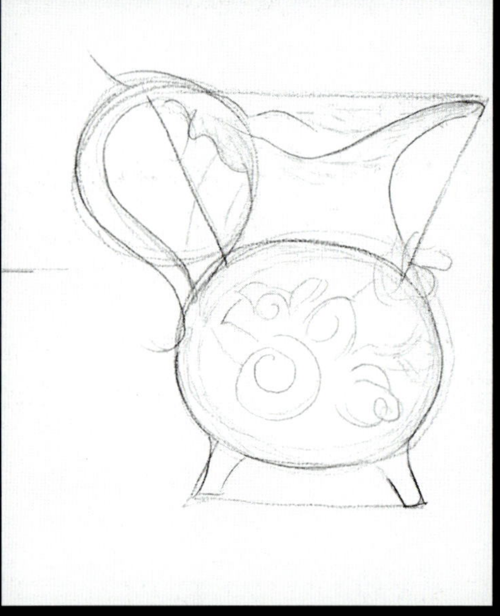

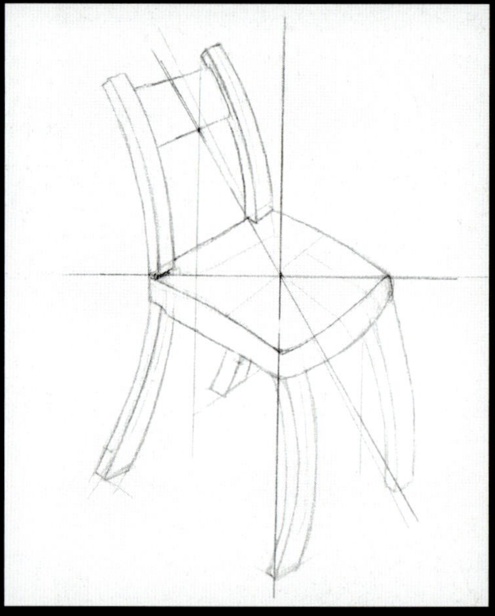

Many times, a straight diagonal line is sufficient to help you understand the configuration of the object that you are drawing.

When the object's shapes are more complex, you can combine straight lines with simple geometric shapes that help define its outline.

Diagonal lines can also be combined with the axes of symmetry. Here, crossed lines help construct a chair proportionally.

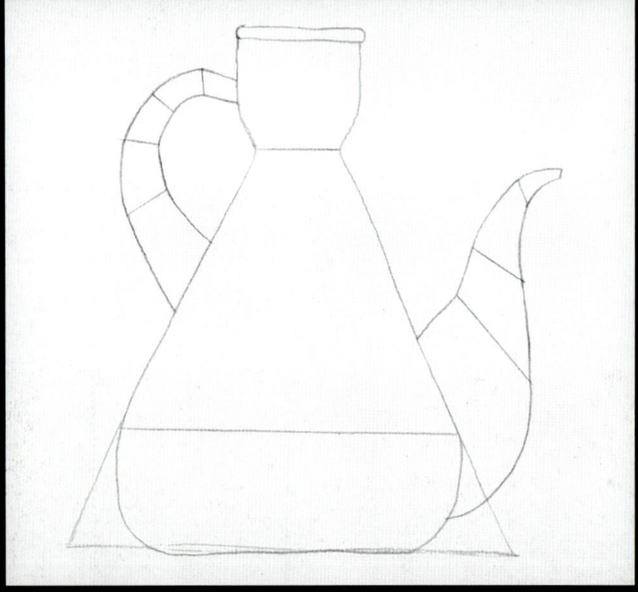

There are some interior lines that, when incorporated into a drawing, can help you better understand how to draw more complex areas, such as the handle and the spout of this oil cruet.

PROPORTION. For every model, it is possible to draw imaginary lines that correspond to its orientation or distance. These lines help with blocking in and with measurement of the proportions. This analytical work is very useful to do before you finalize the drawing.

A CORRECT OUTLINE. Encasing an object inside a box and within the axes of symmetry will help you draw its outline correctly and symmetrically.

FROM BLOCKING IN TO DRAWING. When you are faced with a complex subject, you can approach it in four well-defined phases that will help you come up with a proportionate solution.

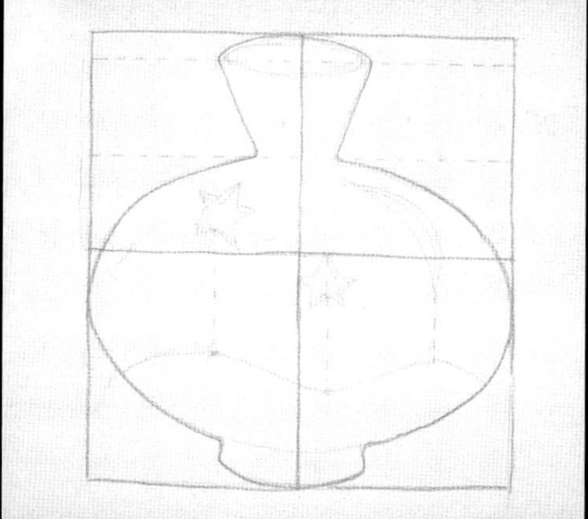

To draw the outline of an object, in this case a vase, copy the left side of the vase as shown in the two boxes on the right, using each box as a guide for blocking in the form.

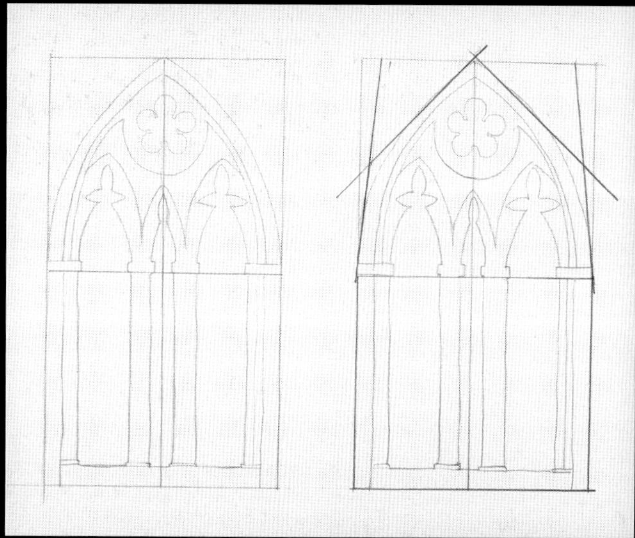

First, draw a box with the model inside. Then, locate the axes of symmetry, which will help you balance both sides of the drawing.

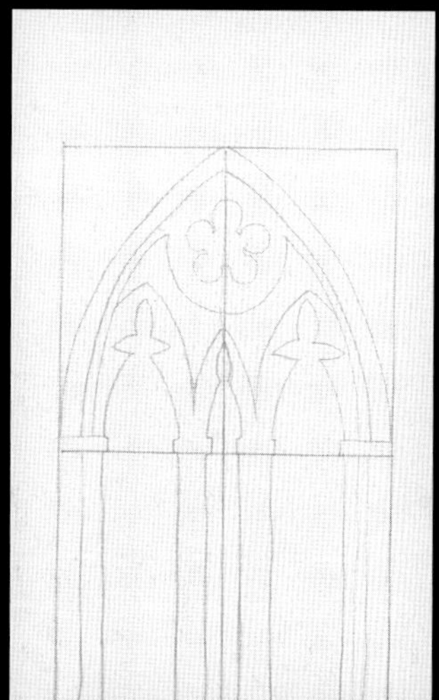

With new lines, study the model's outline in relationship to the initial box, controlling the correct angle of the Gothic arch.

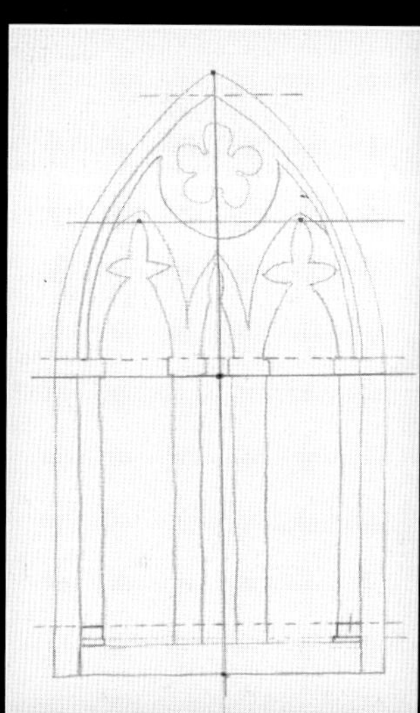

Drawing straight horizontal lines to establish new interior measurements will help you draw the decorative design.

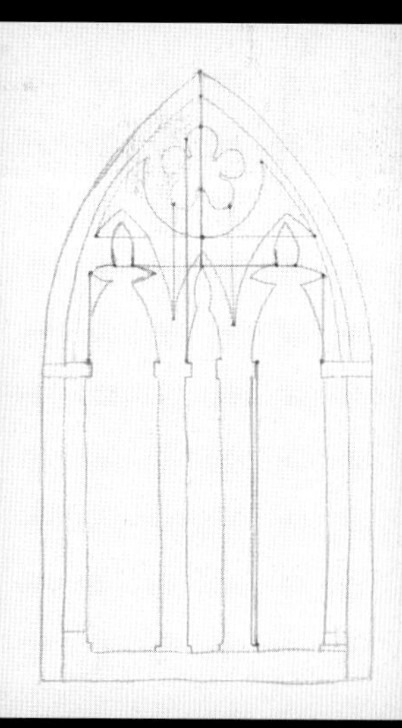

To draw the ornamental elements, it is necessary to study the placement of key points along a line and to make sure that the proportions are correct.

ESTABLISHING MEASUREMENTS. We have shown that reducing the main forms to simple geometric shapes and straight converging lines helps to establish the model's measurements. This permits accurate study of its proportions and the subsequent detailed representation of each of its parts.

8.1

FORMS, LINES, AND DIAGRAMS. Any subject can be accurately represented through the correct construction of lines and simple forms. Begin the process by drawing a few very simple geometric lines that establish the basic proportions of the different objects.

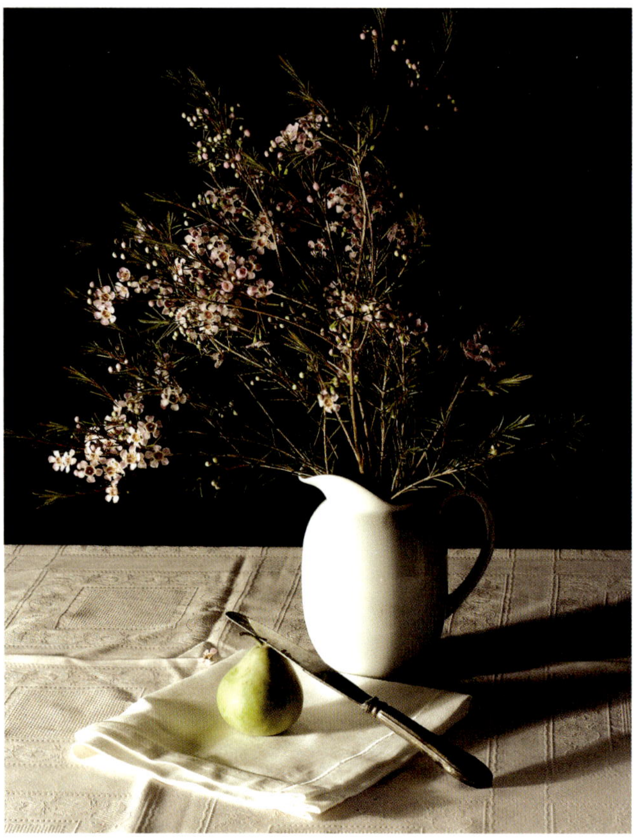

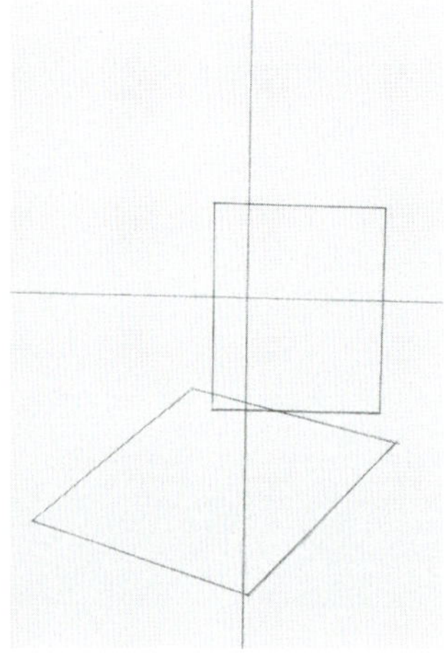

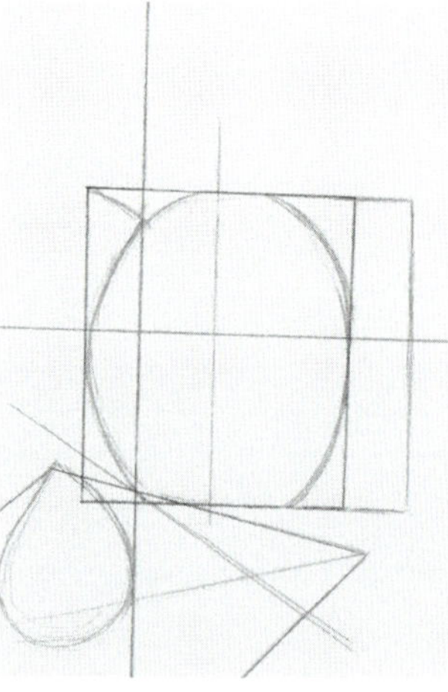

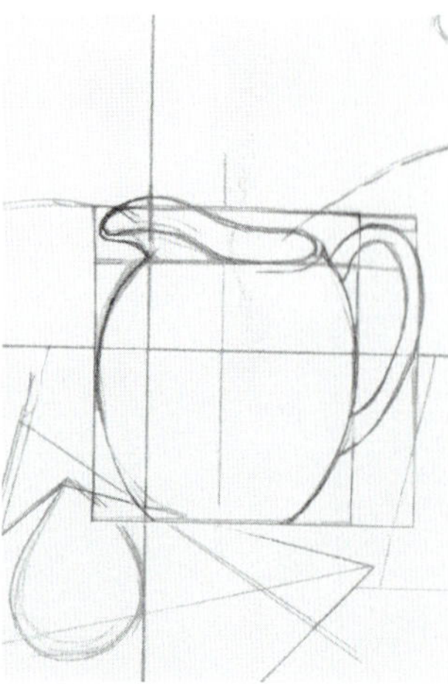

To understand the model's forms, begin with very simple diagrams drawn with a few lines. Two straight lines, one horizontal and another vertical that cross at the center point, are sufficient to define axes of symmetry. The shapes of the vase and the napkin are synthesized from a square and a rhomboid.

The vase is drawn based on a rectangle. If you measure it, you will realize that the space occupied by the handle is approximately one-fifth the width of the pitcher. A rectangle is drawn to its left to indicate this space. The pear extends a little beyond the middle of the pitcher.

To draw the top part of the pitcher you can use almost the same measurement as you used for the handle. A rectangle drawn horizontally contains the opening of the pitcher. A couple of diagonal lines indicate the placement of the knife and the fold in the tablecloth. Now, begin to sketch the space that will be occupied by the bouquet of flowers.

When you attempt a more complex form, begin by making a good diagram; this will give you an advantage when you begin to draw your subject.

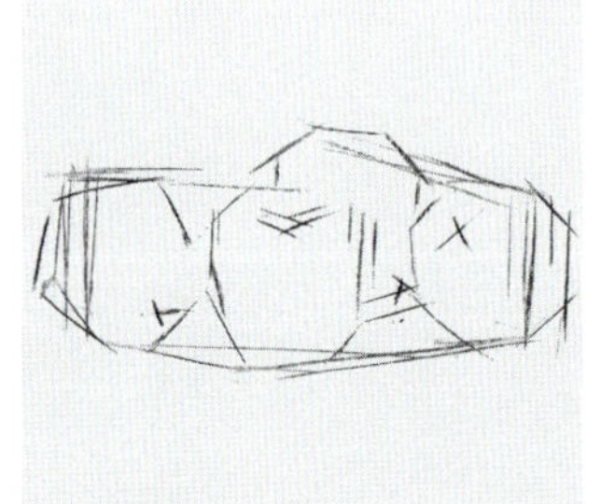

In this phase the work is done with a very sharp pencil. To avoid constant sharpening, rub the pencil against the paper at an angle.

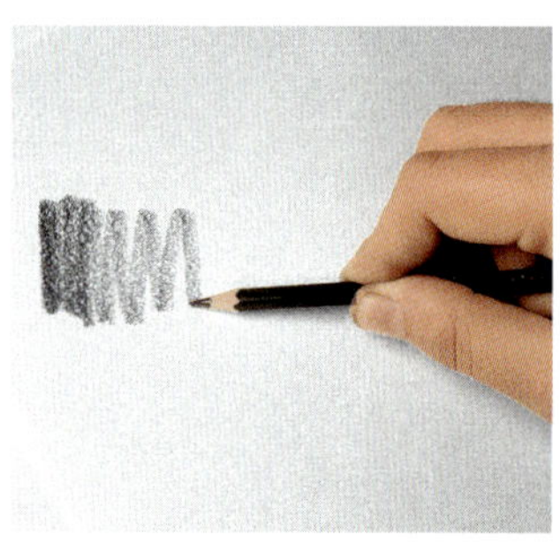

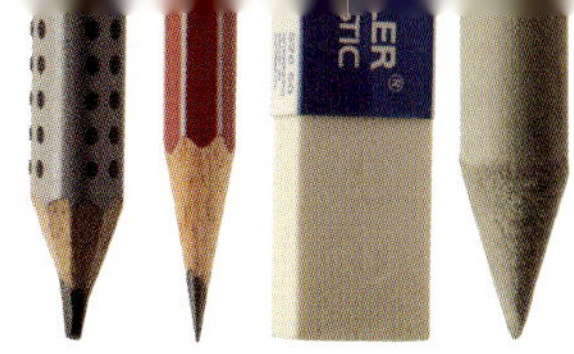

8.2

DRAWING THE WHOLE. The main forms of the model, drawn with a 2B pencil, are based on a very simple diagram. The goal of this stage is for the beginner to understand the importance of working the "whole," (the overall drawing) and paying attention to the shading and details.

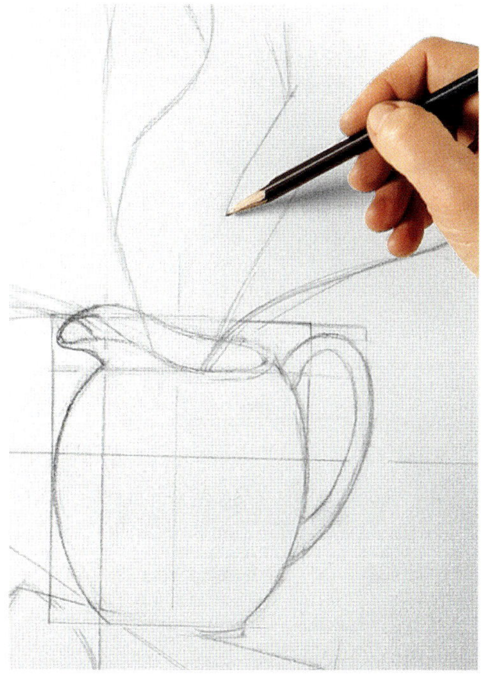

Notice this simple approach to the outlines of the objects and the bouquet's main branches,. New lines are superimposed on the previous ones to provide a first look at the whole. Draw these lines very cleanly to avoid confusion later.

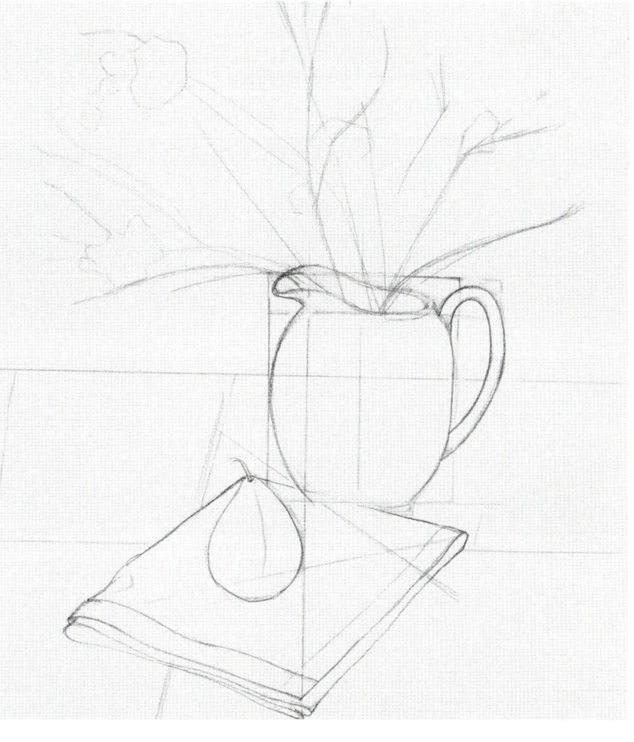

A solid preliminary sketch reinforces the drawing, which becomes surer as you define more parts. This way, it is much easier to indicate the definitive lines of the pitcher, the napkin, and the pear over the preliminary diagram. The stems of the bouquet are also sketched out in this phase.

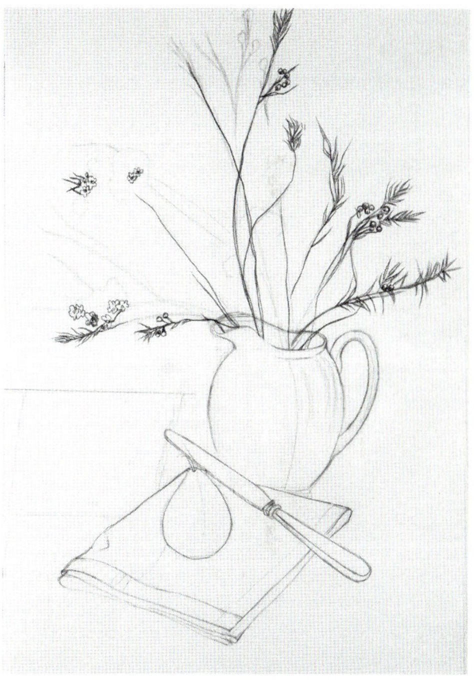

Redefine the structure of the bouquet by darkening the lines. Use the diagonal edge of the napkin to define the placement of the knife. Once the compositional and structural lines are no longer needed, you can easily remove them with an eraser.

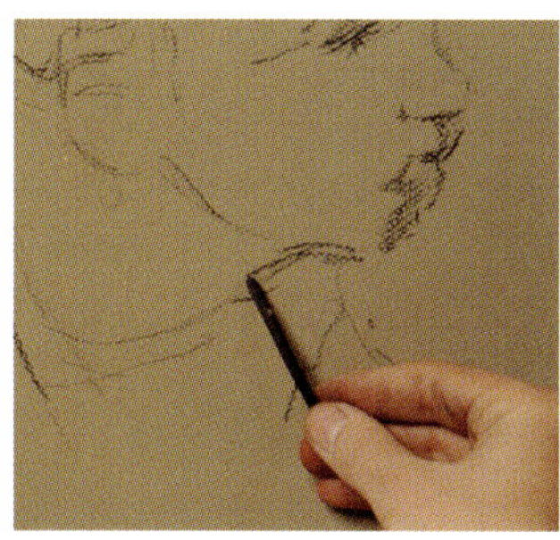

Some professional artists superimpose several lines on the same outline when they draw. A final revision will tell you which version will be the definitive one; highlight it with a heavier and more intense line.

8.3

DEFINING THE PARTS. Now is the time to add the details. Draw them with precision, paying attention to each one of the model's parts: the reflections on the metal, the shaded areas, the foliage, the bouquet's flowers, and the folds of the tablecloth. In this phase, lines are intensified and shaded areas take a more important role in the drawing.

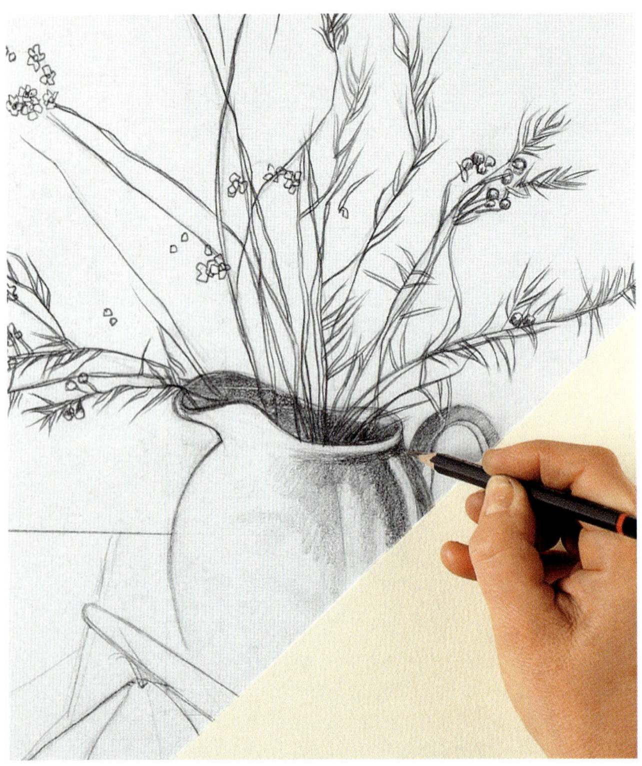

From this point on you should use a 4B graphite pencil. Draw the flowers and the leaves in more detail and apply the first areas of shading. Use a sheet of paper as protection to prevent the drawing surface from becoming smudged as you rub your hand on it.

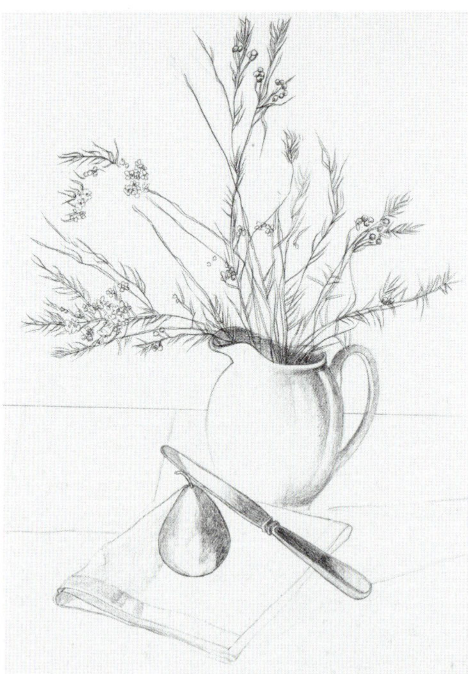

As you progress, draw darker lines each time to de-emphasize the earlier lines that served as guides. Continue the gray shading of the pitcher on the knife and the pear to give them a sense of volume. Apply the shading very lightly so no lines are apparent.

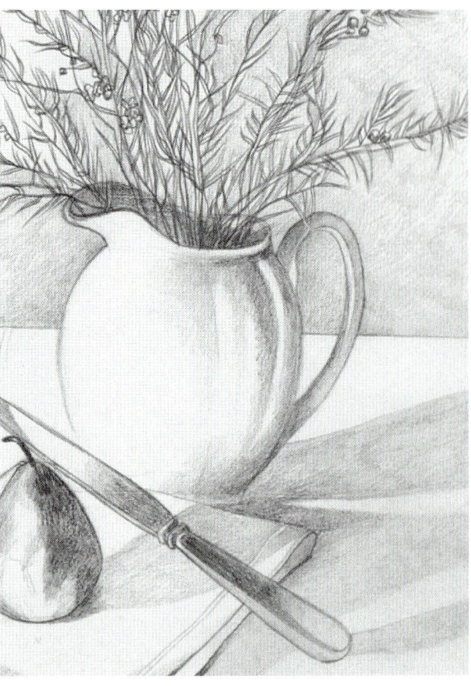

Cover the drawing's background with light shading. Do not press too hard on the paper because the idea is to eliminate these lines by rubbing lightly with a blending stick. Draw the shadows projected on the table with evenly applied gray shading; draw the outlines with a very light line.

Learn to draw volume with a graphite pencil, barely applying pressure on the pencil. This enables you to create very soft modeling without visible lines.

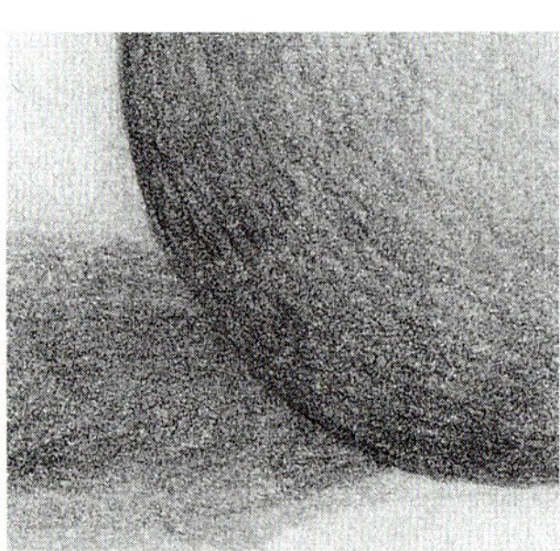

It is also important to practice creating gradations with graphite. This skill will be handy when you paint the model's background.

When you get to this point, you may consider the drawing to be complete; the most important areas of the still life are finished. All that is left is to darken the background, which is between and behind the flowers. For consistency, the projected shadows must be darkened with new shading and the folds of the cloth that covers the table must be better defined. Drawing by Almudena Carreño.

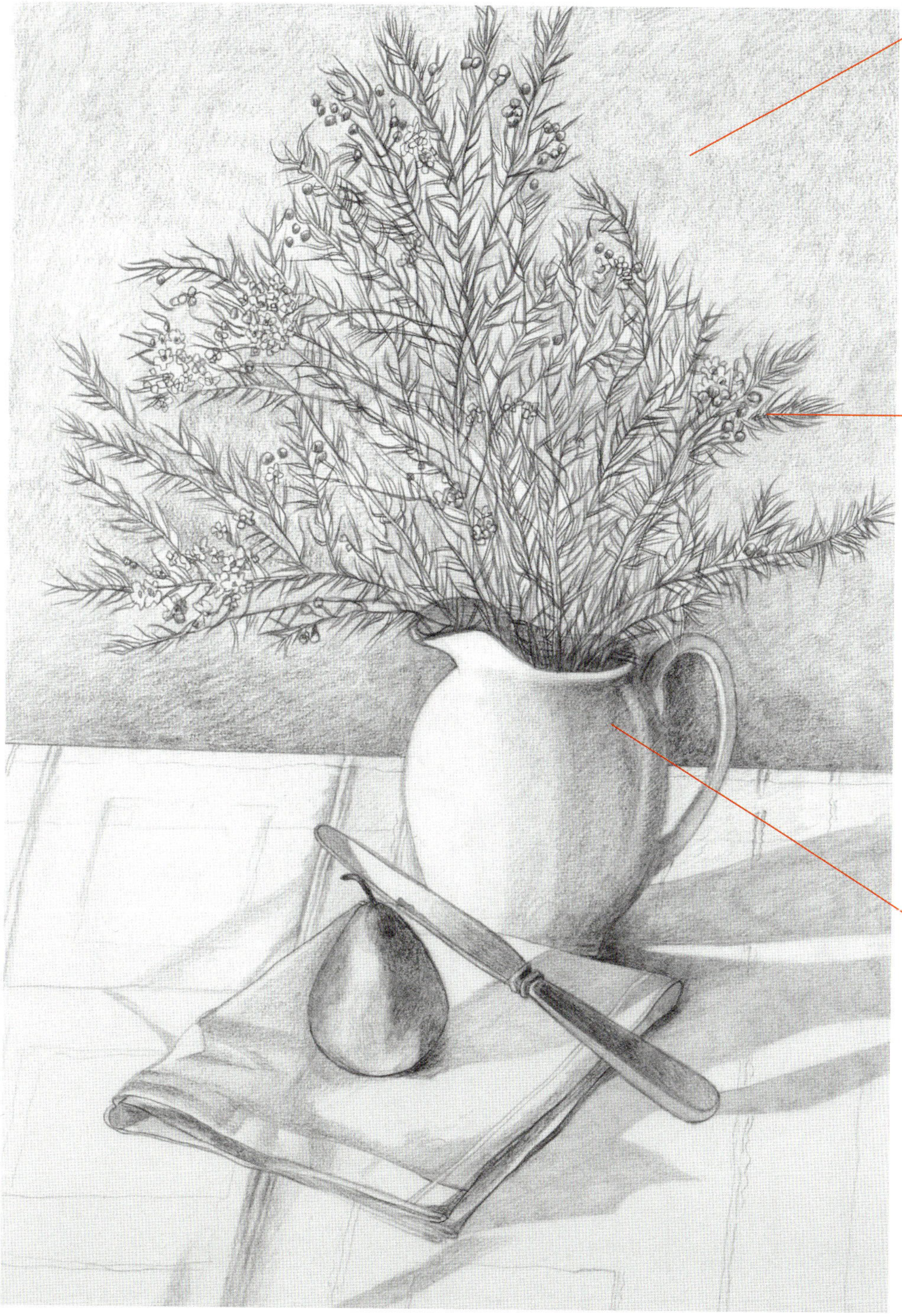

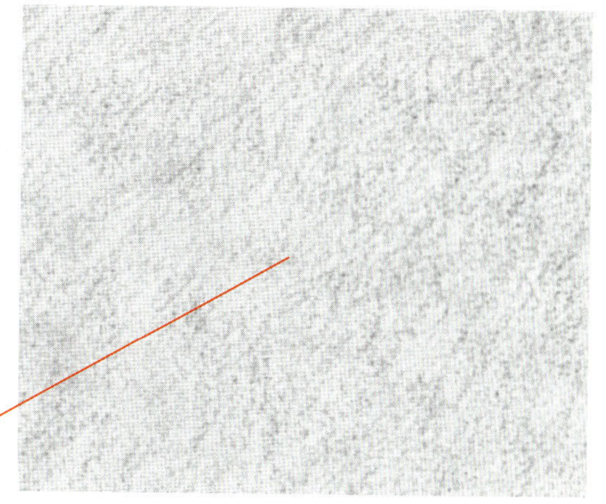

In this final stage, complete the background with very soft shading. Work with a pencil whose point is flat and worn so the graphite can be rubbed and extended over the paper evenly.

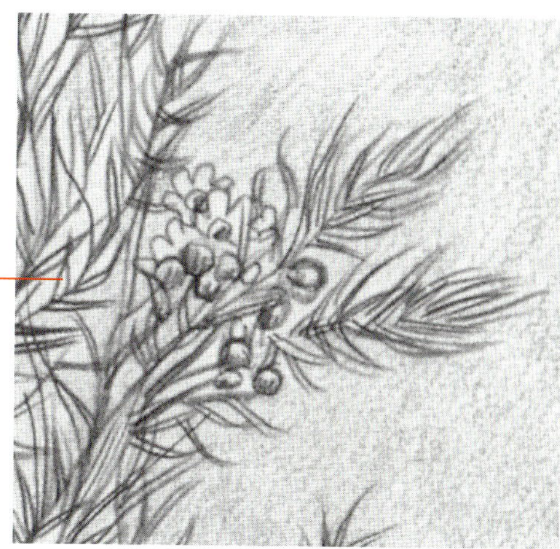

Notice how the details evolve through the process of drawing: The darker the background that surrounds the bouquet, the darker the lines will be that define the leaves and the flowers.

The gradated areas convey a feeling of volume to the objects. Here, a soft gradation defines the pitcher's roundness and its soft and shiny texture.

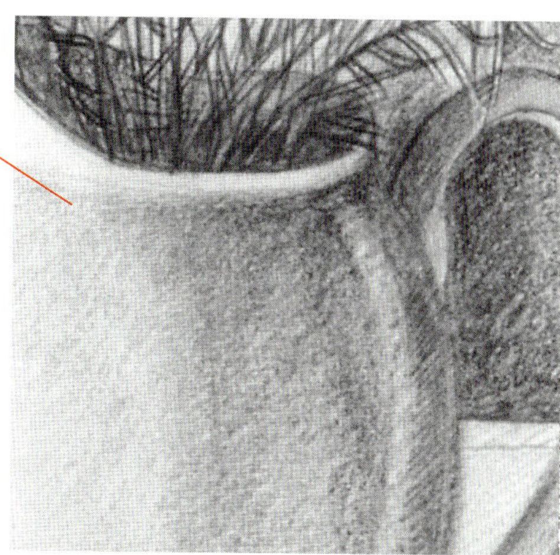

CHOOSING INTERESTING COMPOSITIONS. Often, you will come across discordant elements that distract you from the main subject and that do not add anything interesting to the drawing. One way to find new, interesting approaches is to use a frame, which you can make yourself using two pieces of mat board, each cut in the shape of an L.

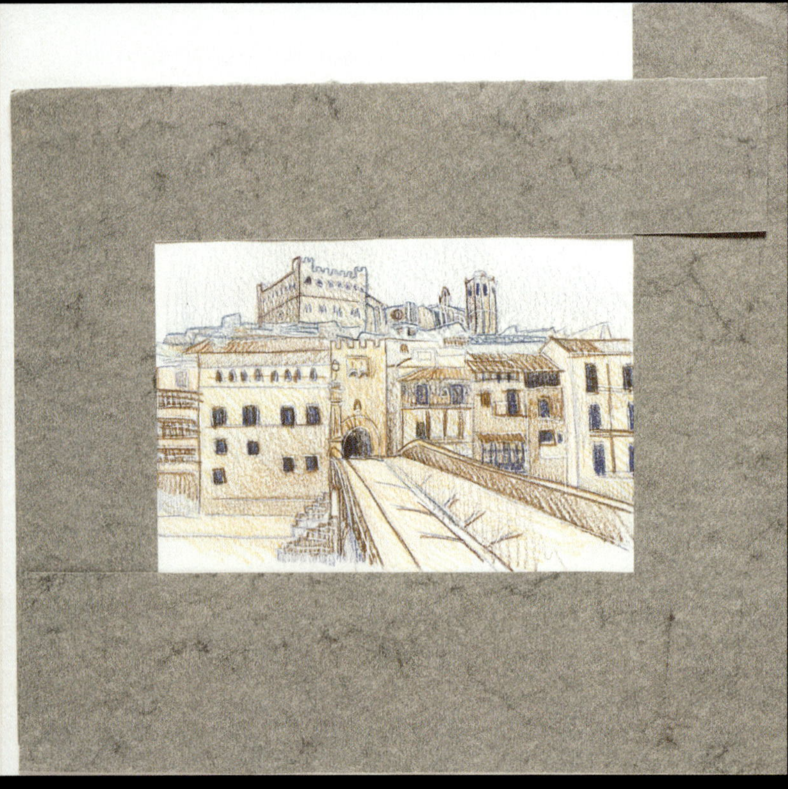

This view of a group of houses has a composition that is excessively monotonous, too static, and without interest.

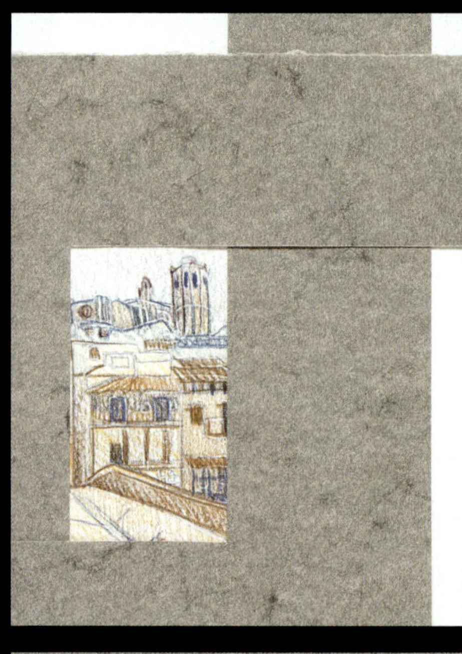

A vertical layout emphasizes the shapes of the buildings much more, even when some of the façades are cut out.

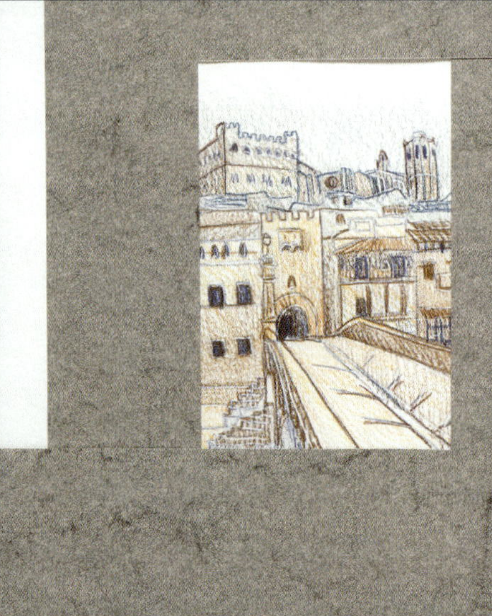

Although this is a centered and balanced composition, the position of the frame provides greater interest than the original layout, emphasizing the vertical effect of the buildings.

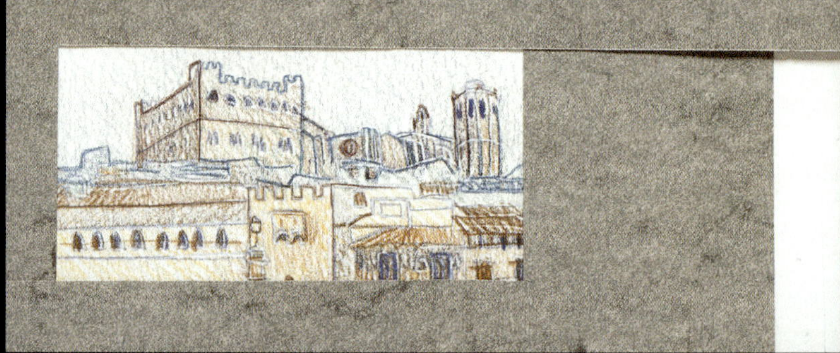

Another way to add interest is to choose a horizontal layout that is based on the upper part of the drawing.

COMPOSITION. Any composition is in some way a selective representation of a theme. Each image is a unique observation and conveys a personal point of view. Drawing sketches offers different ways for selecting a layout and lets you try out different possibilities. Shown below are the most common ones.

EXCLUDING CERTAIN PARTS OF THE DRAWING. There is no rule that dictates the inclusion of an element in a drawing just because it's there. If for compositional or other reasons you need to cut off part of the model or eliminate some elements, you should not hesitate to do so.

BALANCING OUT EMPTY SPACES.
Nontraditional artists often use compositions that are off center and out of balance. They play off the area occupied by the model against an empty space that acts as a counterbalance. The resulting spatial tension adds great interest.

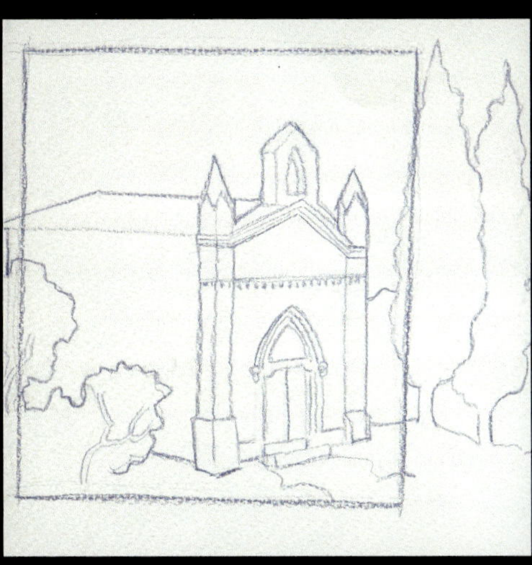

Here the artist has chosen a composition that includes only the small church and excludes all the other elements.

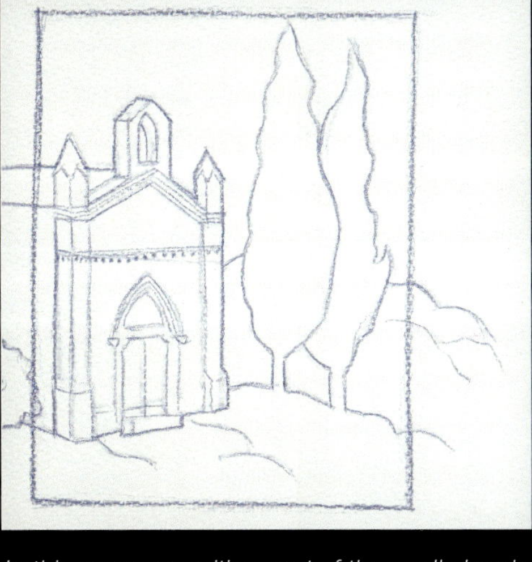

In this new composition, part of the small church has been cut off to include the cypress trees on the right.

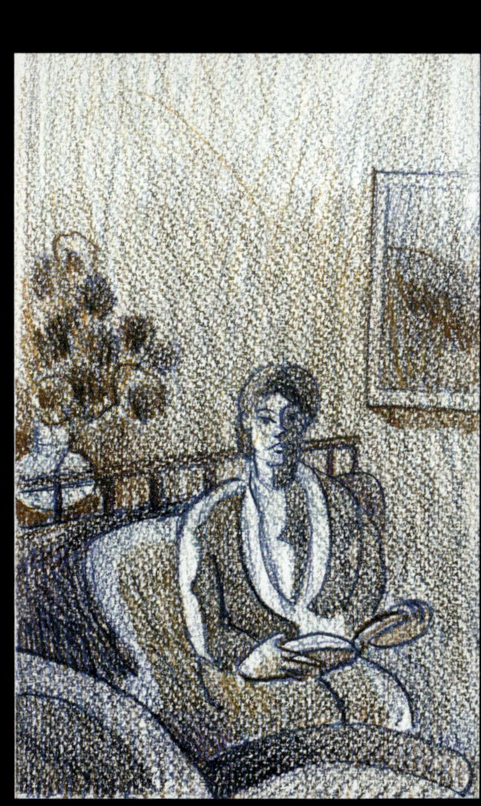

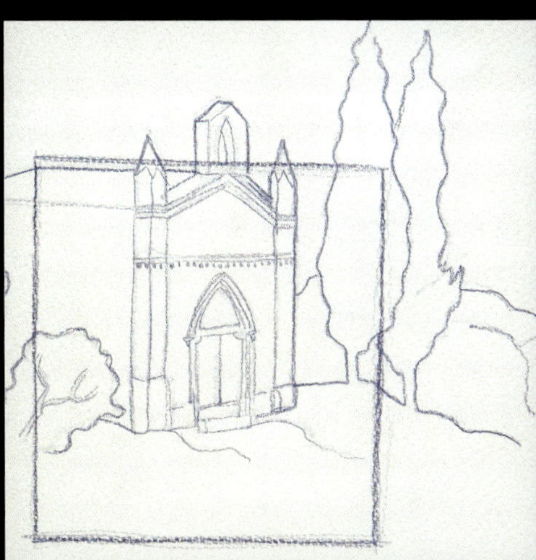

A new composition directs the viewer's attention toward the ground, creating a dialogue between the empty space of the ground and the architectural features of the church's façade.

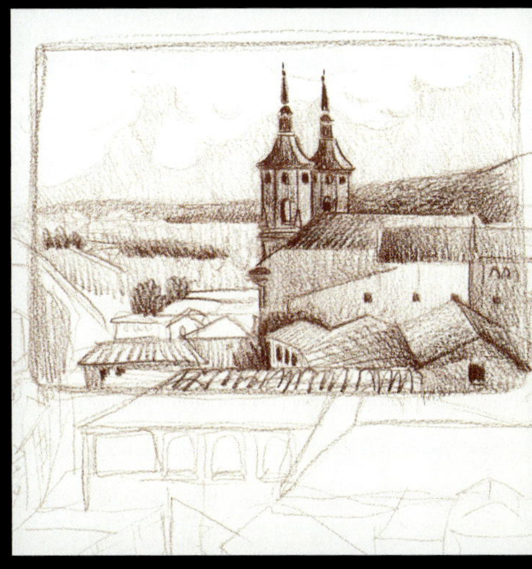

Sometimes, as you draw a subject, you may realize that you are only interested in part of it. If this happens, you must select a new composition and improvise the rest. From this point you can create a sketch that will allow you to work with the theme in more depth.

This vertical format places the model at the bottom of the composition, while the top area is left empty, covered with only a simple gradation.

When drawing, you do not necessarily have to accept the model as you see it. The most important thing is to study it and emphasize some aspects of the subject, minimize others, and eliminate those that are altogether irrelevant.

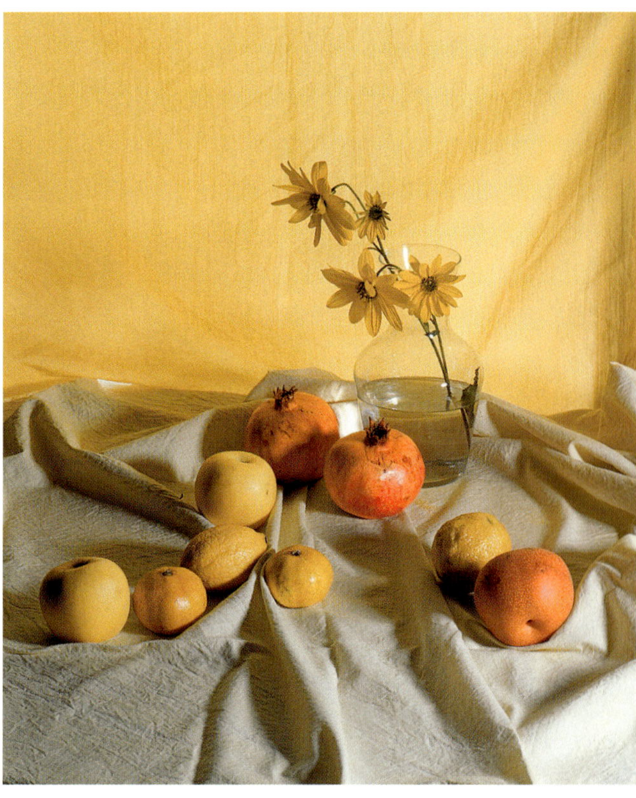

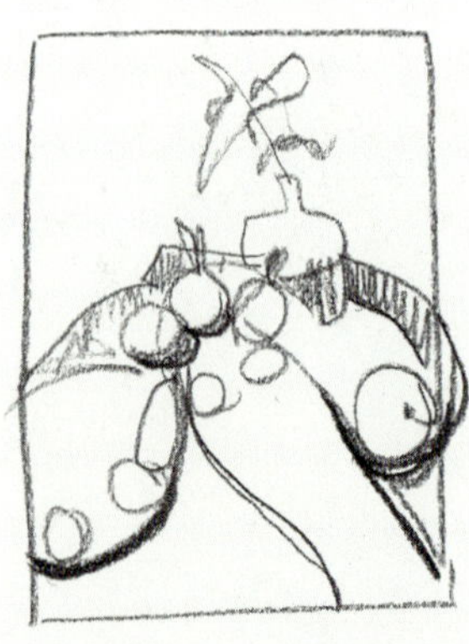

When you analyze the drawing you may notice that the pieces of fruit are all in a line. In this sketch the layout crops the subject, resulting in this composition. The fruit is placed along a curved line, forming arabesques.

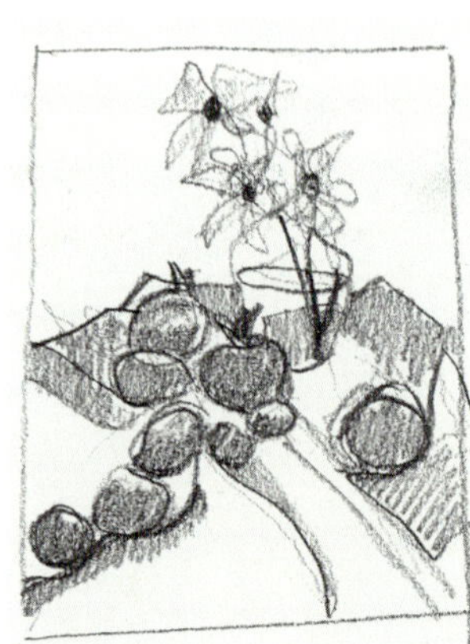

Although it has a layout similar to that of the previous one, this sketch focuses on an analysis of light and shadow, marking the darkest areas with gray shading.

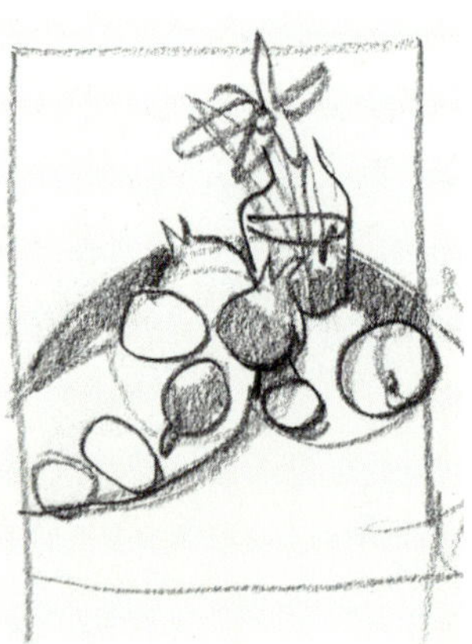

This sketch is yet another study of compositional elements. To create variations, the artist simply shaded several pieces of fruit and reinforced the tablecloth's folds with shaded areas. However, the shading is too fragmented and dispersed.

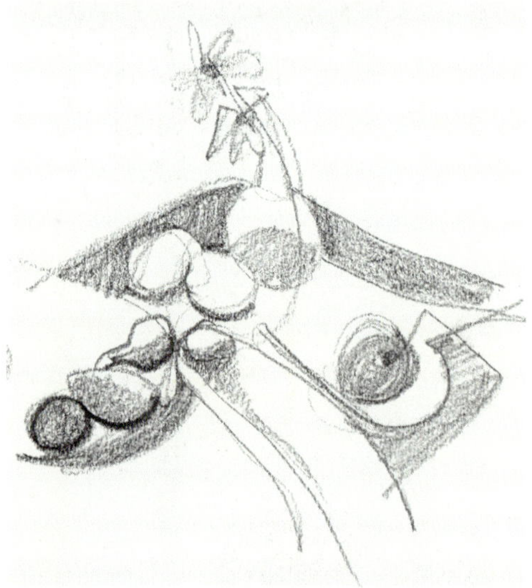

After a final study, it looks like this is going to be the definitive layout. The fruit is placed along the two compositional curves. The pitcher with the flowers breaks up the symmetry because it is located somewhat to the right, and the bottom part is drawn as an empty space.

ANALYZING COMPOSITION AND LAYOUT. In essence, a drawing's composition and layout make reference to the artist's attitude toward the model—to the way he or she sees the subject, chooses its most interesting parts, and organizes and combines all the elements that form part of the work. Therefore, it is a good idea to make many preliminary studies to experiment with the formal disposition of the model.

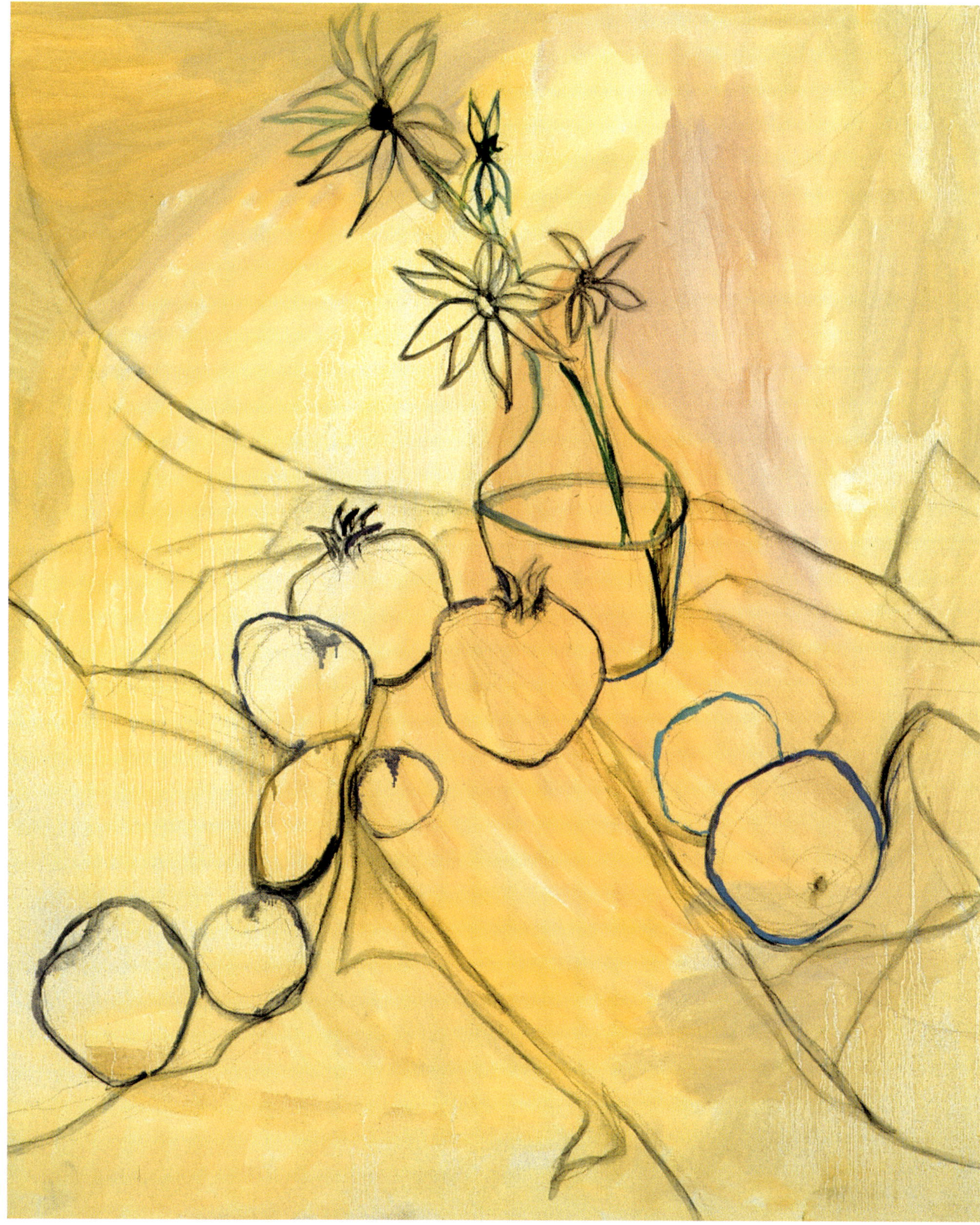

From the previous sketches, the artist arrived at a synthesis of the model interpreted with basic lines, respecting the order of the objects placed on the table while slightly modifying their distribution and size.

A DIFFERENT LAYOUT. There are some traditional compositional layouts that should not be disregarded, but it is also very interesting to interpret some fragments of a scene from a personal perspective. This is the approach of the following exercise. This layout, instead of concentrating on the view from the balcony, which would be the conventional approach, focuses instead on the effects that the light creates on the room's floor. The interior is drawn with sanguine chalk, which is applied the same way as charcoal, but it adheres to the paper better.

9.1

THE INTERIOR SPACE. The choice of layout, the absence of furniture, and the perspective view of the floor tiles make it easy to represent this interior scene with a simple perspective sketch.

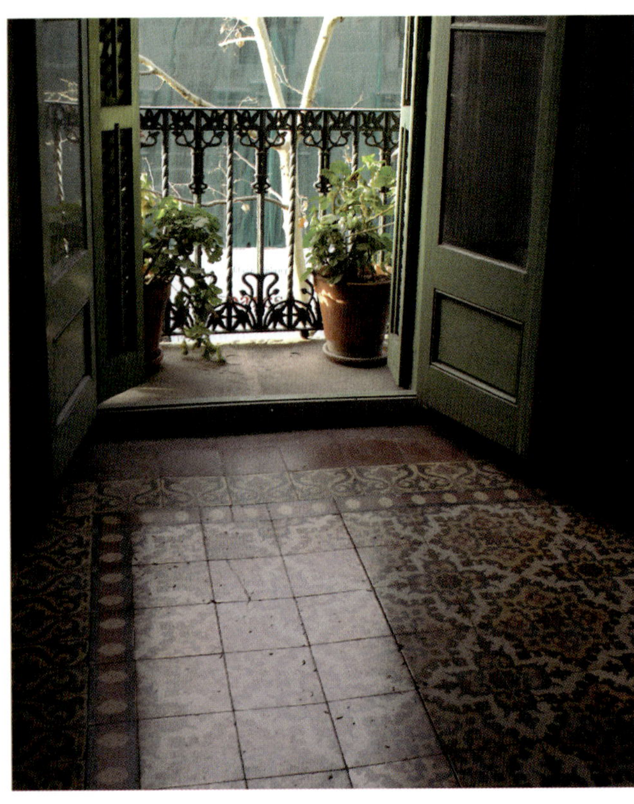

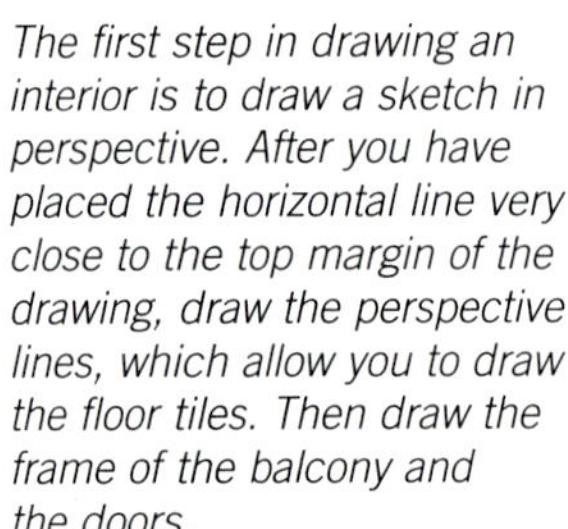

The first step in drawing an interior is to draw a sketch in perspective. After you have placed the horizontal line very close to the top margin of the drawing, draw the perspective lines, which allow you to draw the floor tiles. Then draw the frame of the balcony and the doors.

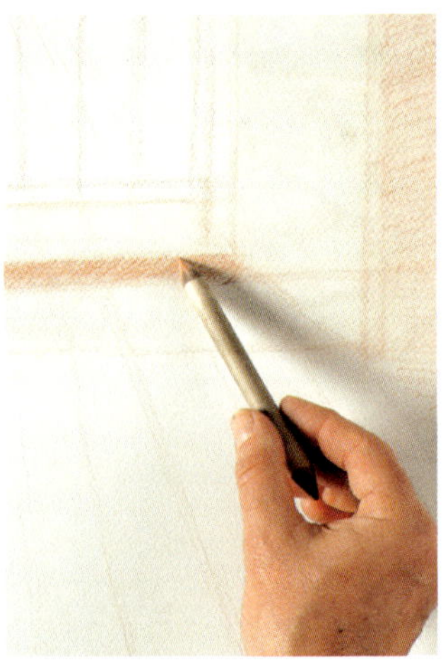

Cover the back wall and the doors with light shading. The pressure applied with the sanguine, whether in stick or pencil form, should be minimal. Avoid hatching to make blending easier later. You will do this by rubbing lightly with a blending stick.

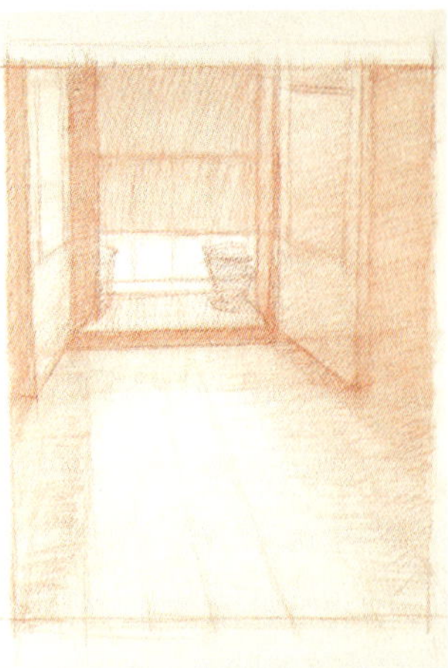

In its early stages the drawing should have even, homogeneous tones. The lines should be very light, barely standing out against the shading. Here, only the lighted areas are left uncovered: the doors, the panes of glass, the bottom part of the composition, and the floor.

It is possible to draw with the blending stick when it is very full of sanguine. In some cases, it is employed as a useful drawing tool that creates very soft shading.

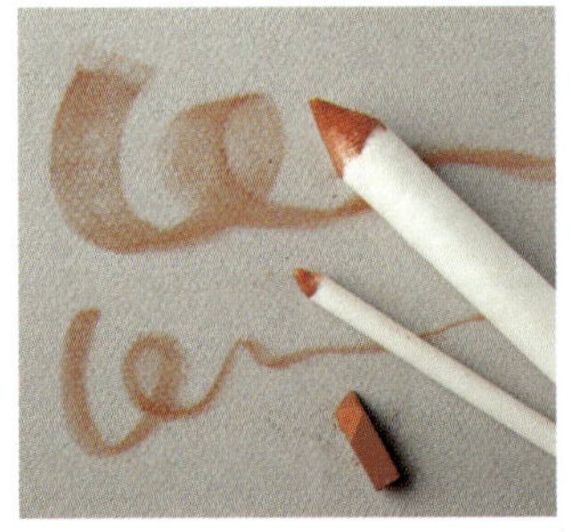

Create the preliminary drawing and the initial shading by drawing softly with the tip of the pencil or the sanguine chalk. The tool should barely touch the surface of the paper when shading so your marks will be very light.

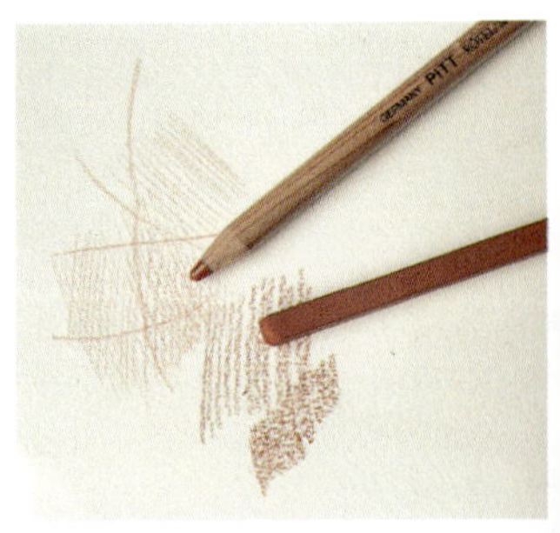

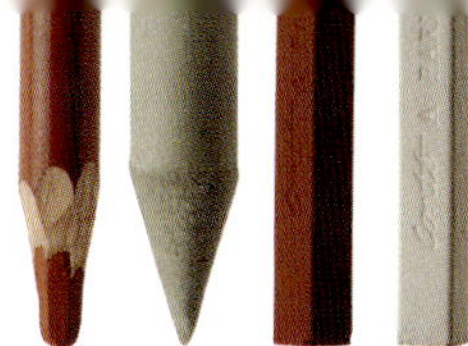

9.2

SHADING AND MODELING. The technique of modeling with sanguine is based mainly on tonal gradation and blending. It is important to pay attention to light and reflections, because they differentiate the planes and spaces of the interior.

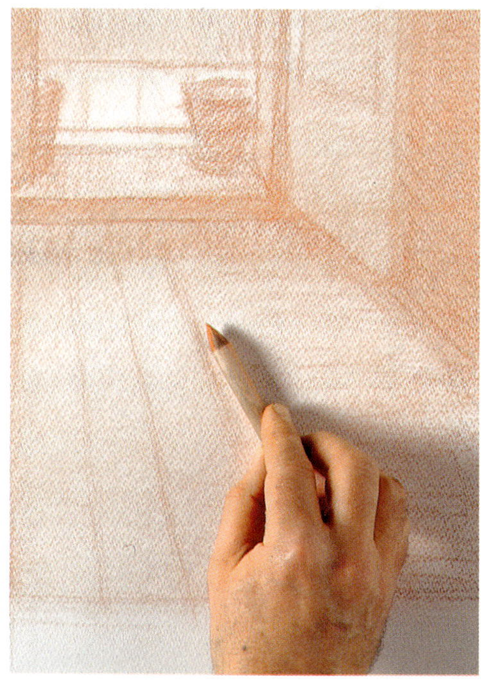

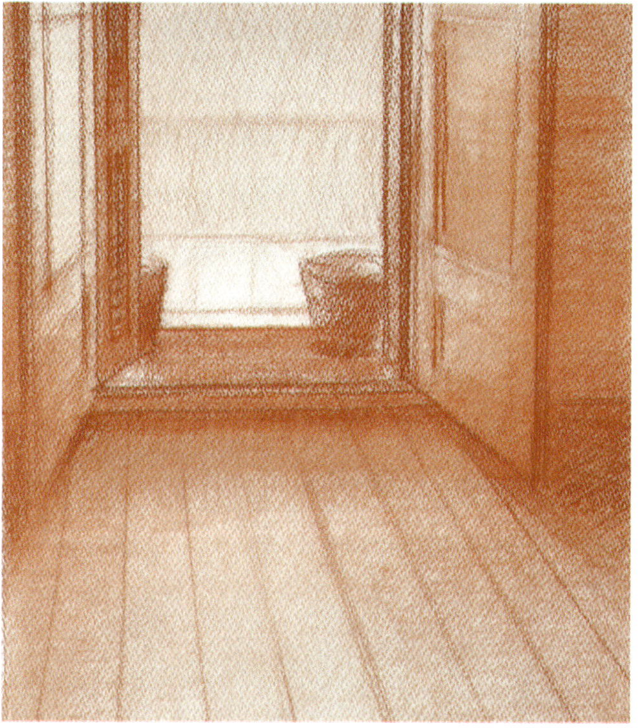

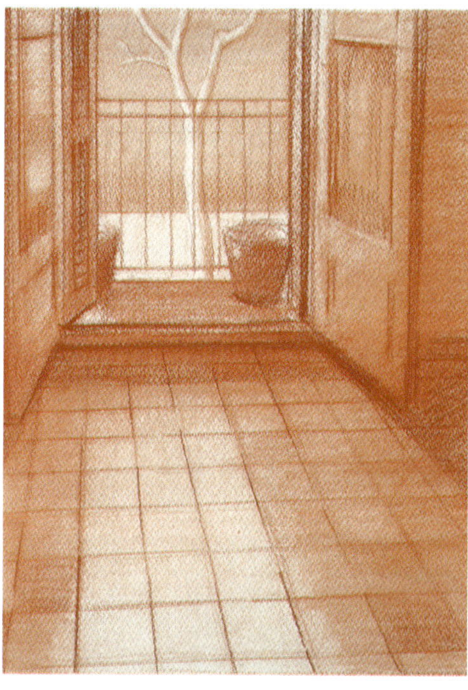

Darken the previous shading slowly and progressively, leaving the most illuminated areas blank. Then, to integrate the light areas with the shaded ones, rub the entire surface of the paper with the side of the blending stick to remove the boundaries between areas of light and shadow and cover any spots of the paper that may have been left uncovered.

When the first values are completely developed, begin to plan the intermediate tones, work the gradated areas of the floor, and darken the outlines of the doors. Work on the background wall, where the shadows need to be intensified with the sanguine stick.

Draw the lines of the balcony, the railing, and the doorframe and darken the lines of the floor tiles. With a sanguine pencil, draw the tree in the background, which stands out thanks to the shading around it. The modeling does not look heavy, but instead is light and atmospheric, a result of the tone of sanguine.

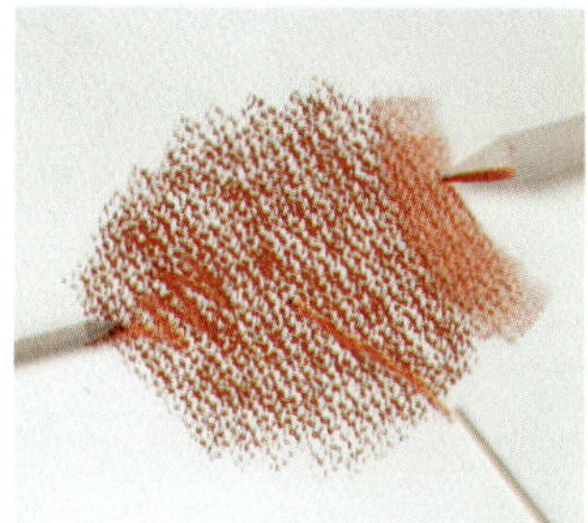

To create diffused shading, first apply shading with sanguine. Then, rub this shaded area with the blending stick to make it denser and more diffuse.

9.3

DRAWING THE ORNAMENTAL ELEMENTS. Once the tonal values have been resolved, the final phase consists of clarifying the details, including the ornamental elements of the railing and the pattern of the floor tiles.

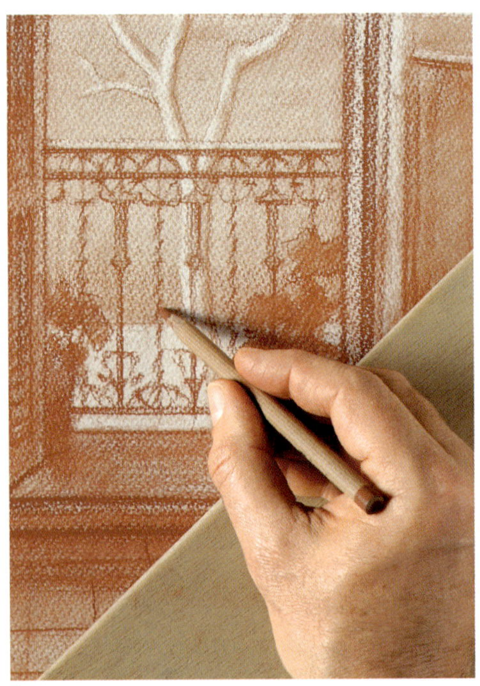

Emphasize contrasts by shading and outlining the dark areas with a sanguine pencil. Touch up the tree's outline and finish the flowerpots on the balcony, which are silhouetted against the light, with very dense shading and hatching. Rest your hand on a sheet of paper to avoid getting the drawing dirty when you rub your hand against it.

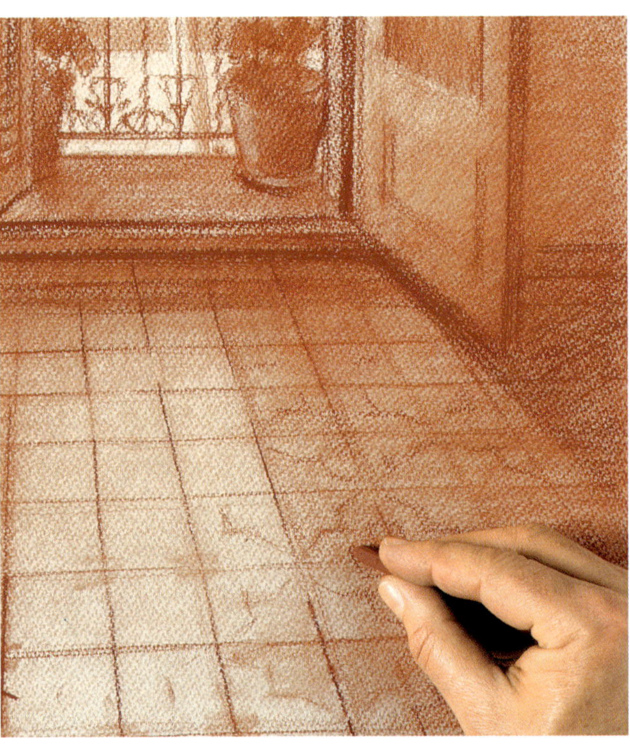

With the tip of the chalk stick, draw the ornamental motifs of the floor tile. It is not necessary to completely draw the tiles; it is sufficient to outline a few of them with sketched lines, applying very light pressure. In this case, it is more interesting to suggest the remaining tiles than to draw them in detail.

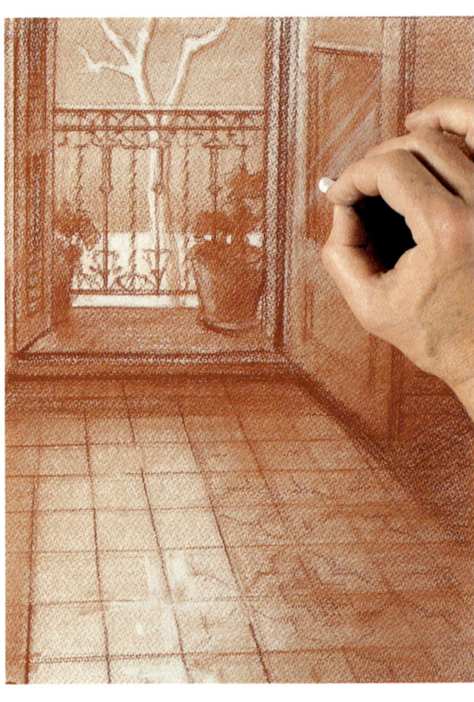

Use the white chalk to create the most important highlights to the doorframe and the windowpanes. They will stand out dramatically because you have covered the entire surface of the paper with light sanguine color during the drawing process. Using the tip of the chalk produces more intense highlights.

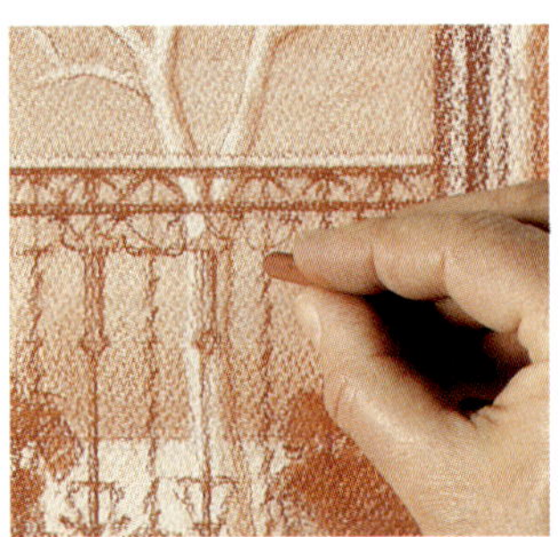

Detail the ornamental motifs of the iron railing with the tip of the sanguine stick. It is important to pay attention to the model in order to replicate its forms correctly.

Do not touch up the drawing or work the details too much. A quick drawing that leaves some areas unfinished gives the work a freshness that is lost when the drawing is too finished.

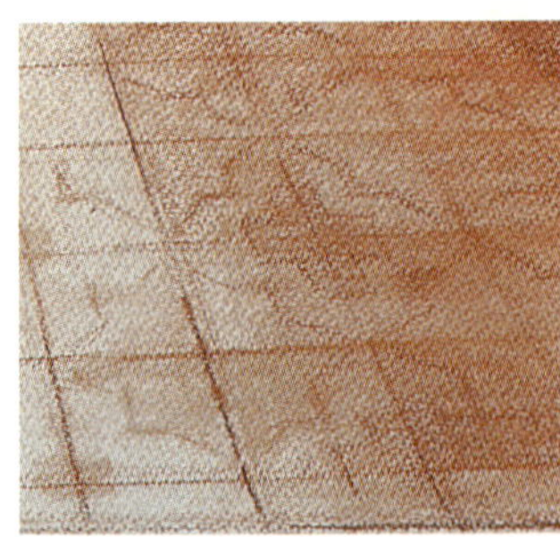

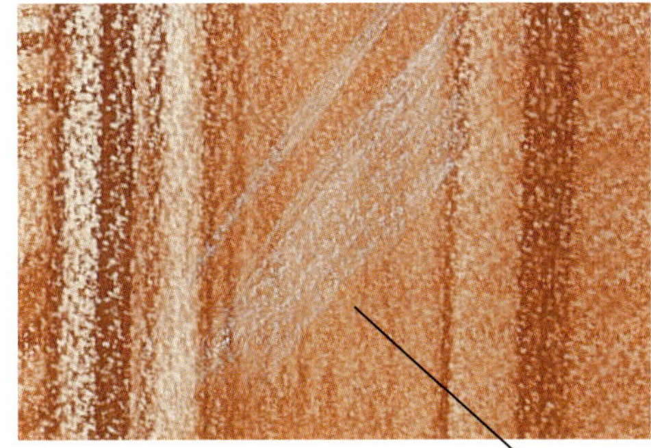

Darken the outlines that you wish to emphasize. This treatment only works when it is very carefully placed and does not extend indiscriminately over the entire drawing.

The success of sanguine resides in the warmth and softness that it brings to the drawing. Additionally, it is a medium that is easy to control and creates rich tonal gradations. A very convincing drawing of an interior theme that is based on the contrast of light and shadow can be achieved by alternating three or four values. Drawing by Carlant.

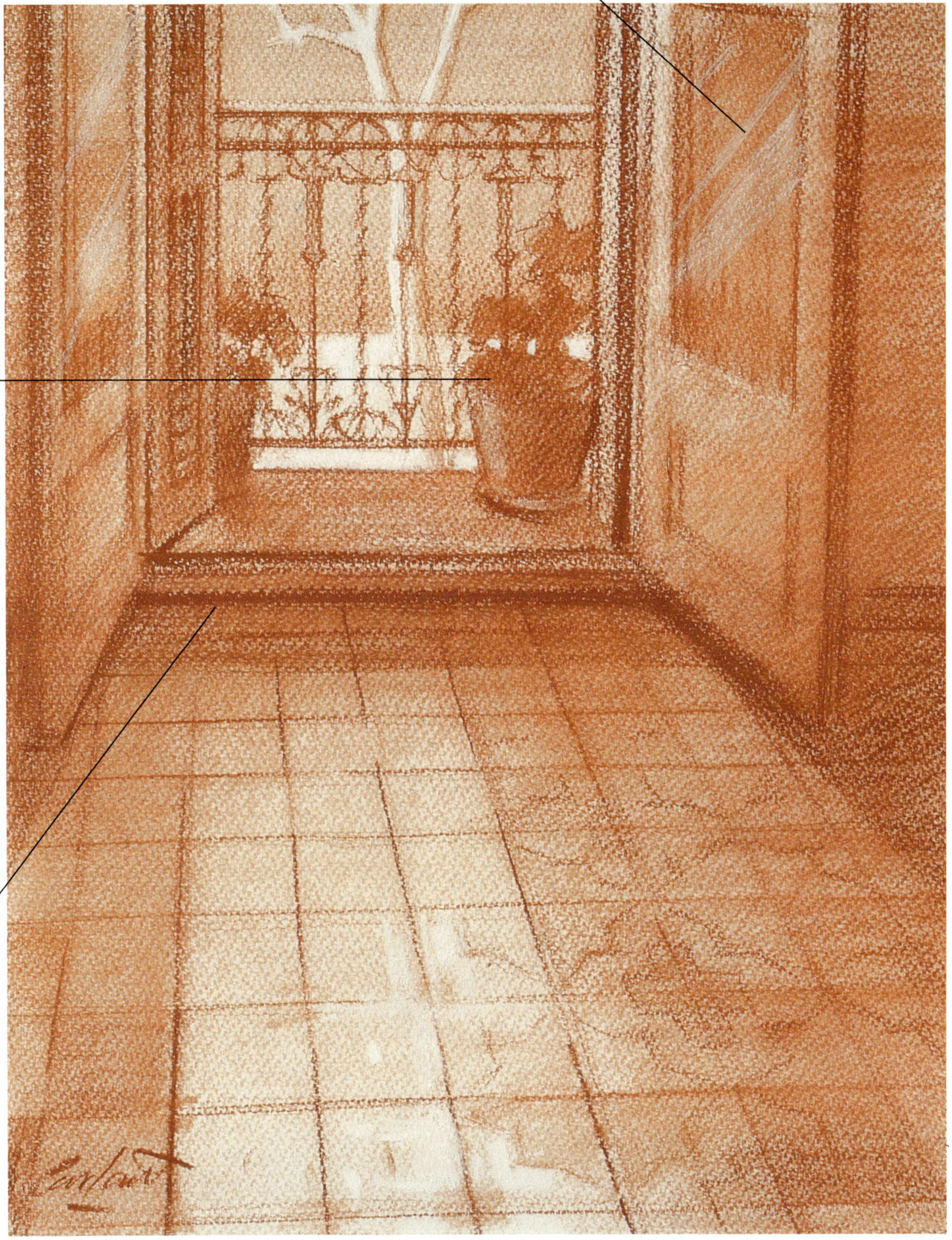

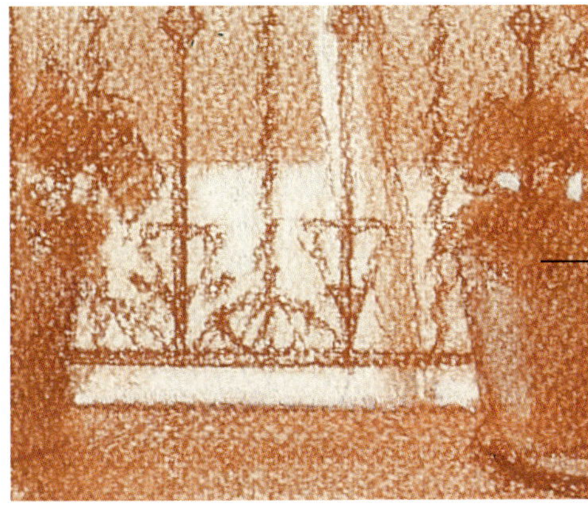

A few parallel lines are enough to describe the texture of the glass. Work done with white chalk has to be very well thought out; if too many highlights are applied they will lack relevance.

The effect of light coming from the street is created through contrast. This makes the lighter tones, when placed next to darker ones, appear much lighter.

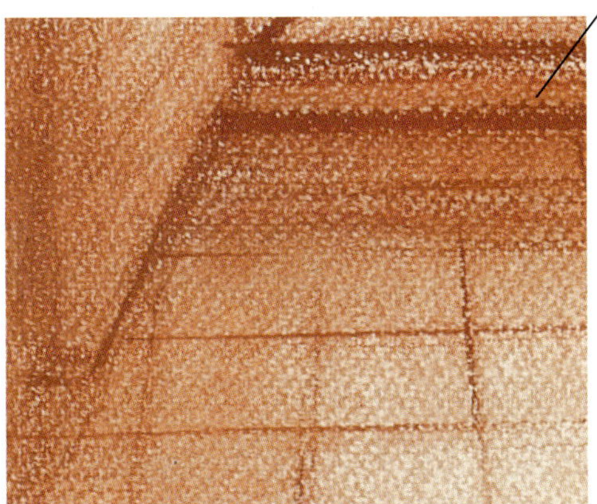

THE GEOMETRIC APPROACH. When you draw an object from a model, sometimes you have to simulate the depth that the eye sees by using intuitive perspective or some geometric method. You should become familiar with the graphic language used to geometrically represent three-dimensional forms in different projection systems, and their application in sketches and freehand perspective drawings.

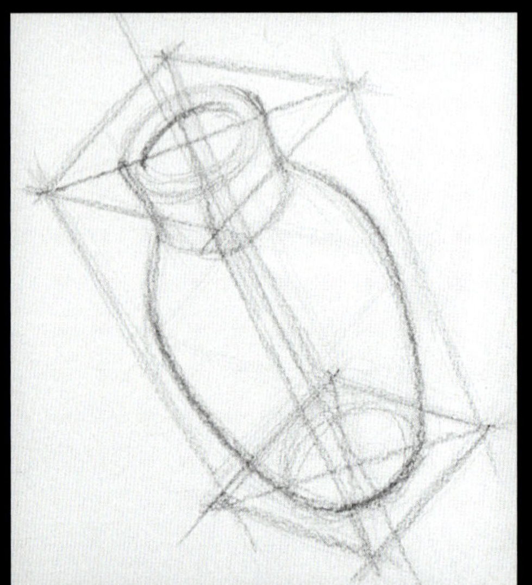

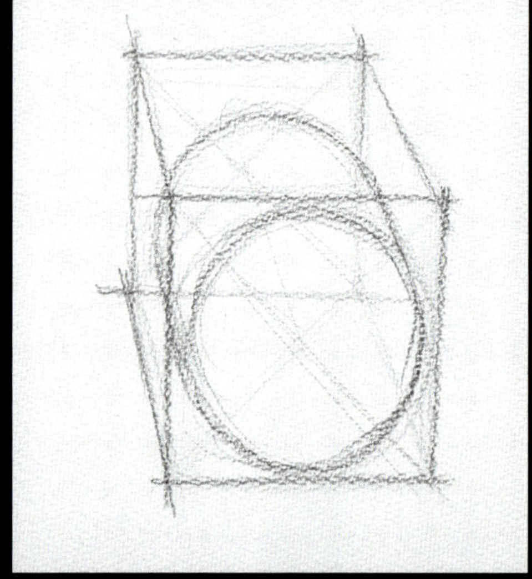

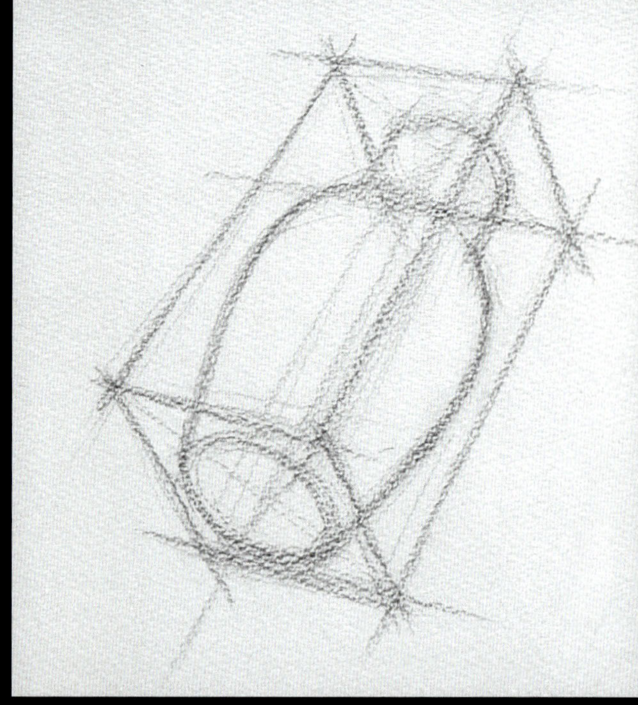

If you have difficulty drawing a tilted object with obvious perspective or foreshortening effects, it is best to draw it in a box. By using this box as a guide, you can draw the object from any angle.

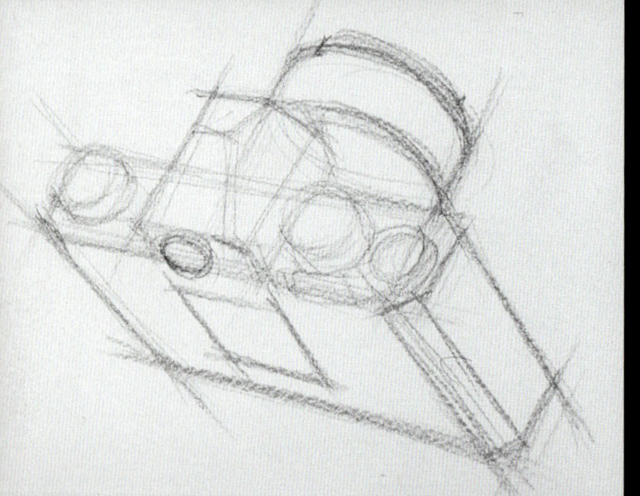

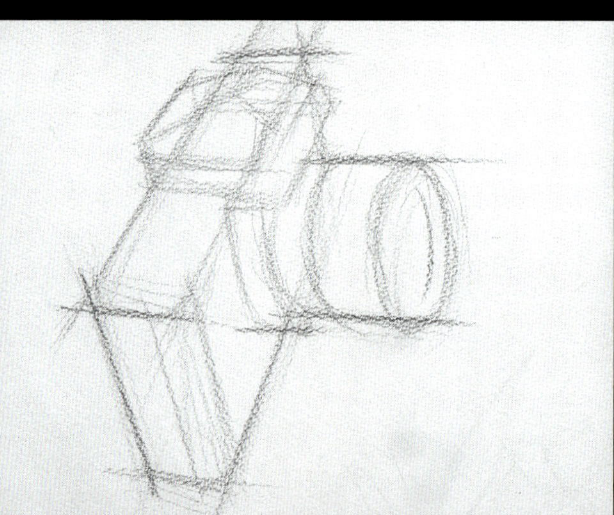

This imaginary box defines and synthesizes the three-dimensional effect of the object. Changing the point of view and rotating the box will allow you to draw the object without ever losing the perspective effect.

FORESHORTENING. This is the influence of the perspective effect on an object that extends directly toward the viewer. It creates a very evident contrast in scale between the object's closest and farthest parts. It can be seen in the way of representing an object so that it is arranged perpendicular and angled in respect to the viewer.

OVERSCALED PARTS. The art of foreshortening consists of representing an object from a point of view so that its dimensions are modified by the perspective. Such effects require the artist to enlarge forms nearest the viewer to accentuate the effect of perspective on the model.

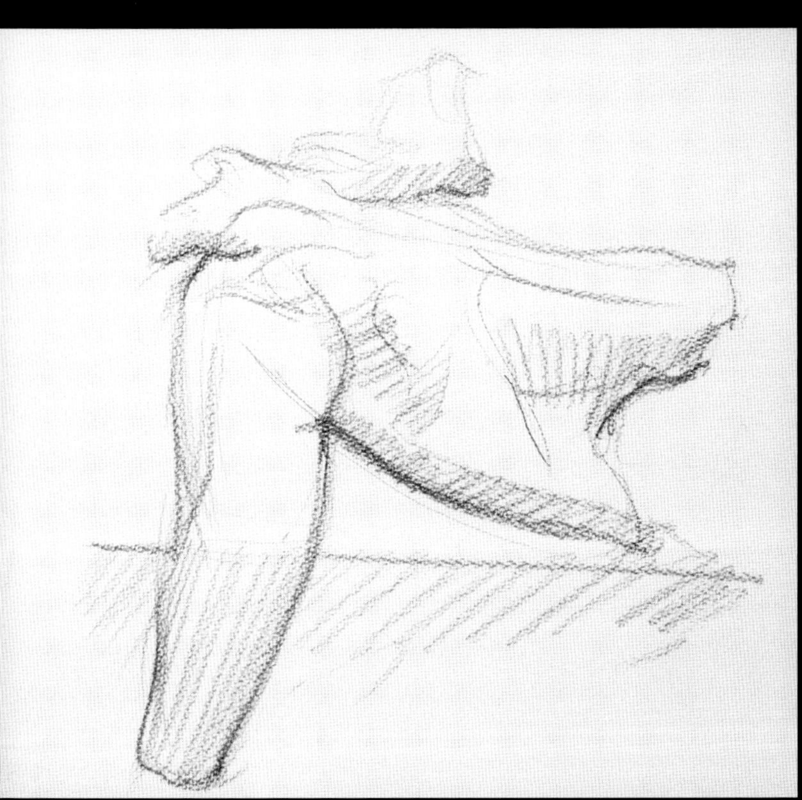

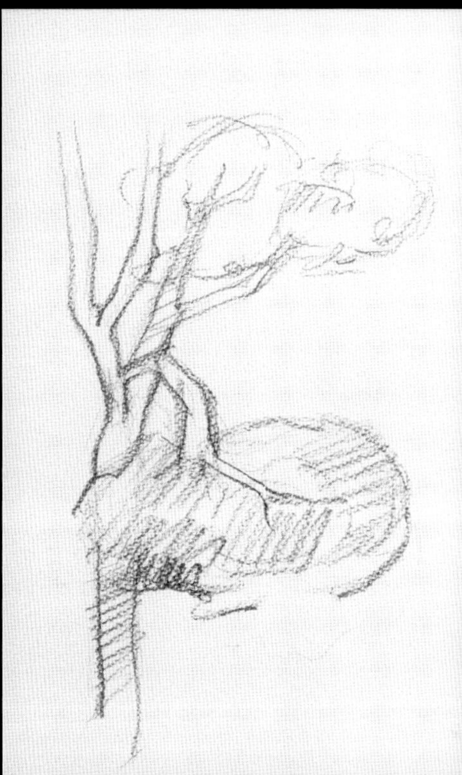

Foreshortening alters the proportional relationships of an object. The part of a foreshortened sweater that is closest to you will be overscaled; in this case the sleeve, altered by perspective, looks larger than the rest of the sweater.

The same thing happens to a tree that has a branch that visually advances toward the viewer. Knowing this, you should enlarge the branch in relation to the rest of the tree.

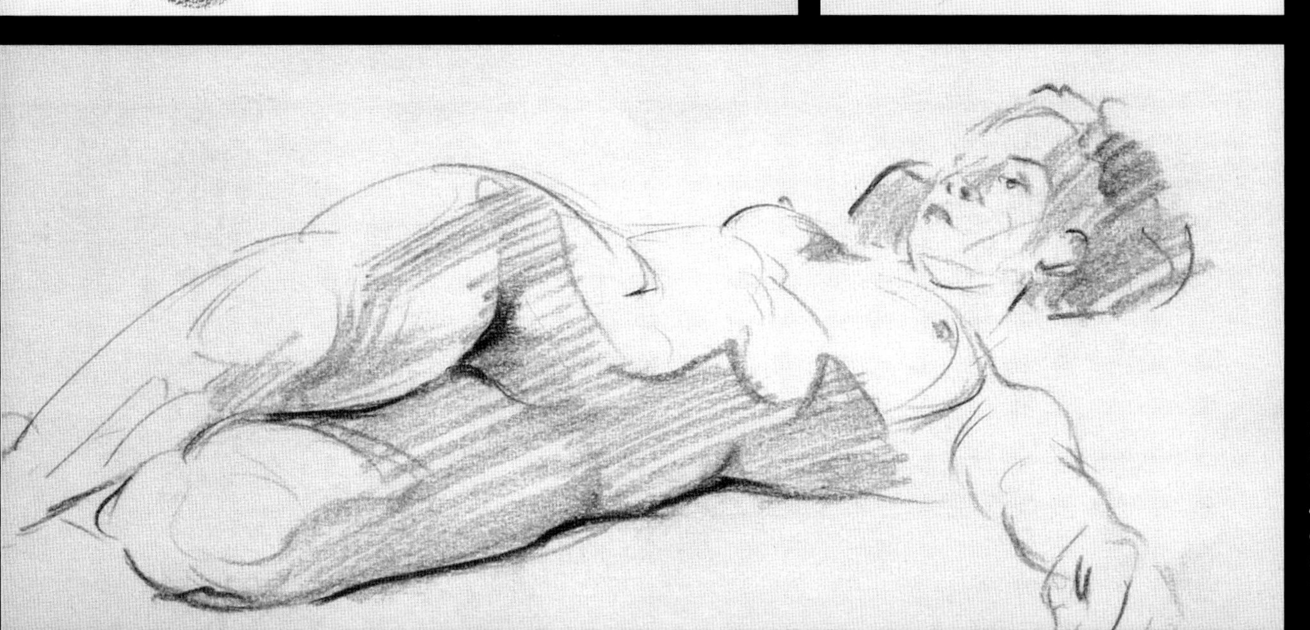

In drawings of the human figure it is typical to encounter foreshortening in some parts of the body. Usually a leg or an arm will look too large or deformed, giving the impression that it is moving toward the viewer.

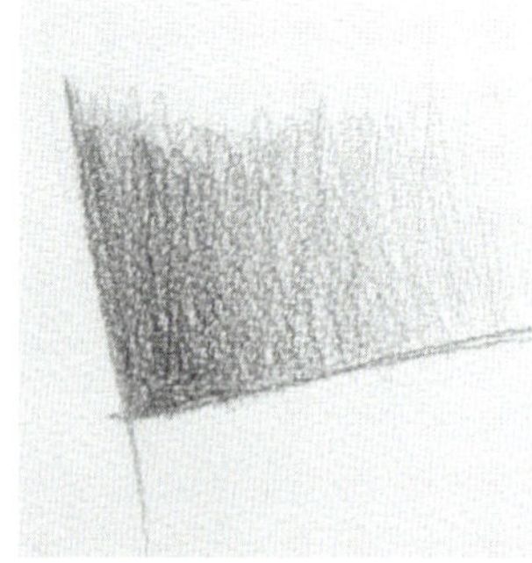

In shading this Cubist model you can use flat shading or create tonal gradations to make small volumetric fragments that impart a spectacular effect to the composition.

To fragment the image, it is important to destroy the continuity of the object's outlines, for example, by making cuts or by rearranging its parts as if they were autonomous and could move by themselves.

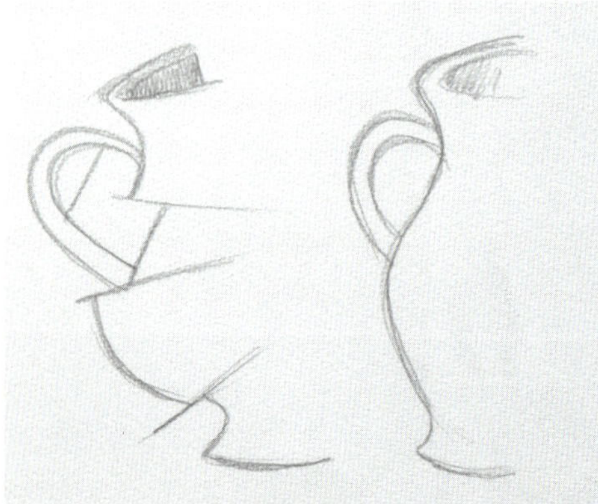

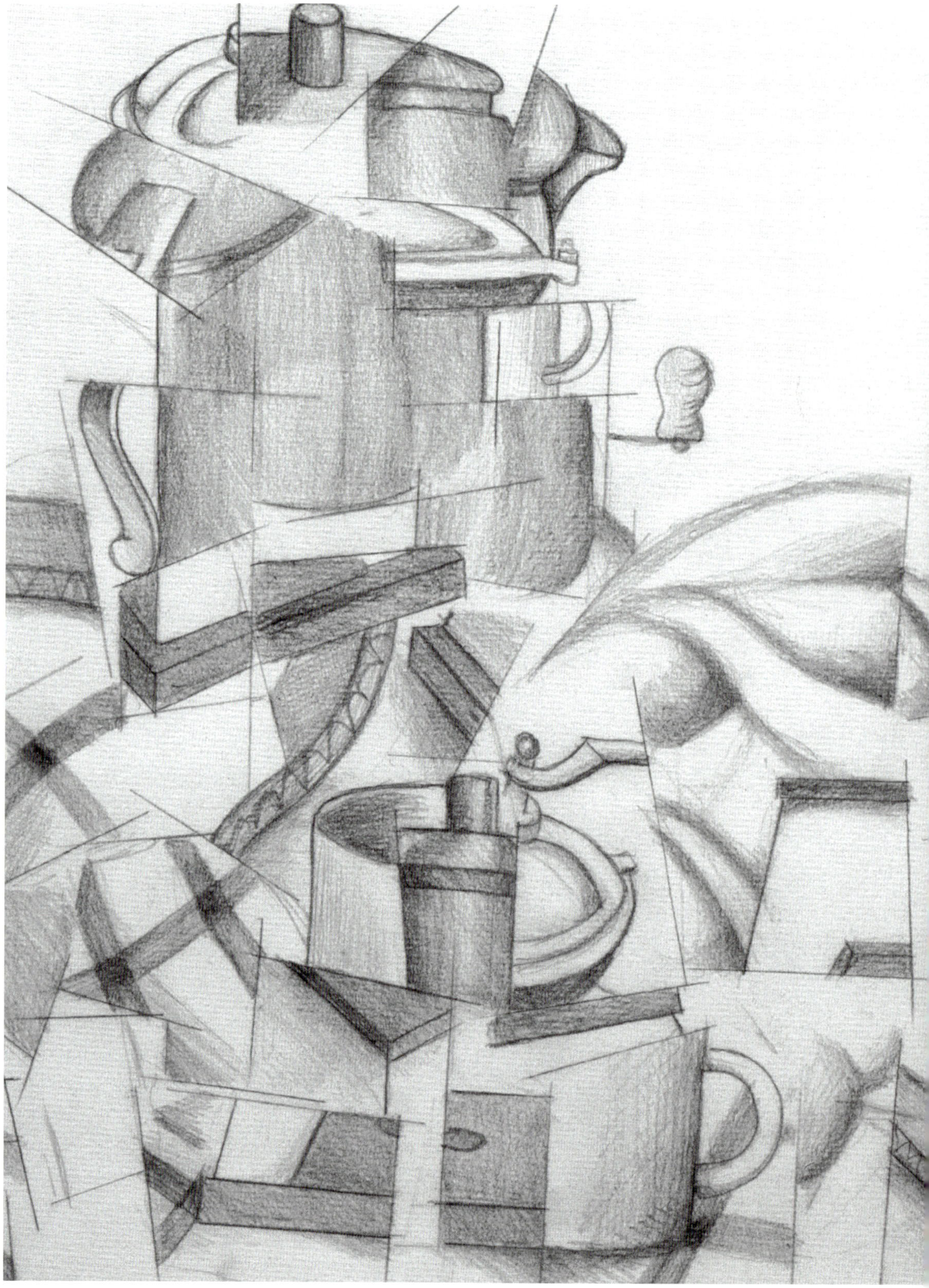

SIMULTANEOUS POINTS OF VIEW. The eye is not static; it is constantly in motion and moves unconsciously from one part of the scene to another to focus on a small area with each movement. Therefore, in drawing it is important to "see around the object" in order to better understand the model. This idea caused Picasso to simultaneously incorporate several points of view of a model in one drawing. This is how Cubism was born.

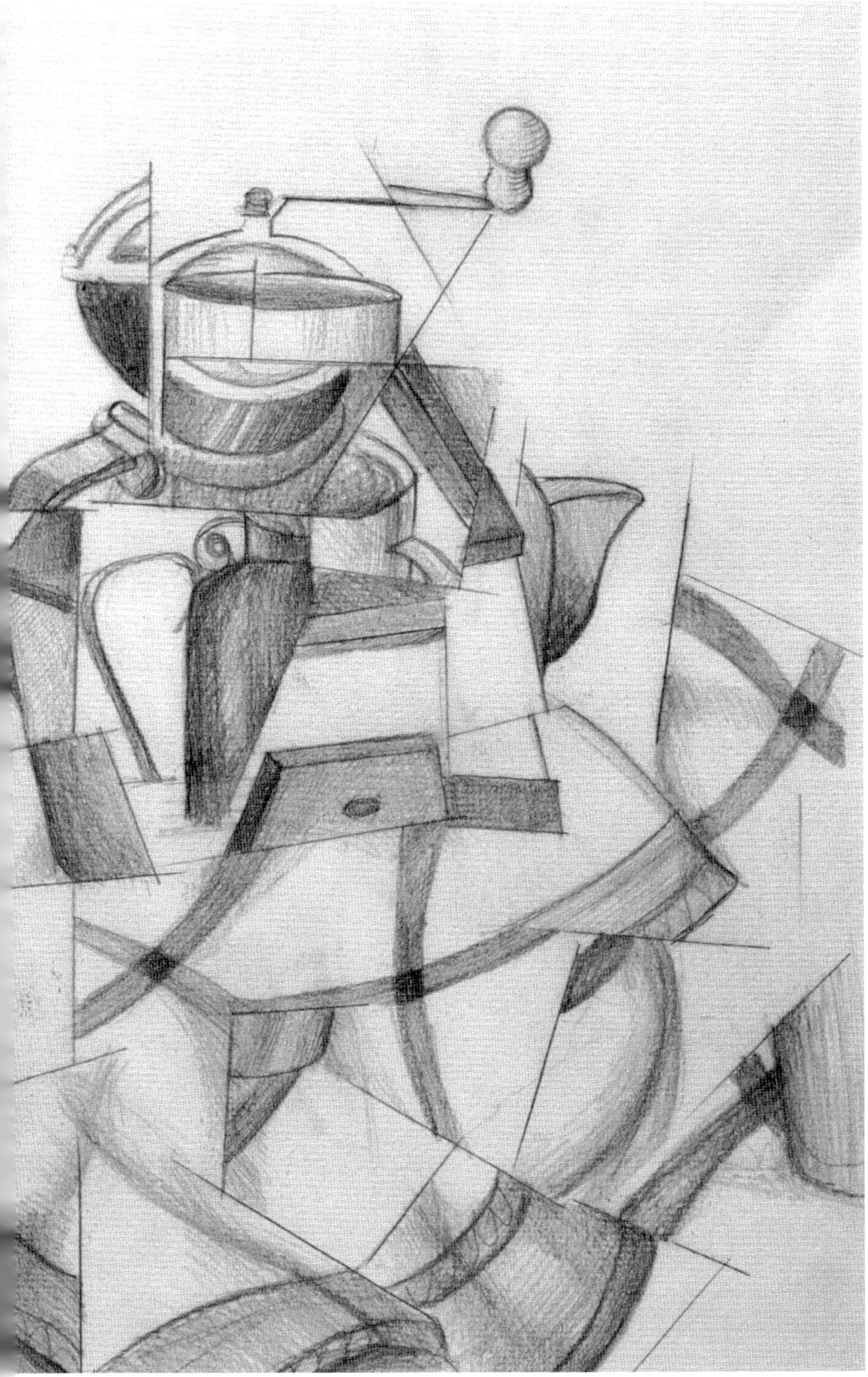

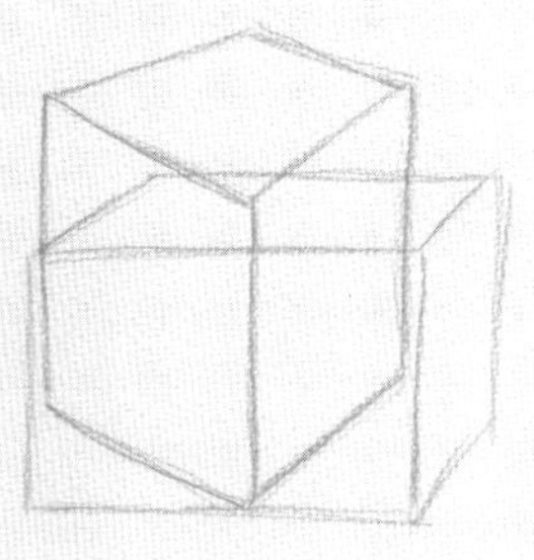

Cubism is based on the incorporation of several overlapping points of view of the same model. To understand how this works, draw the same quadrangular form from two different viewpoints. Then, overlay the two drawings.

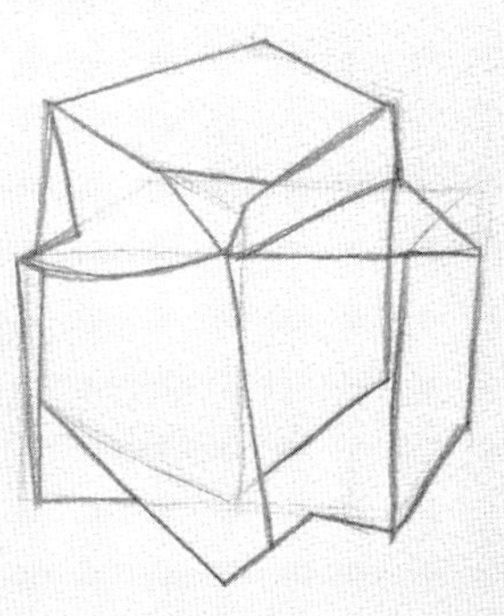

Fuse the two geometric forms, altering some of their shapes.

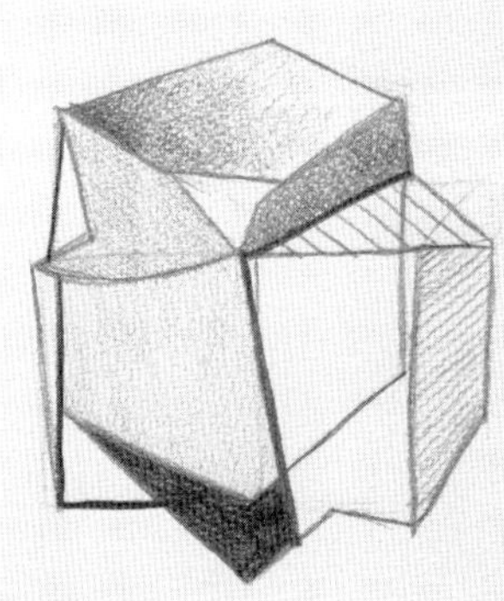

Shade them in any way you wish. The result is a Cubist form.

Cubism creates a fragmented and dynamic view of the subject, like a puzzle in which each piece takes on a life of its own.

Light and Contrast

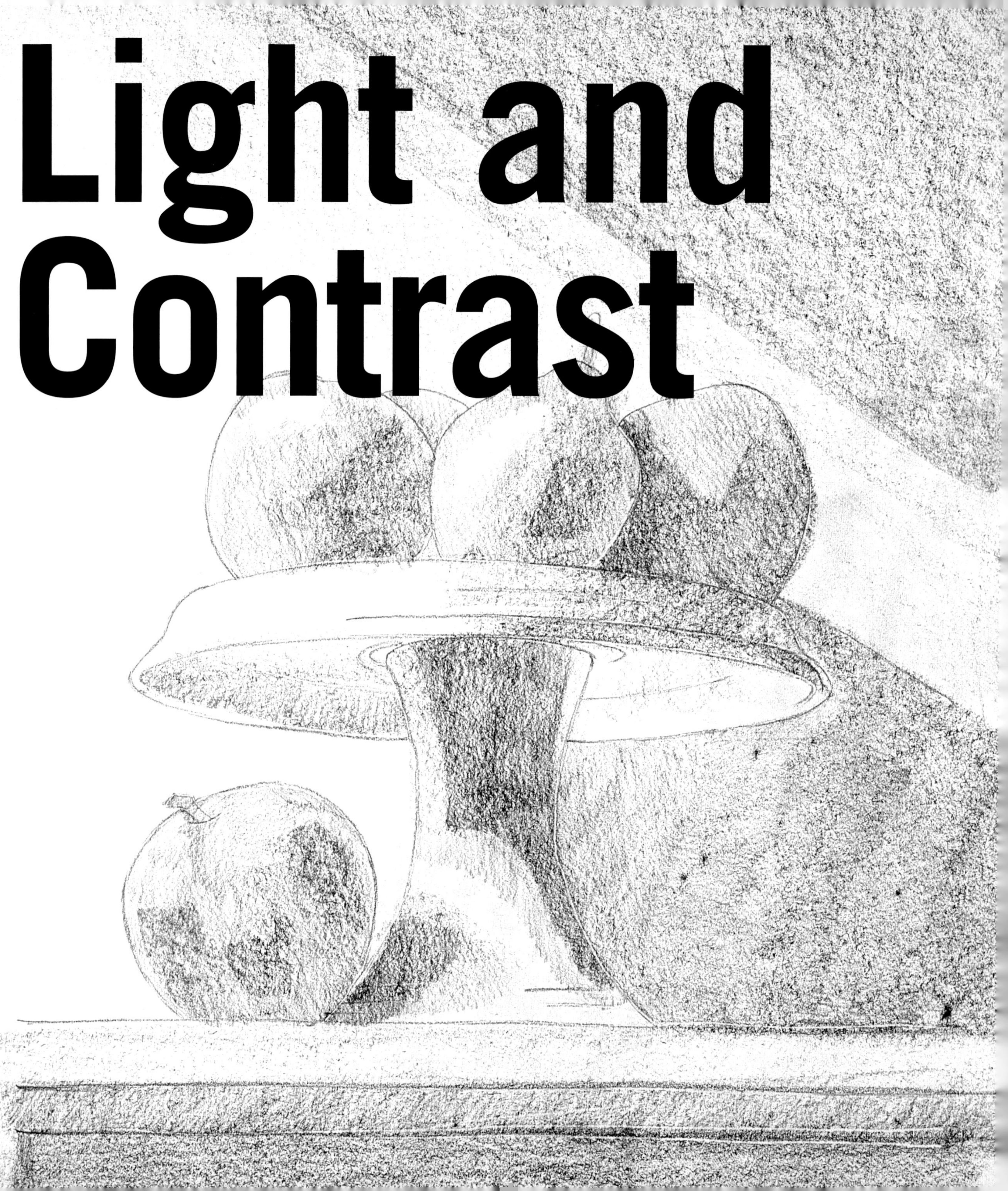

The line is the clearest and most descriptive element
in a drawing. Everything can be defined with the
utmost precision using lines, and it is no surprise
that architects, engineers, topographers, and other
professionals who plan, design, and represent aspects
of reality always work with lines. But there is one thing
that a line cannot define, at least completely: light. To
represent light and its opposite, shadow, something
more than line is required: shading, tones, and
contrasts between the light parts and the dark parts.

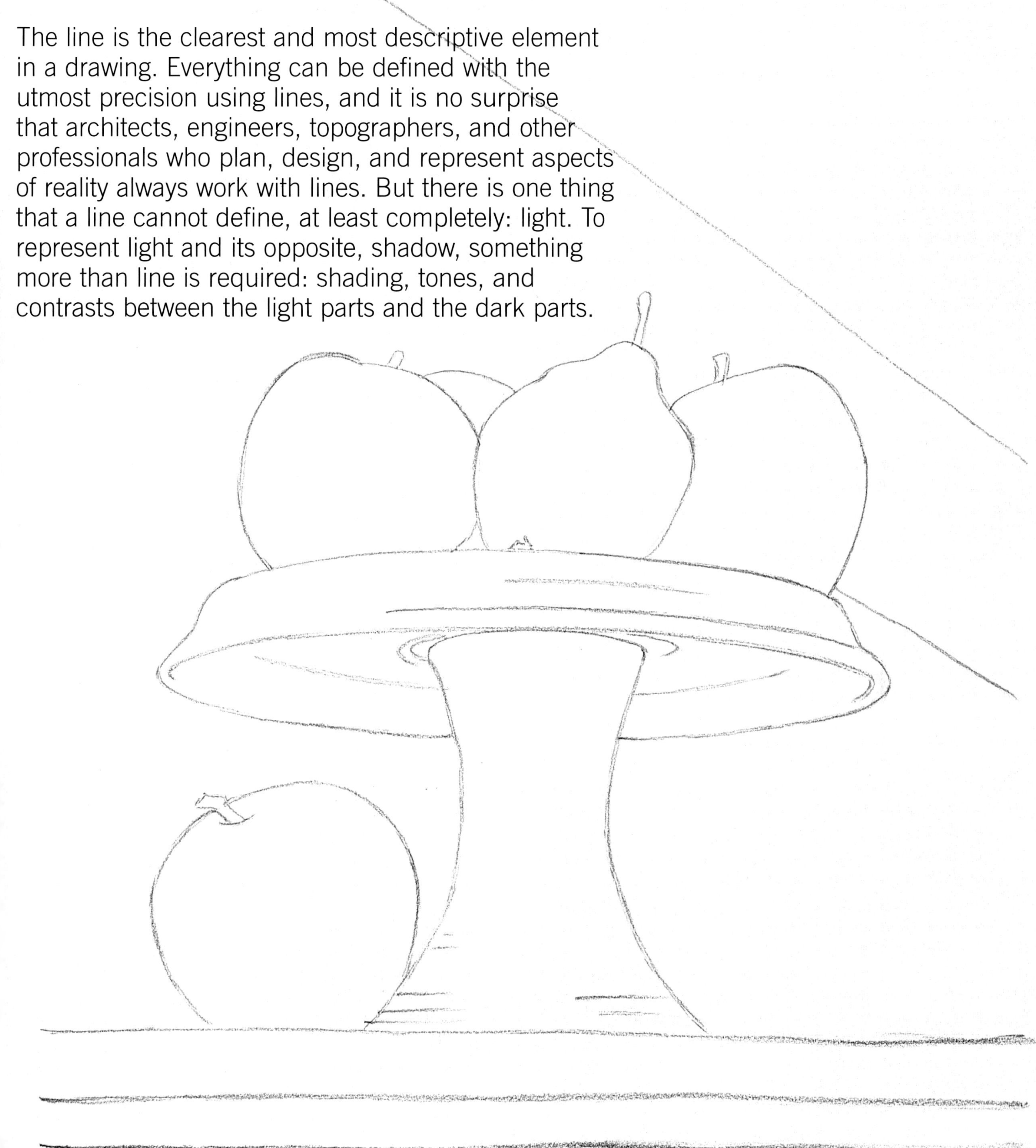

DRAWING SHADOWS. You are going to draw an urban subject, starting by structuring its shadows with vine charcoal. In this exercise you will make a detailed study of light and tonal values. It is very important to lay the drawing out perfectly before beginning its definitive resolution. The reflections and lightest areas must be reserved; that is, from the beginning the paper must be left white and untouched where the brightly lit areas are.

10.1

OUTLINING THE ZONES. The basic sketch of the model is easy to make; first, draw the subject with the point of the charcoal to create an approximate form. Then, color the shaded wall of the building with the flat side of the stick. After lightly blending with your hand, you have finished the layout of the subject.

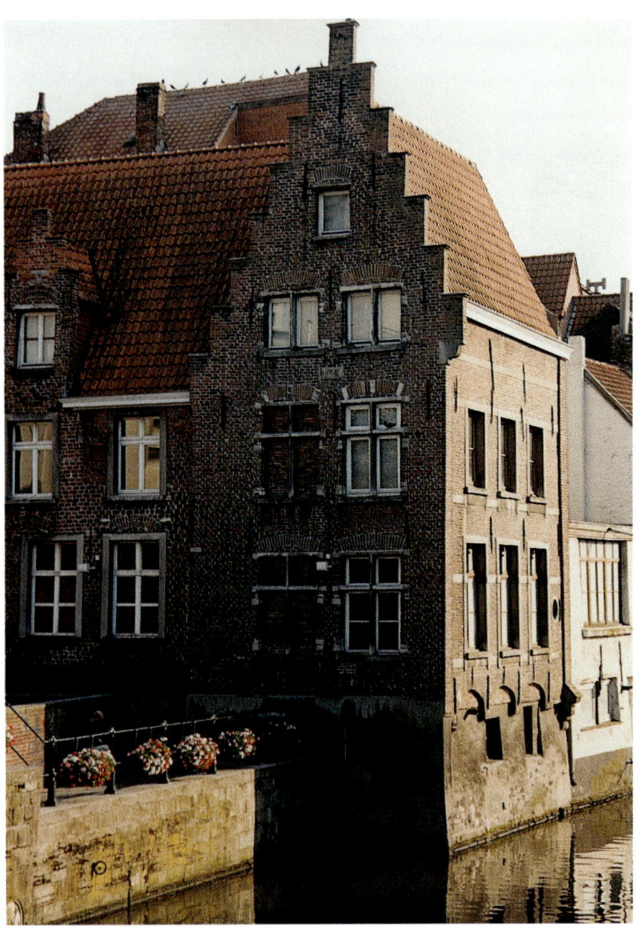

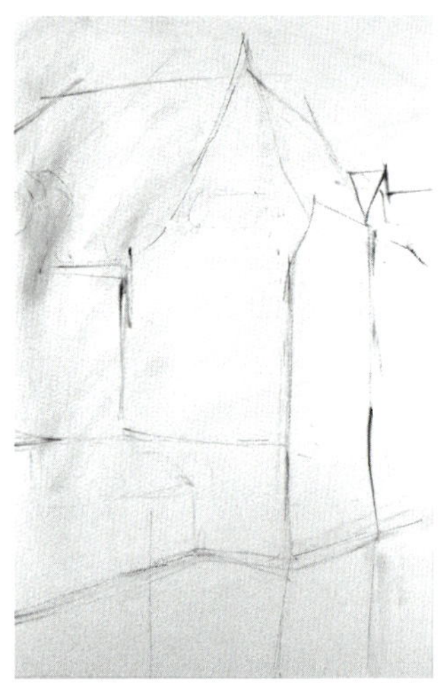

Make the framework of the drawing using the point of the charcoal. With just a few lightly drawn lines, indicate the outline of the building. This stage of the drawing requires special attention, since all later steps will be based on the results of this one.

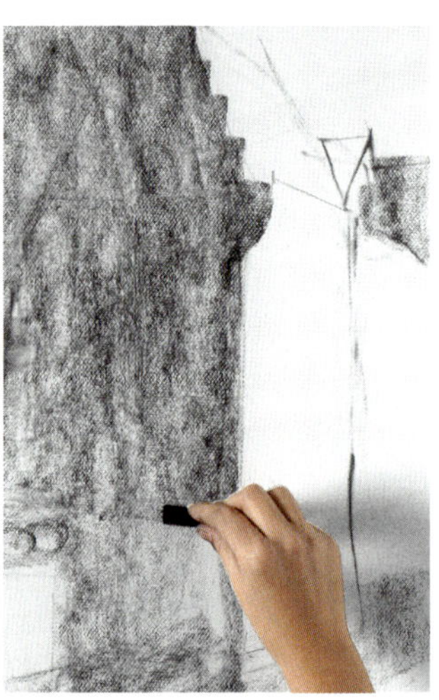

Cover the wall with shading using the side of the charcoal stick. Apply even pressure without making lines on the paper; remember that sometimes vine charcoal has a grain that does not make a mark but will scratch.

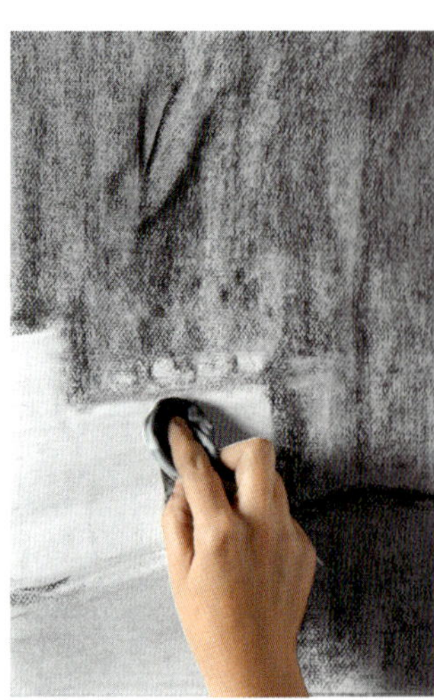

If the tone you obtain by softly rubbing the charcoal like this is still light, you can apply successive layers, rubbing it each time until you achieve the desired tone. Next, mark the outlines of the illuminated façades with a kneaded eraser to create more contrast.

This is the best way to hold the charcoal stick when making your line sketch.

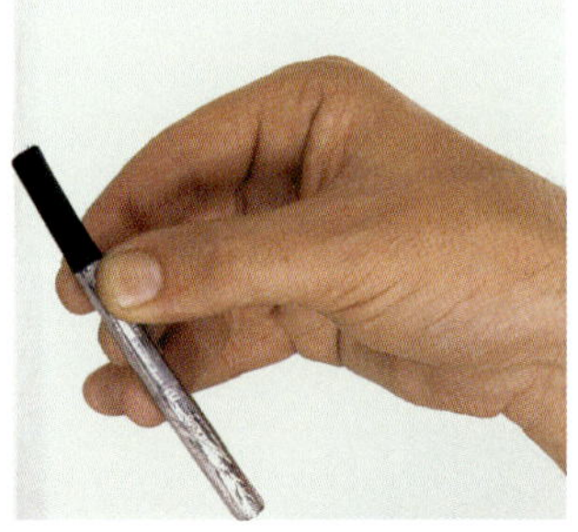

Your fingertips should be covered with charcoal dust. This way, when you begin blending you will not remove the powder already deposited on the paper, but will spread it on the paper as desired.

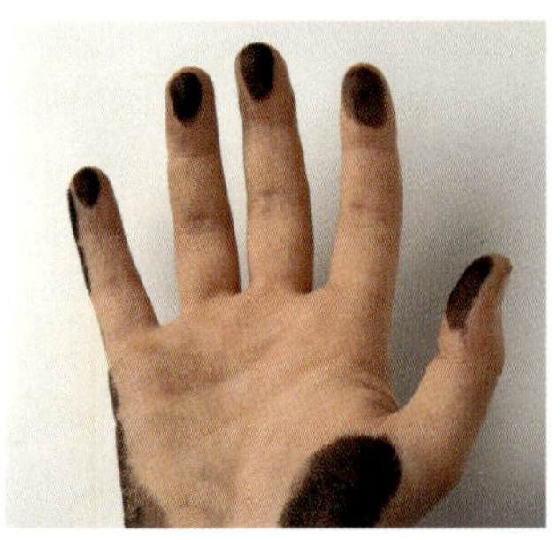

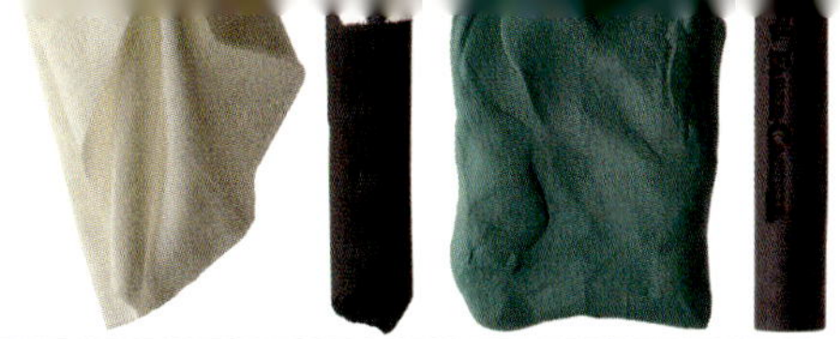

10.2

MODELING WITH THE HAND. When the paper is covered with pigment it can be modeled with your fingers, which are able to easily pick up the charcoal dust. This technique makes it possible to use your hands to reduce or grade tones at any time.

Once the façade is shaded, wipe it lightly with your hand to make the shading more even and eliminate any traces of lines. The area of the illuminated roof also looks shaded and blended, but with a much lighter gray.

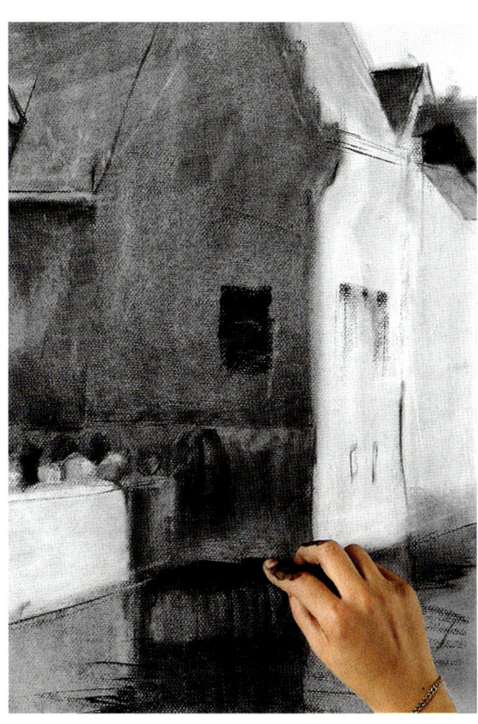

In a charcoal work, there are always fine outlines, thin, light, linear marks on the roof or contrasting spaces at the base of the building that indicate reflections on the surface of the water. These lines are made with a stick of vine charcoal with a sharp point.

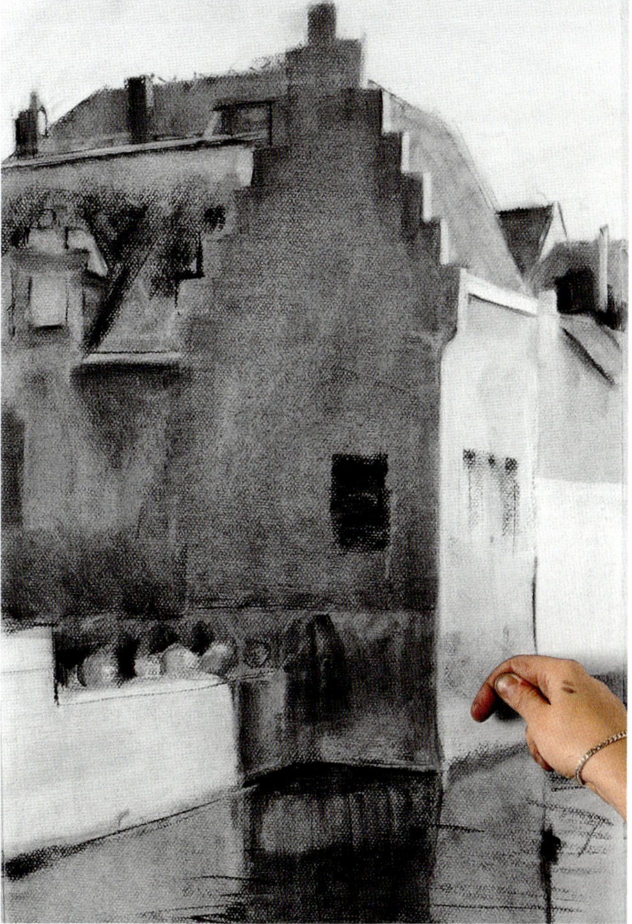

Now, blend the shading on the illuminated façade, barely rubbing with the side of your finger. Wipe your fingers very lightly over the charcoal powder on the paper to spread it without removing it.

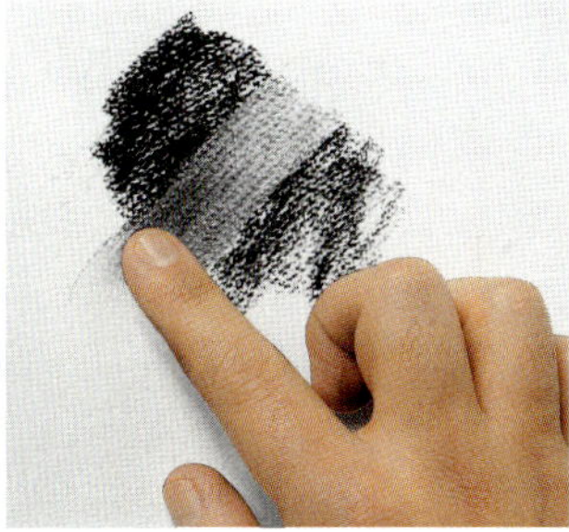

If you apply a lot of pressure with your finger on the drawing surface, you will wipe away the charcoal dust. You can avoid this danger by working very lightly.

10.3

DETAILS AND ERASING. At this stage, the cotton rag and the kneaded eraser become very important. These tools, which can do so many things, are perfect complements for charcoal drawing.

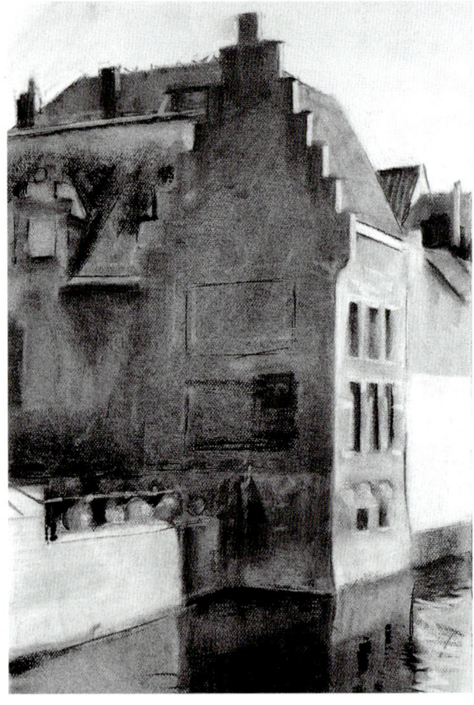

Draw the darkest shadows of the windows and the reflection projected on the water with the point of the vine charcoal. Then draw new lines on the shaded area to mark the locations of some of the windows. Apply these lines lightly.

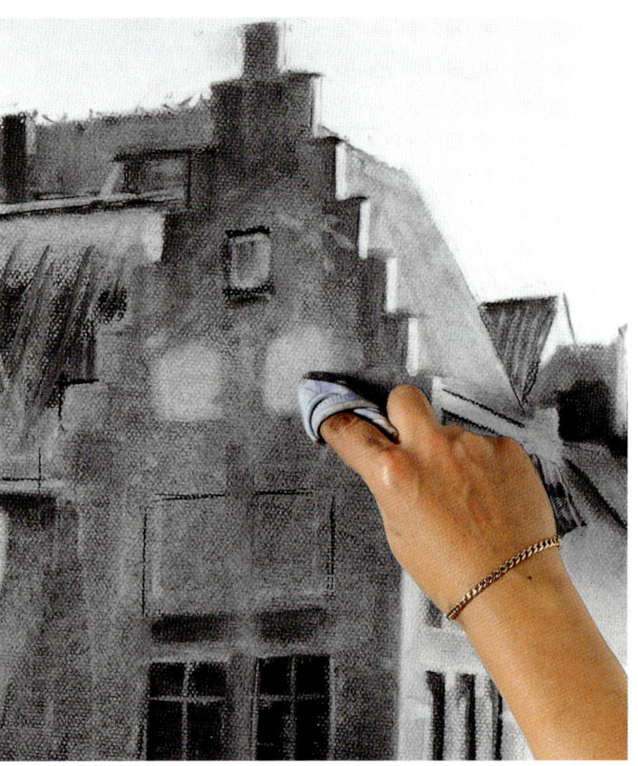

Lighten the upper windows of the façade. Vine charcoal is very unstable and easy to erase. Just rub the areas that you wish to correct with a clean rag so that the charcoal dust is removed.

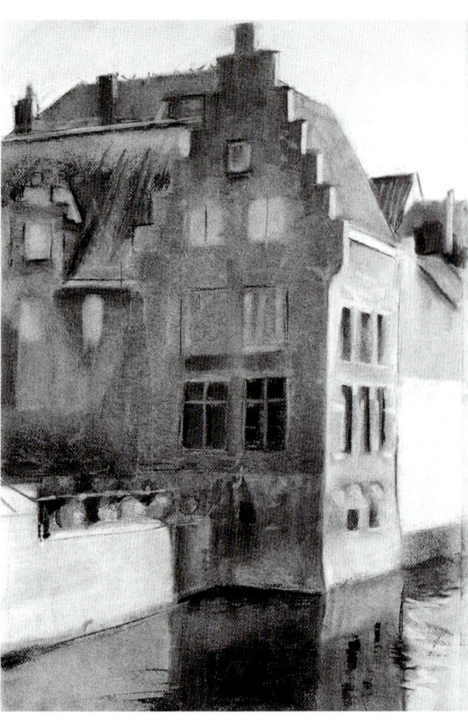

Make the thinnest lines with a corner of the eraser. All that is left to do is to draw an occasional line with a stick of compressed charcoal to sharpen the forms of the windows and the roof.

It is easier to remove charcoal powder with a cotton rag if it is not overworked; if it is, no matter how hard you rub you will not be able to remove the layer of pigment.

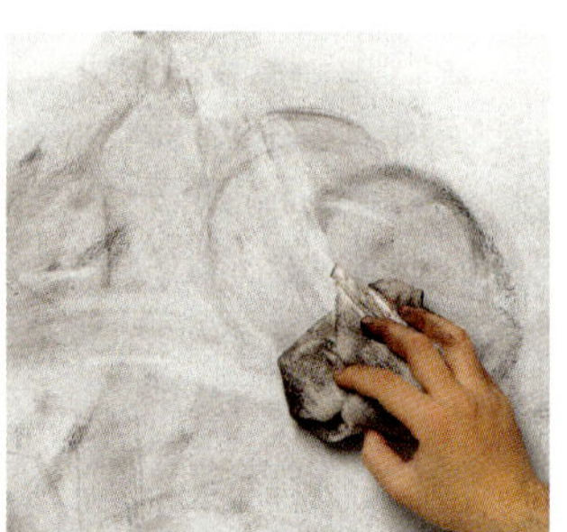

A blending stick can be used on small areas that are too small to rub with a finger.

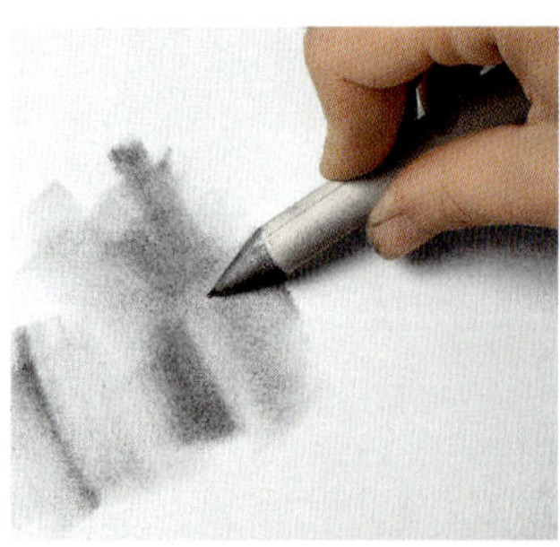

The final result is a work containing the basic characteristics of a charcoal drawing: meticulous blending with the hands and a cotton rag to model the volumes, dark tones made with repeated applications of charcoal, and highlights made with the eraser. Drawn by Mercedes Gaspar.

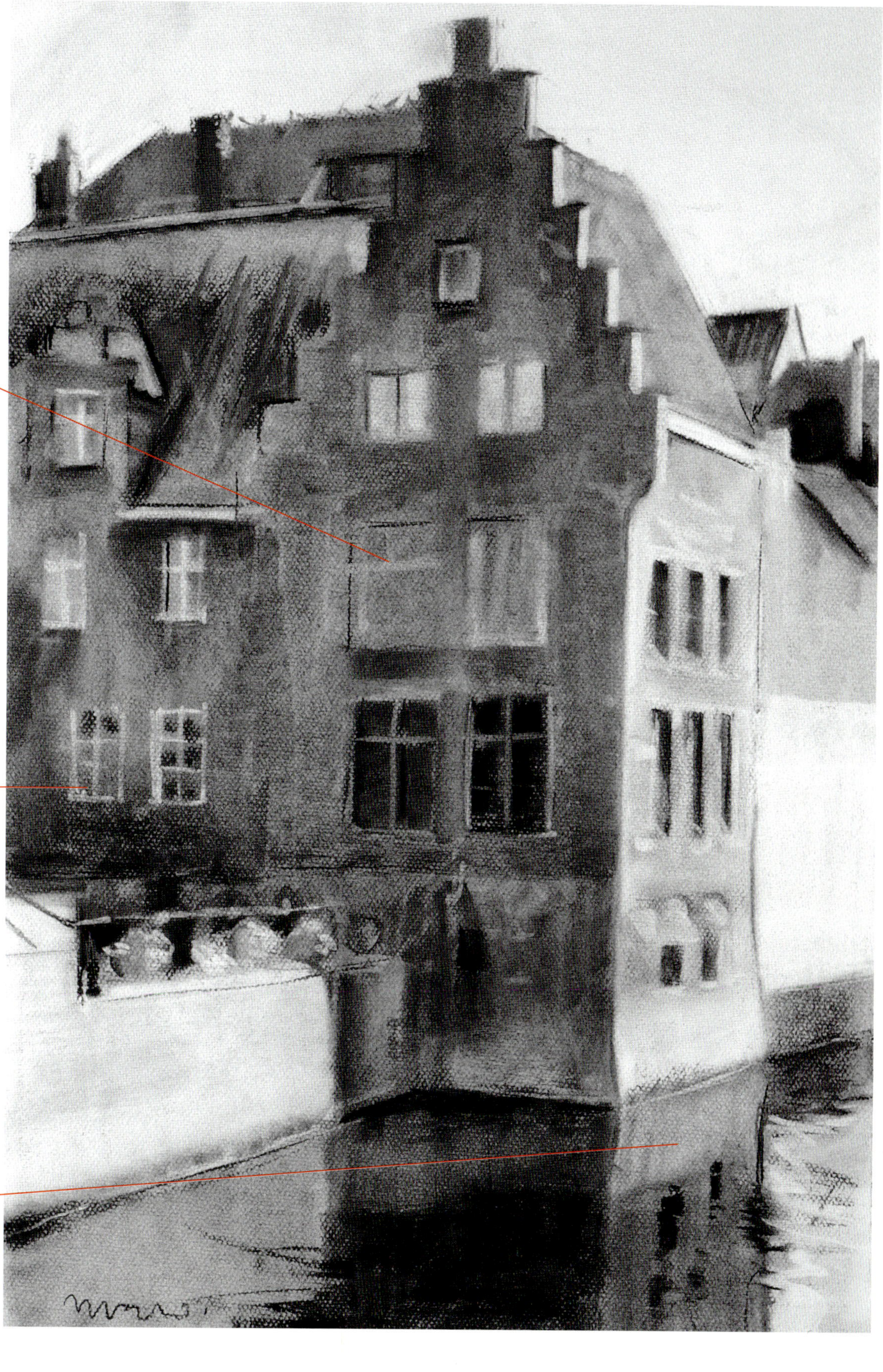

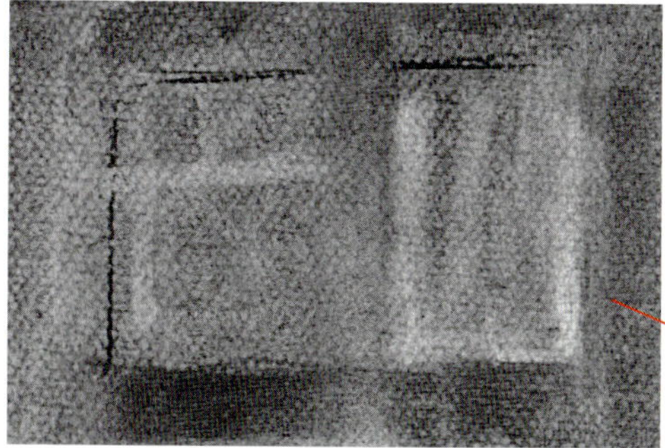

It is not necessary to completely draw the windows when drawing building façades; they can simply be indicated. Often a suggestion is more interesting than a detailed drawing.

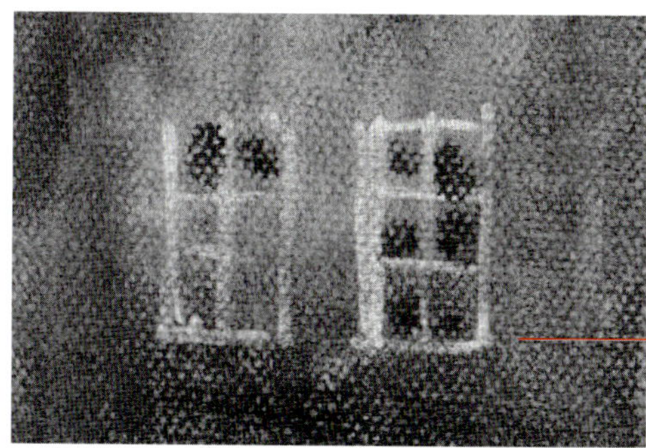

Use an eraser for small spaces, making outlines, highlighting, and drawing light areas.

The reflections of a body in water are always vertical, with zigzag outlines and darker tones than the actual object.

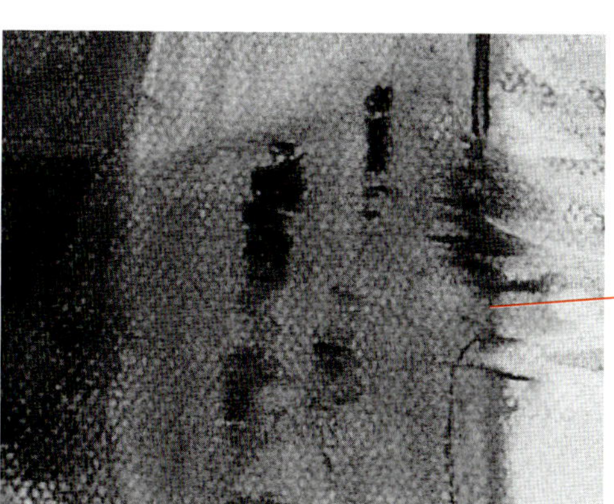

BLOCK SHADING. This exercise is a good way to learn the technique of shading. By juxtaposing areas with different flat tones you can represent changes in light and volume in a simple and direct way.

11.1

PREPARATION. Choose some simple elements; for example, a fruit stand with an assortment of fruit. It is important to combine objects of different colors to see how color can be translated into a range of grays. Once you have arranged the objects on a shelf with a neutral background, adjust the direction of the light and decide on the framing of the subject.

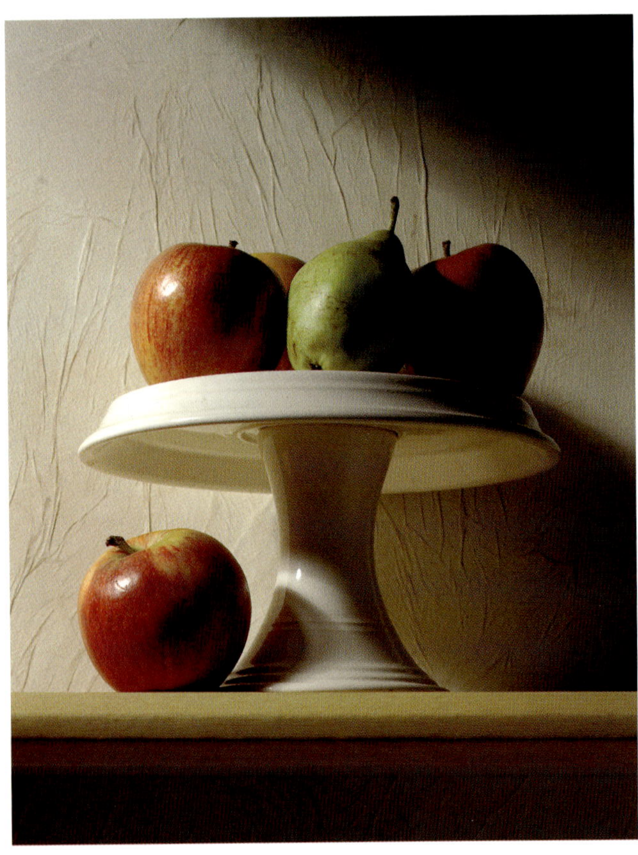

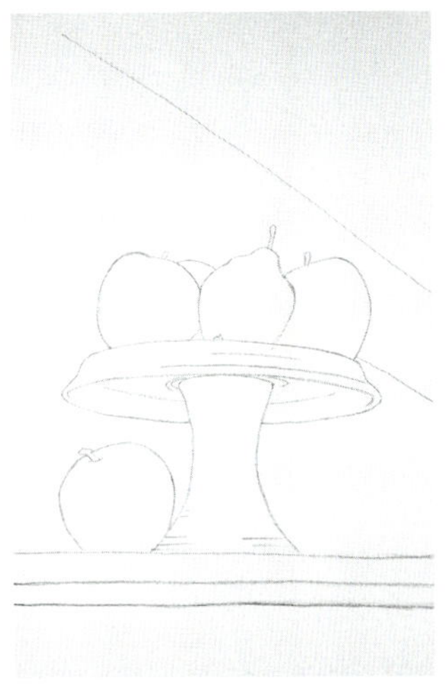

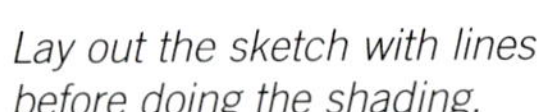

Lay out the sketch with lines before doing the shading.

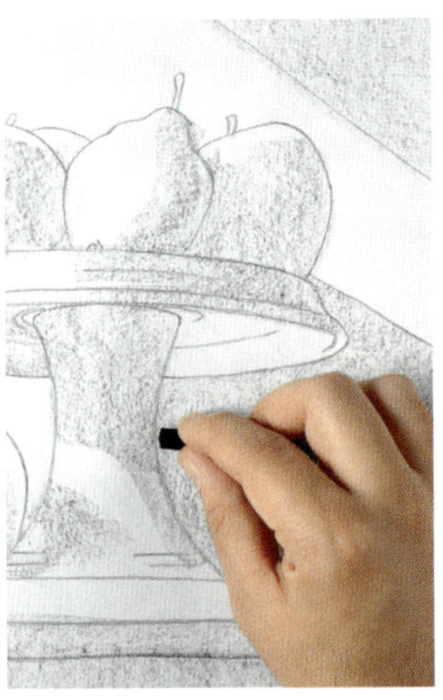

The first step is to clearly differentiate the illuminated areas from the shaded ones. Use the side of a stick of black chalk to create the shading.

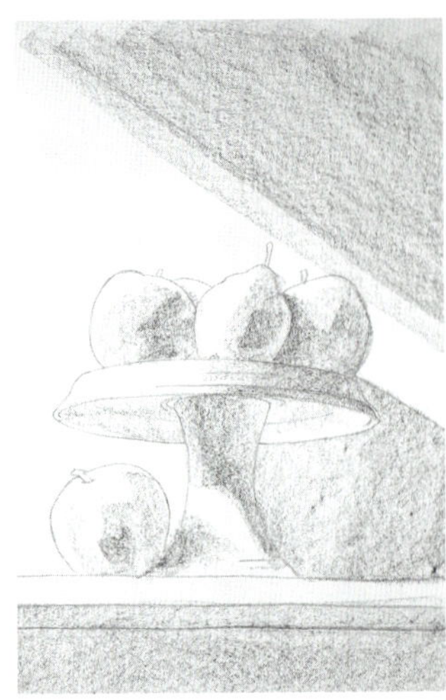

Add a second value, pressing harder on the paper with the side of the chalk stick. This allows you to differentiate two gray tones.

When one gray tone is laid over a previous one it darkens the original gray and reduces the visible texture of the paper.

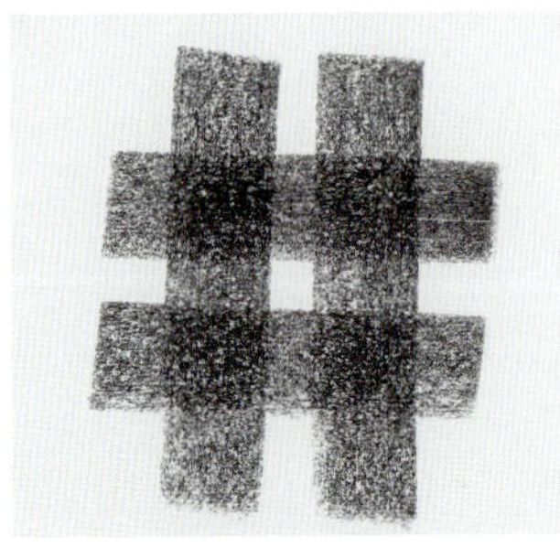

It is a good idea to rub your chalk sticks on a separate piece of paper first; if you do not do this, your strokes may be streaky and broken and negatively affect the final drawing. The shading should always be uniform.

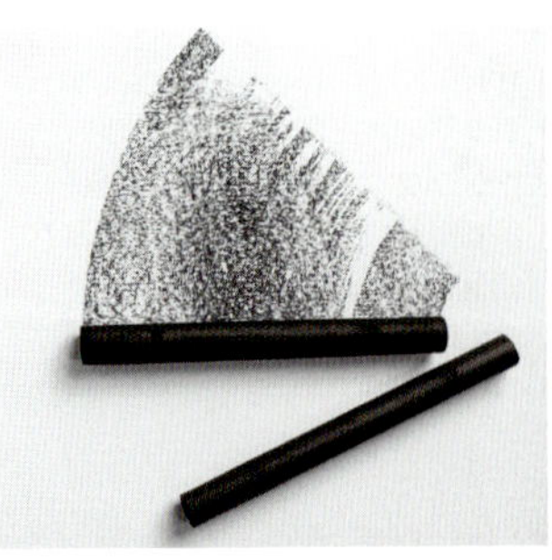

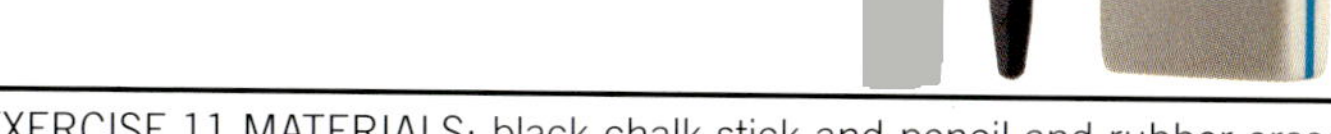

11.2

INCREASING CONTRAST. Strong tonal contrasts define the forms and focus attention on them. Contrasts are created where two differently illuminated areas come into contact; this makes it possible to differentiate the planes based on their position relative to the light source.

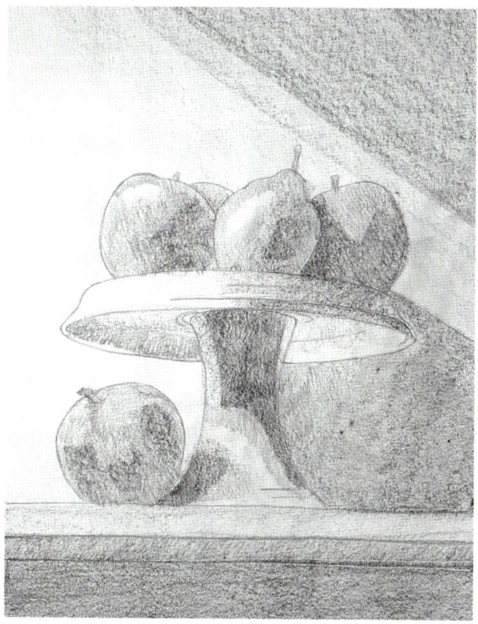

If you apply a third value to the previous drawing, progressively increasing the pressure on the side of the chalk stick, you will create a drawing in which the shadows look very synthesized. Although the contrast still is not enough, it is already possible to notice a clear volumetric effect.

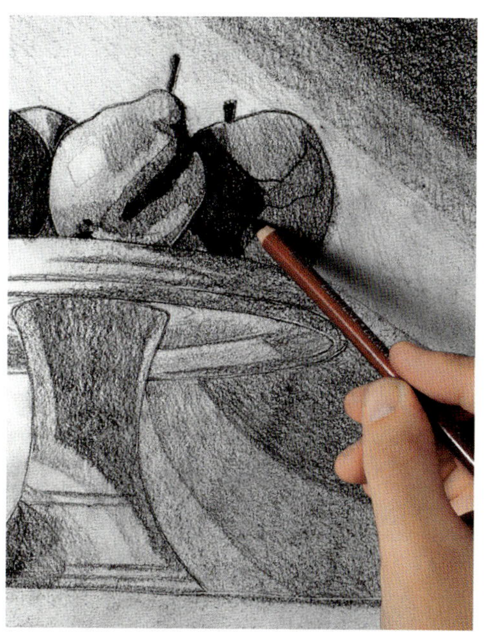

Now use a sharpened soft chalk pencil to shade the darkest areas with nearly pure black. This creates a contrast with the range of intermediate tones that you previously applied. Remember that the shaded areas should be clearly separated from each other.

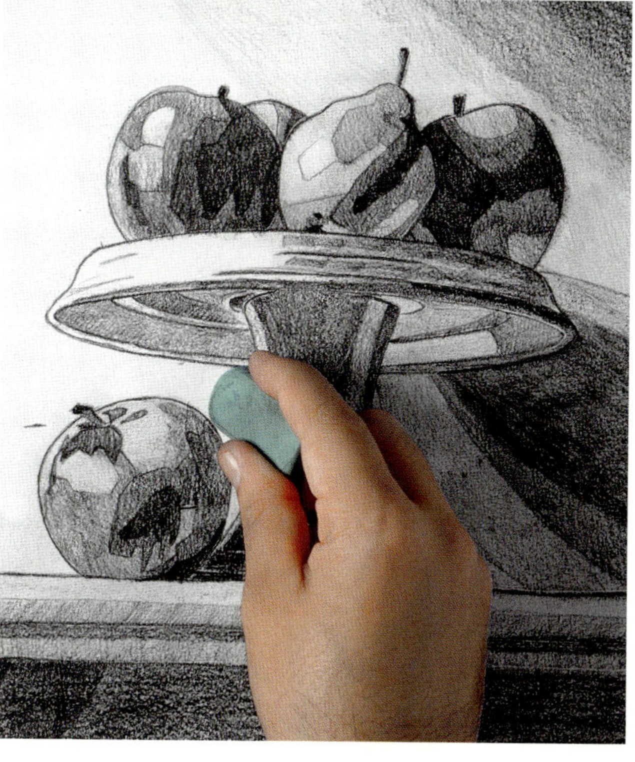

The less light that shines on different areas of the still life, the darker they will be. You can increase the contrast where you think it is needed by lightening the illuminated parts with a rubber eraser.

When you draw the medium tones and the darker shadows, it is good not to press too hard on the paper. This protects the grain, which many artists feel is attractive.

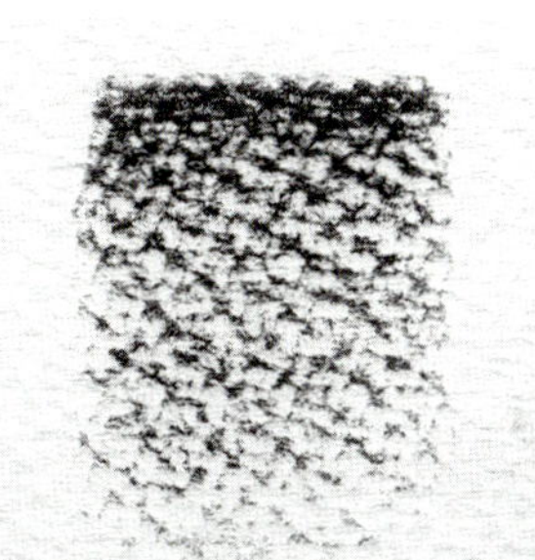

The success of a well-drawn outline often resides in covering the background that surrounds the model with dark shading. The objective is to emphasize the shapes through tonal contrast.

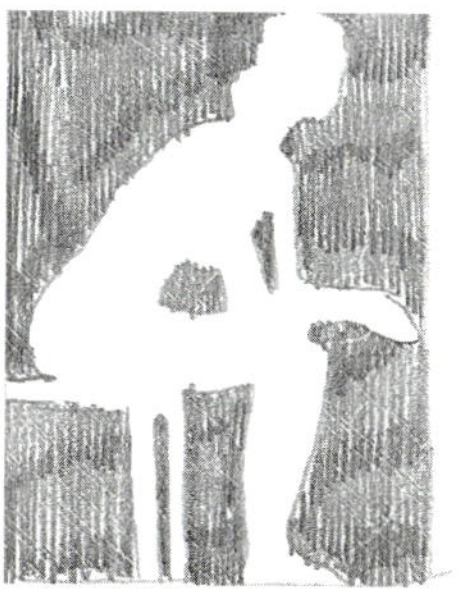

THE VALUE SCALE. Making gray scales with different techniques is a method many beginners use to master a wide range of values. The more shading a subject has, the greater the distance between the black and the white; that is, it will contain a larger number of different values.

It is a good idea to practice wide tonal ranges to guarantee the quality of shading in your drawings.

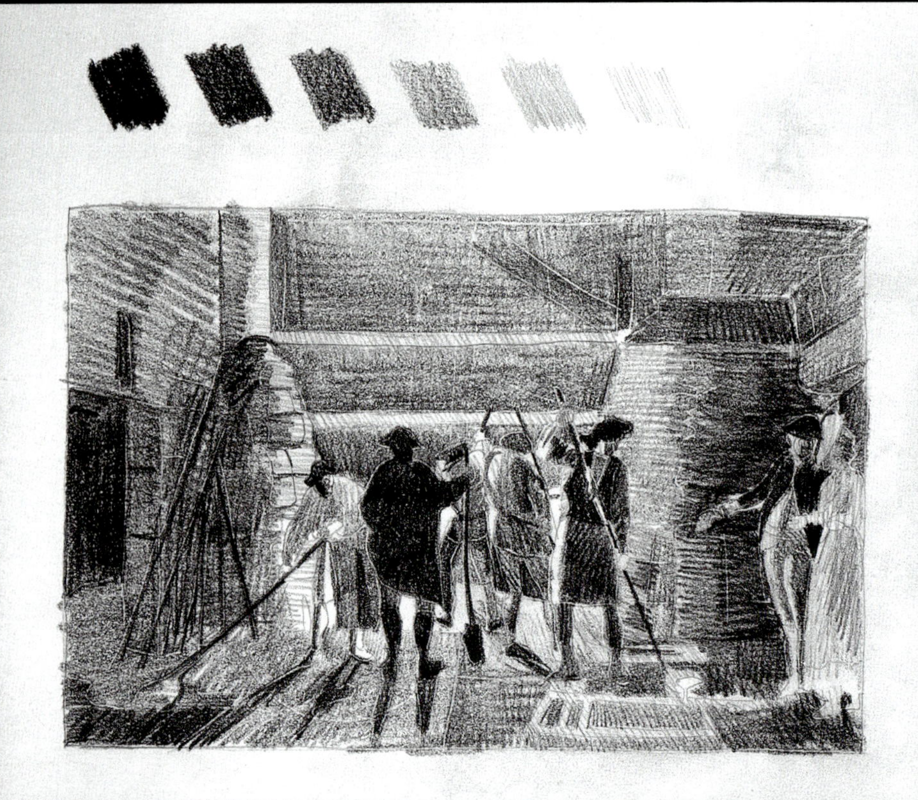

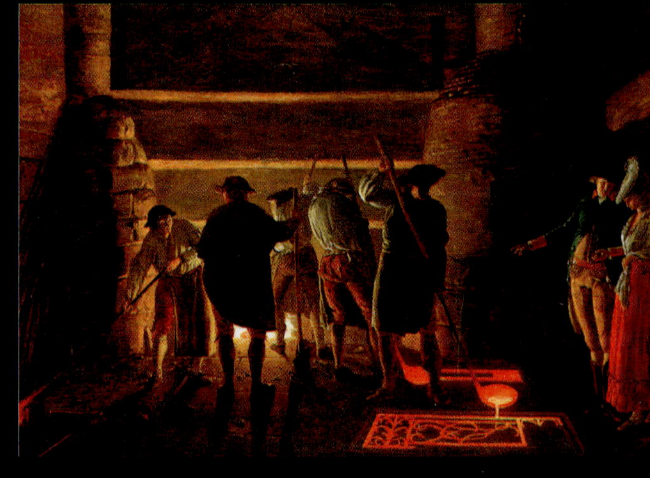

The original painting Visit to the Foundry, *by Léonard Defrance (Valón Art Museum, Liège, Belgium), has been reduced to a monochrome study consisting of six values.*

VALUES. Up until now we have used various terms, such as gradation, intensity, and tone, when referring to light and shadow. All these words make reference to the same visible reality: the different appearance of light and shadows in a drawing, with some areas seeming lighter and others darker. From now on, to avoid confusion, we will use a single concept: *value*. A shaded drawing is composed of different values and each one of them represents a degree of light or shadow.

To illustrate the previous explanation it is a good idea to make some abstract compositions, based on sketches, that only take into consideration the areas of middle tone and shadows. Your approach should be very geometric and without any details. Let's look at some examples.

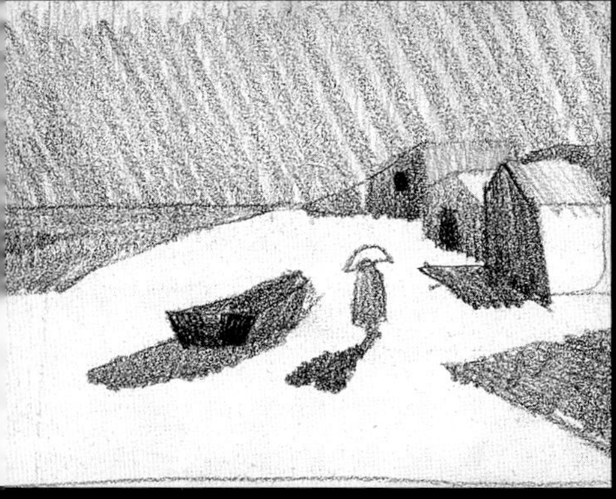

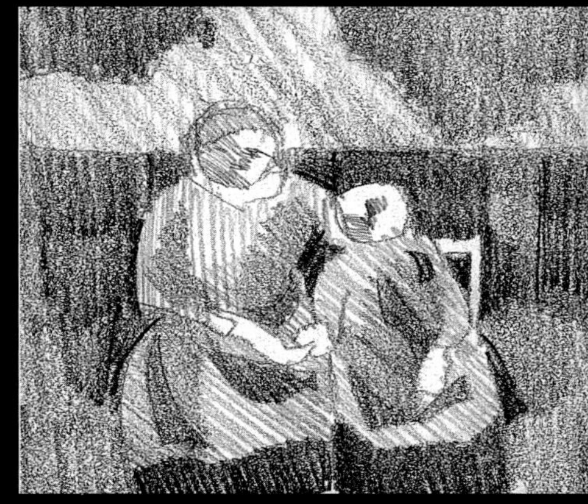

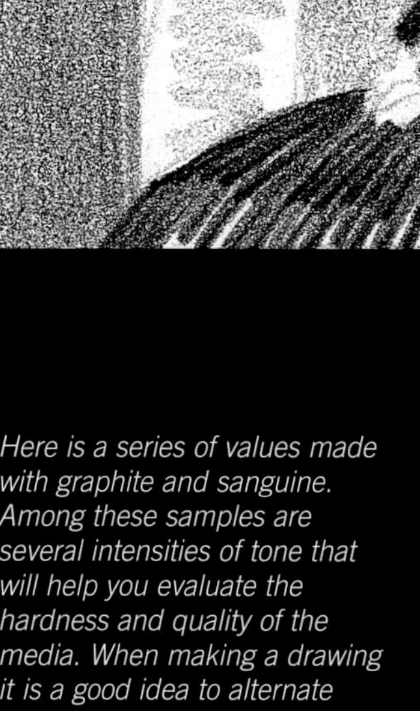

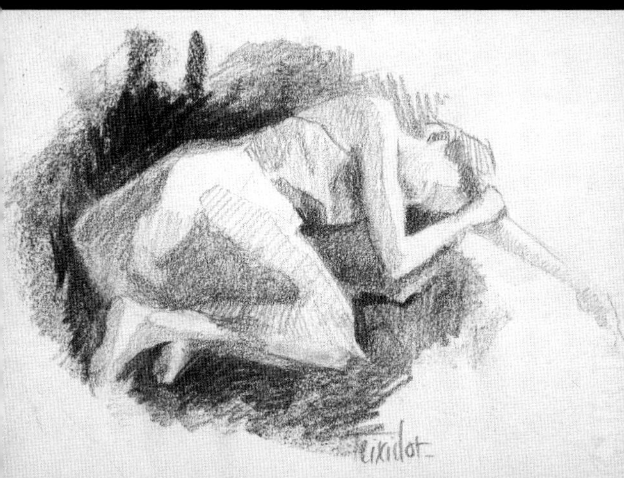

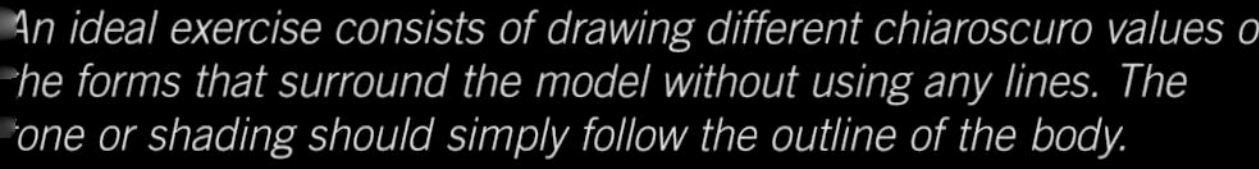

An ideal exercise consists of drawing different chiaroscuro values of the forms that surround the model without using any lines. The tone or shading should simply follow the outline of the body.

Here is a series of values made with graphite and sanguine. Among these samples are several intensities of tone that will help you evaluate the hardness and quality of the media. When making a drawing it is a good idea to alternate among leads of different hardnesses.

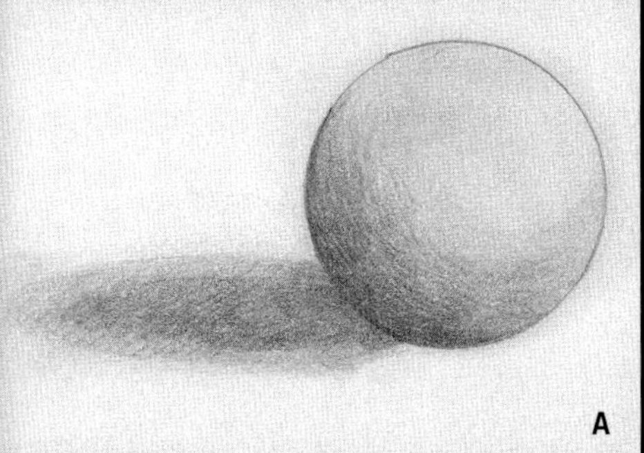

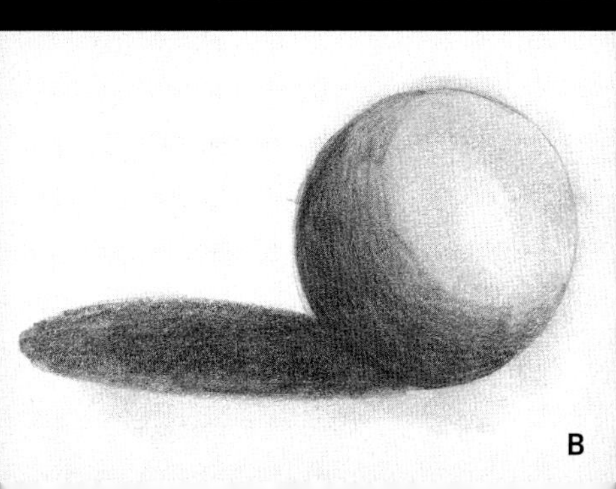

Once you are clear about the concept of value you can attempt simple exercises like this one, which consists of creating the effect of relief on a sphere by adding shading. The first step is to make the sphere gray and project the shadow with light and flat shading. In the second step, darken the shadows that indicate the outline of a crescent on the sphere and an ellipse on the projected shadow.

A

B

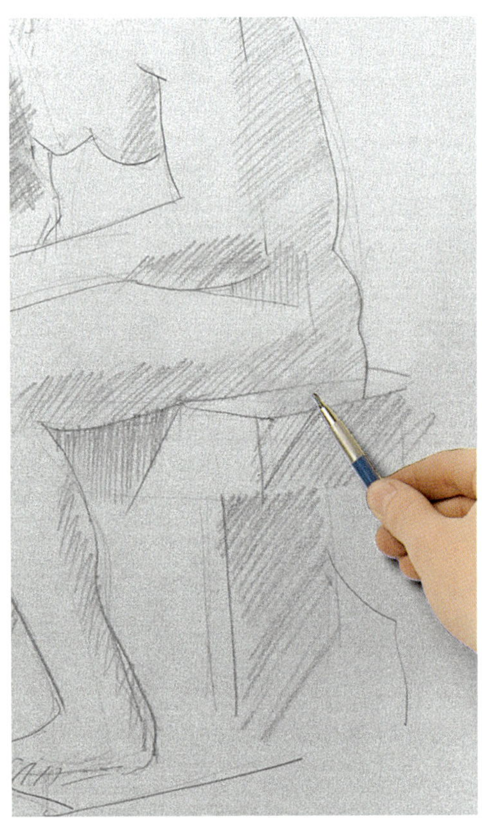

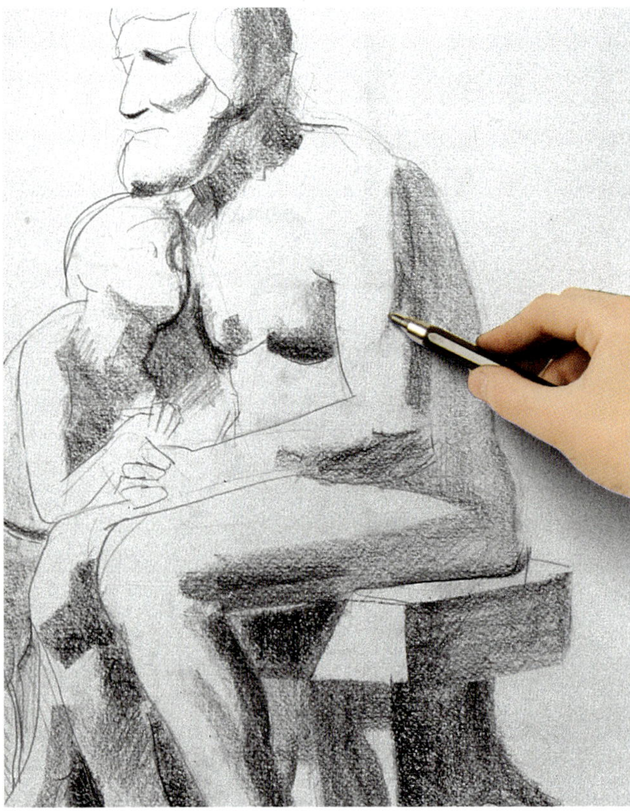

Tones, like many other aspects of a drawing, have a greater effect if they are simplified. Think in terms of three main values: dark, medium, and light.

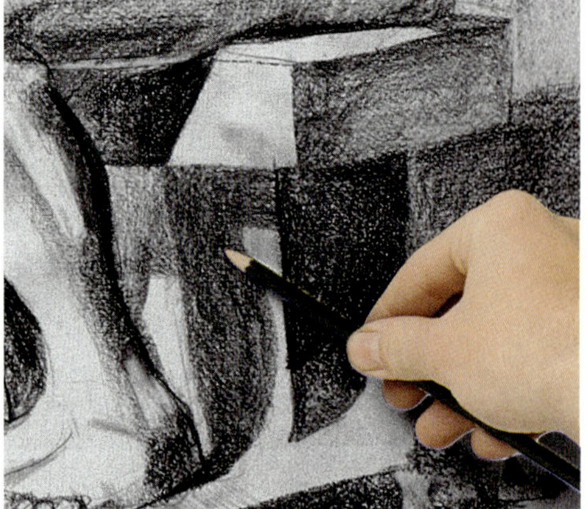

You should make the first lines of shading with a pencil or graphite lead. Use parallel lines set at a 45-degree angle; the distance between them will determine the darkness of the tone.

With the side of the lead, darken the initial shadows more and emphasize the most important ones.

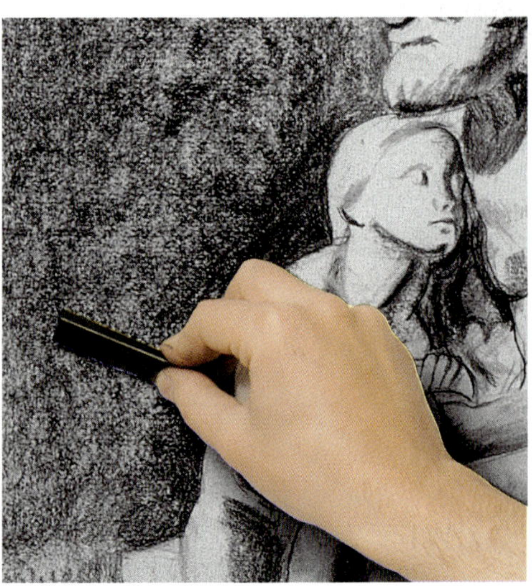

It is possible to alternate among various media in the same drawing to achieve different gradations of gray. Sticks always make very uniform, but less dark, values.

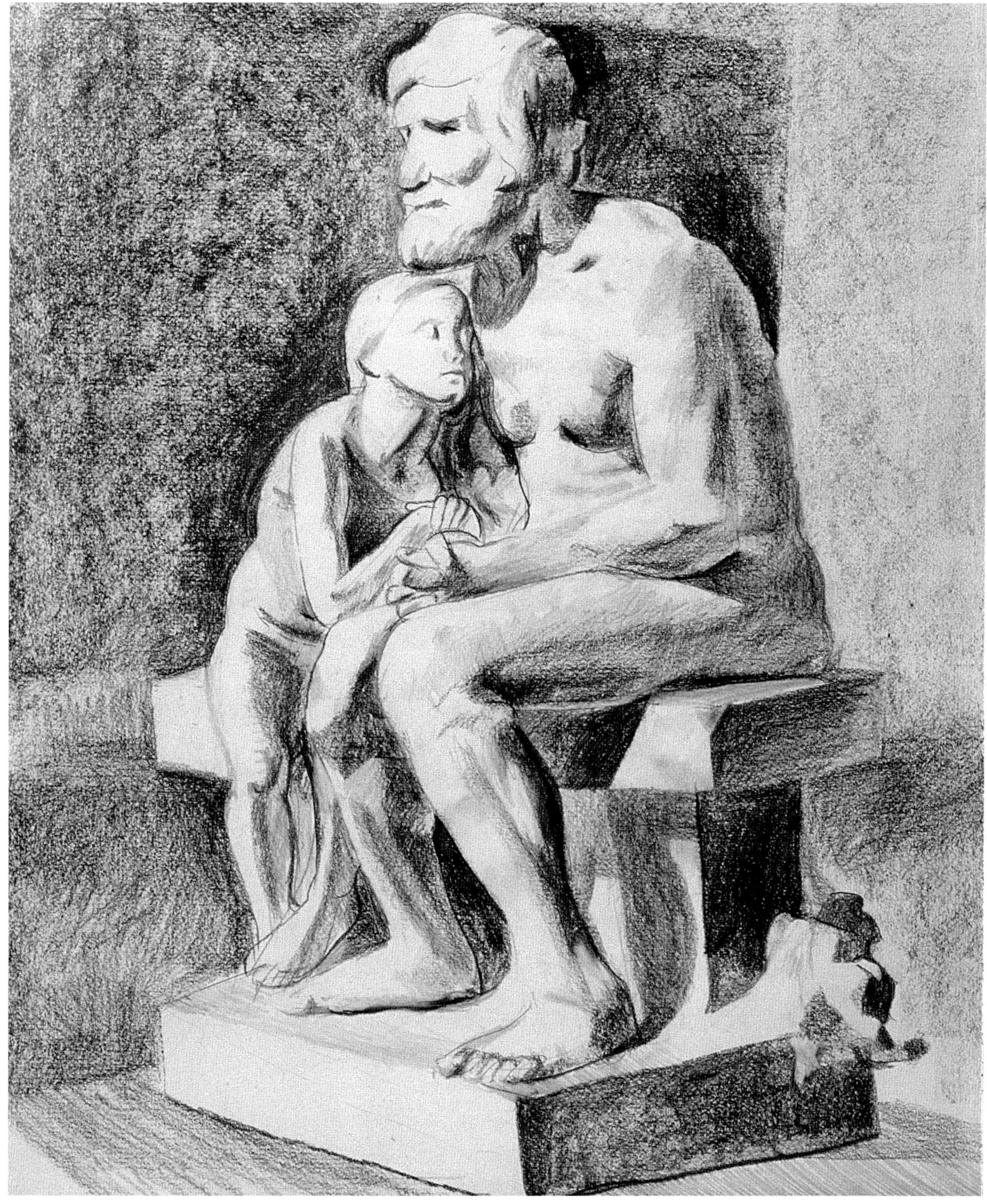

The tone is based on variations of light and darkness in the drawing, and suggests the three-dimensionality of the model. With most media, variations in tone are achieved by changing the pressure applied to the paper.

GRADATIONS. In the following exercise, you are going to practice gradating. You will draw a subject using only gradations, without resorting to flat shading, since all shadows will consist of decreasing tones. The base of the gradated stroke will be drawn with lines that begin with a dark tone and gradually become lighter until they disappear into the white of the paper. You will use a pair of blue oil-base pencils, one light and the other dark, to do this exercise.

12.1

A VERY LIGHT LINE. As always, the first stage consists of sketching the subject with light lines that set up the composition and become the basis of the drawing. The result must be a very clean and linear drawing that will act as a guide and that can be easily shaded and gradated.

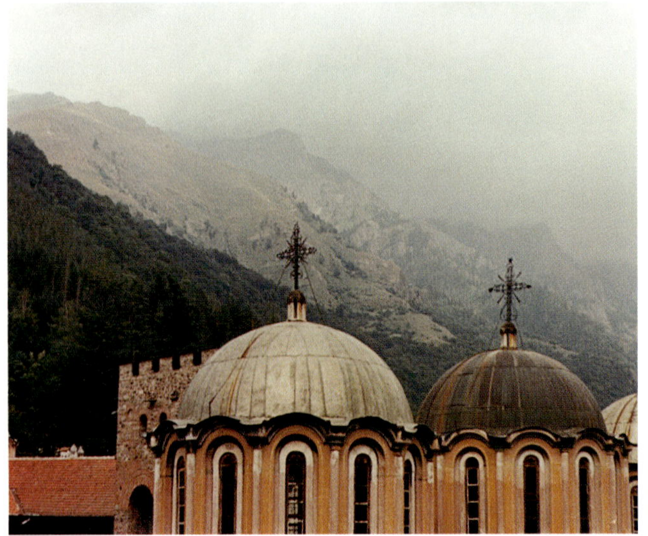

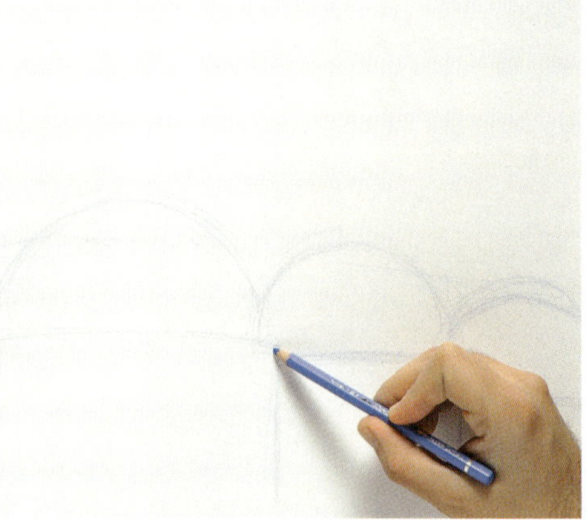

We draw the model with the light blue pencil, using simplified geometric forms. You should hold the pencil in the middle to obtain a light, fluid line. In this first step you will only draw the most basic lines. These form the infrastructure of the buildings and the planes that comprise the mountains in the background.

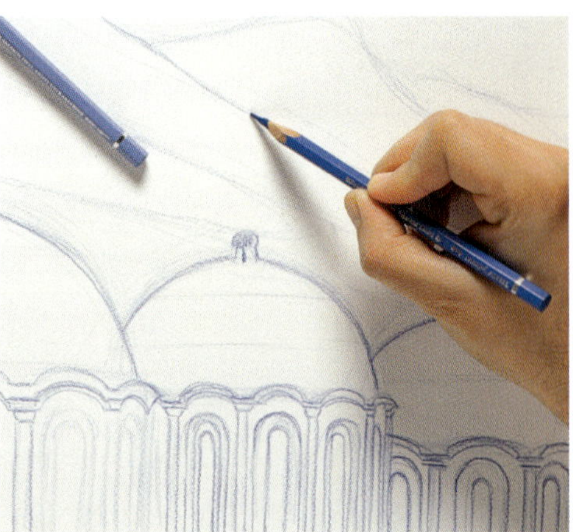

Redraw all the lines with the darker pencil. This ensures the correction of the initial sketch with new, darker lines that will be visible during the entire development of the drawing. As you draw, adjust the form to match the model and add architectural details.

When sketching with oil-base pencils, it is a good idea not to press too hard, since they are very hard to erase in case of an error.

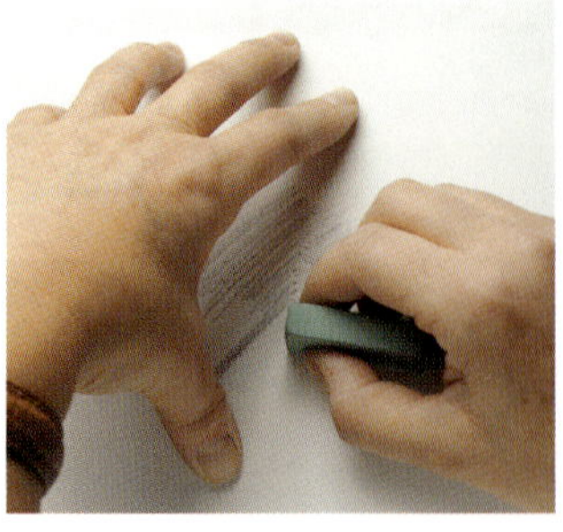

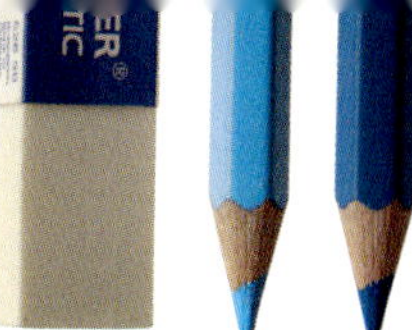

12.2

GRADING THE MOUNTAINS. Apply the first gradations to the mountains to convey the effect of distance. Begin with darker gradations at the lowest part, making them flatter and more unfocused as they move away from the foreground.

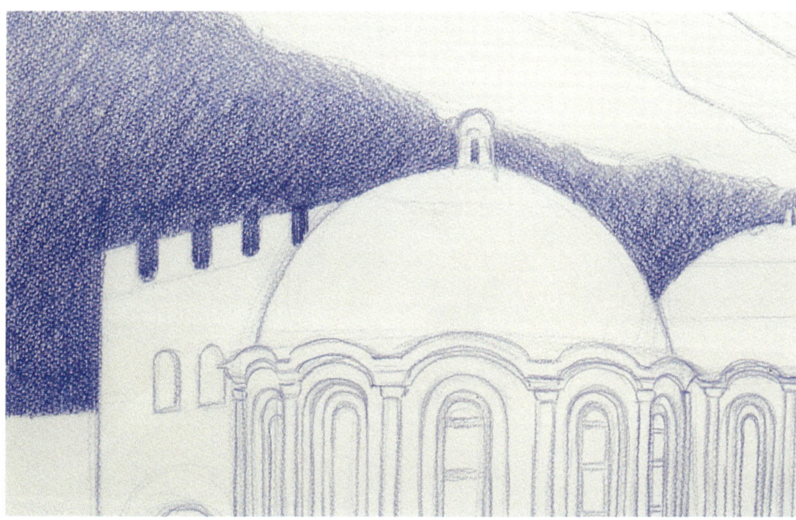

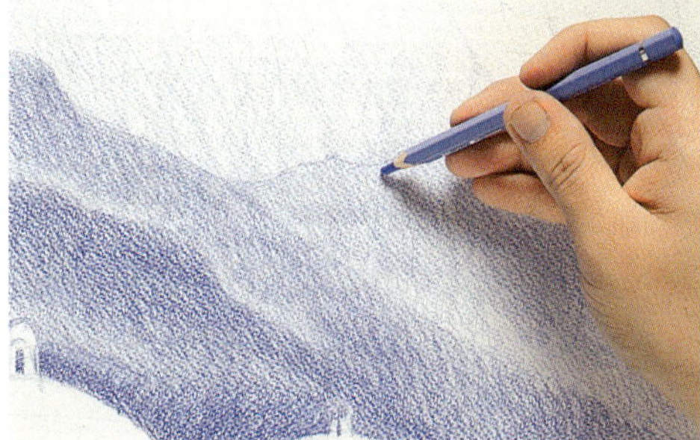

The two most distant planes are the lightest and least defined. For this you must use the light pencil again, making two new gradations with the same technique as you used for the previous plane. On the last mountain, make the lines looser so they spill into the sky to break up the edge of the mountain and integrate it into the atmosphere.

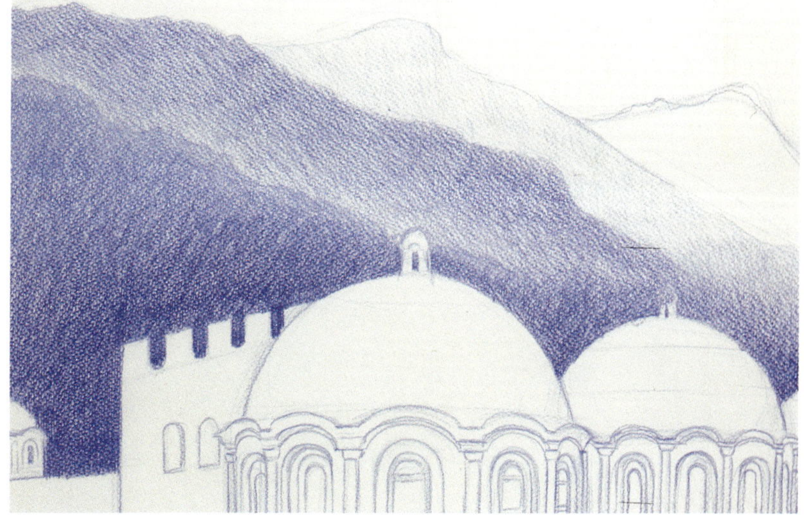

Start by grading the shape of the mountain closest to the viewer. First, draw the outline of the building with a uniform, dark blue tone. Grade up to the upper outline of the mountain, so that the lightest shading is at this edge.

Resolve the second shape in the same way. This time, the gradation is inverted: the lightest part corresponds to the lowest part in the area where it intersects with the shape below it. Here, the shading becomes darker as it moves up the paper.

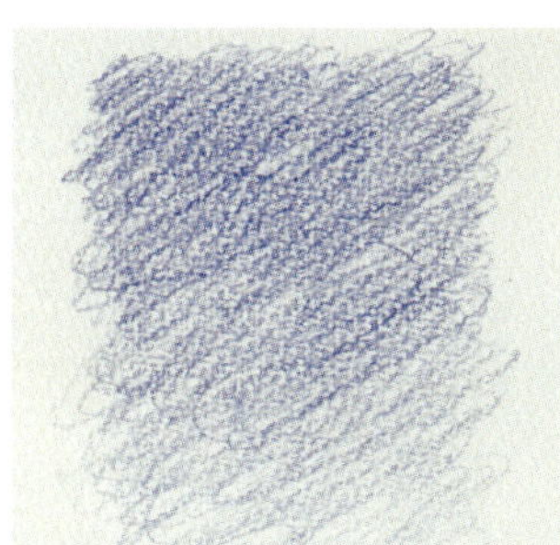

The gradations of the mountains in the foreground show a succession of short, overlaid lines going in the same direction.

12.3

ARCHITECTURAL GRADATION. As you move on to the foreground the gradation is more precise, since it must combine with more definite lines and architectural details. Here, gradations help explain the architecture by emphasizing each one of its details without sacrificing the volumetric effect.

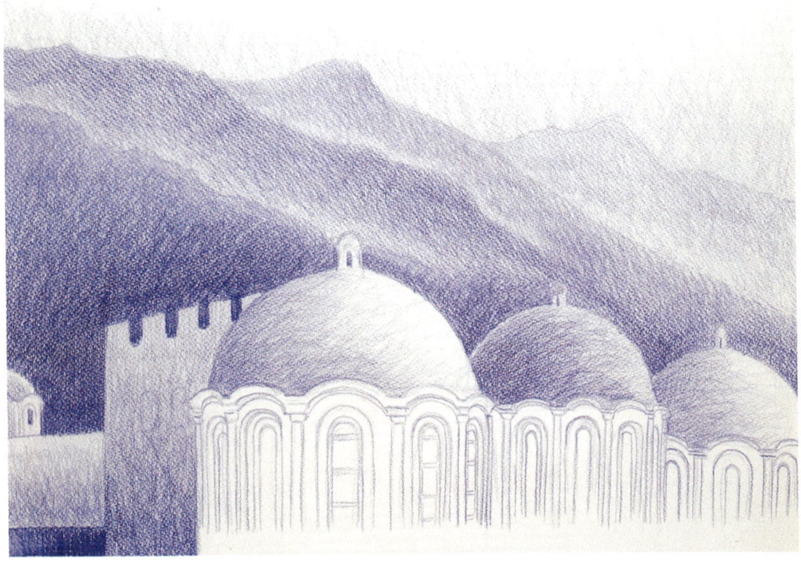

Continue grading the tower and the roof on the left very lightly. The lightest area will be in the upper part so it will contrast with the darkness of the mountains. Work on the hemispherical forms of the cupolas, whose success depends on your ability to control the pressure of the pencil as you gradually color from the darkest tone to the next-lightest one.

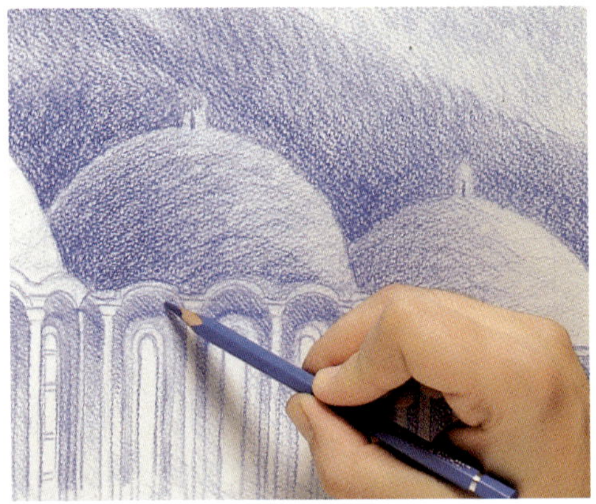

Very carefully, since the area you wish to grade is so small, color the undersides of the arches, leaving the columns and the windows to be colored later. It is a matter of controlling the darkness of the line and the density of the hatching.

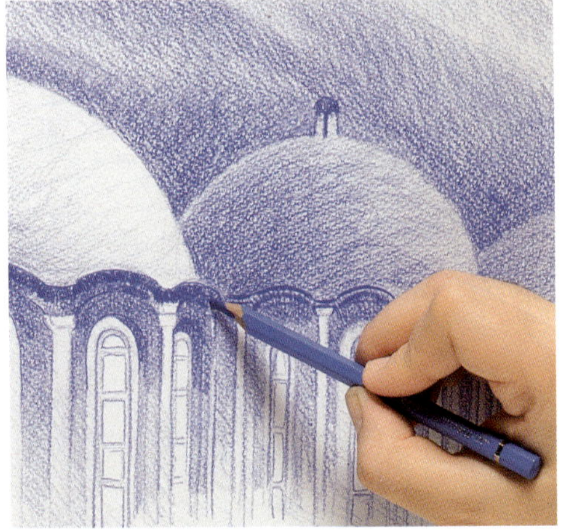

Apply the darkest tones to the parts of the shadow that are between the cupola's columns. Pressing the sharpened pencil harder to make darker lines, color the curves of the roof and the tower's openings.

Among tonal values, white is the lightest tone and a very important reference value. Try to leave the white of the paper free of color to represent this value in the proper areas.

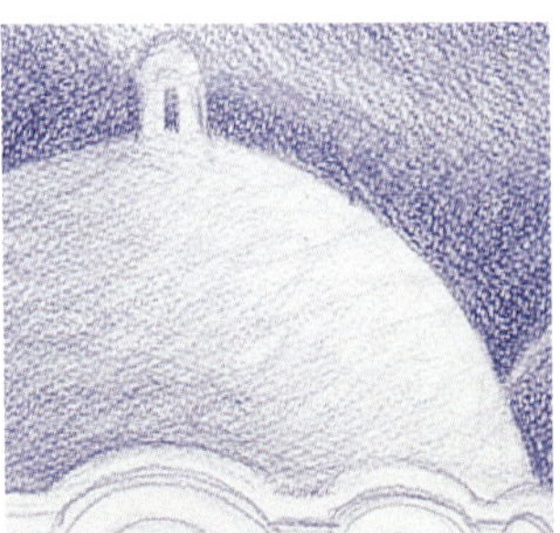

Architectural gradation often employs cross-hatching to give the foreground more solidity.

54

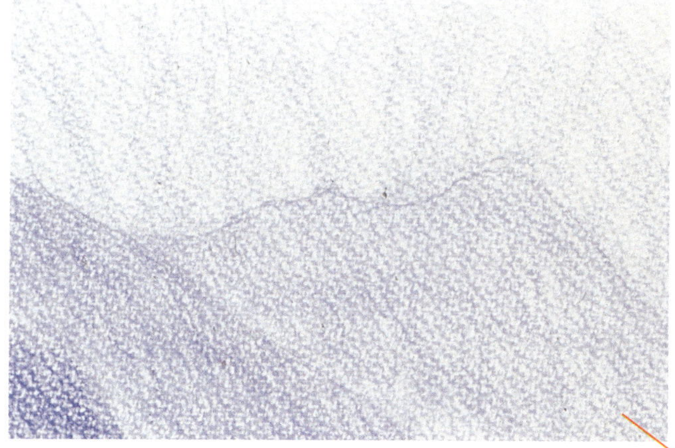

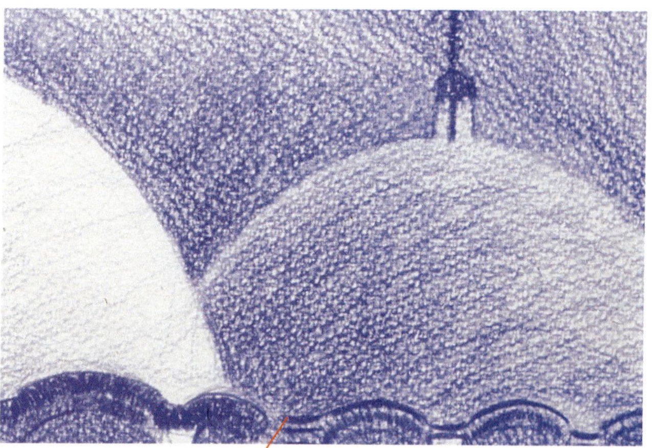

Apply a succession of light, wide, well-spaced lines with the light blue pencil to integrate the outline of the mountains with the sky in the background. This effect produces a hazy, atmospheric feeling around the last mountain shape.

The direction of the lines should always enclose the volume of the surface that they describe. The lines are curved on a spherical surface.

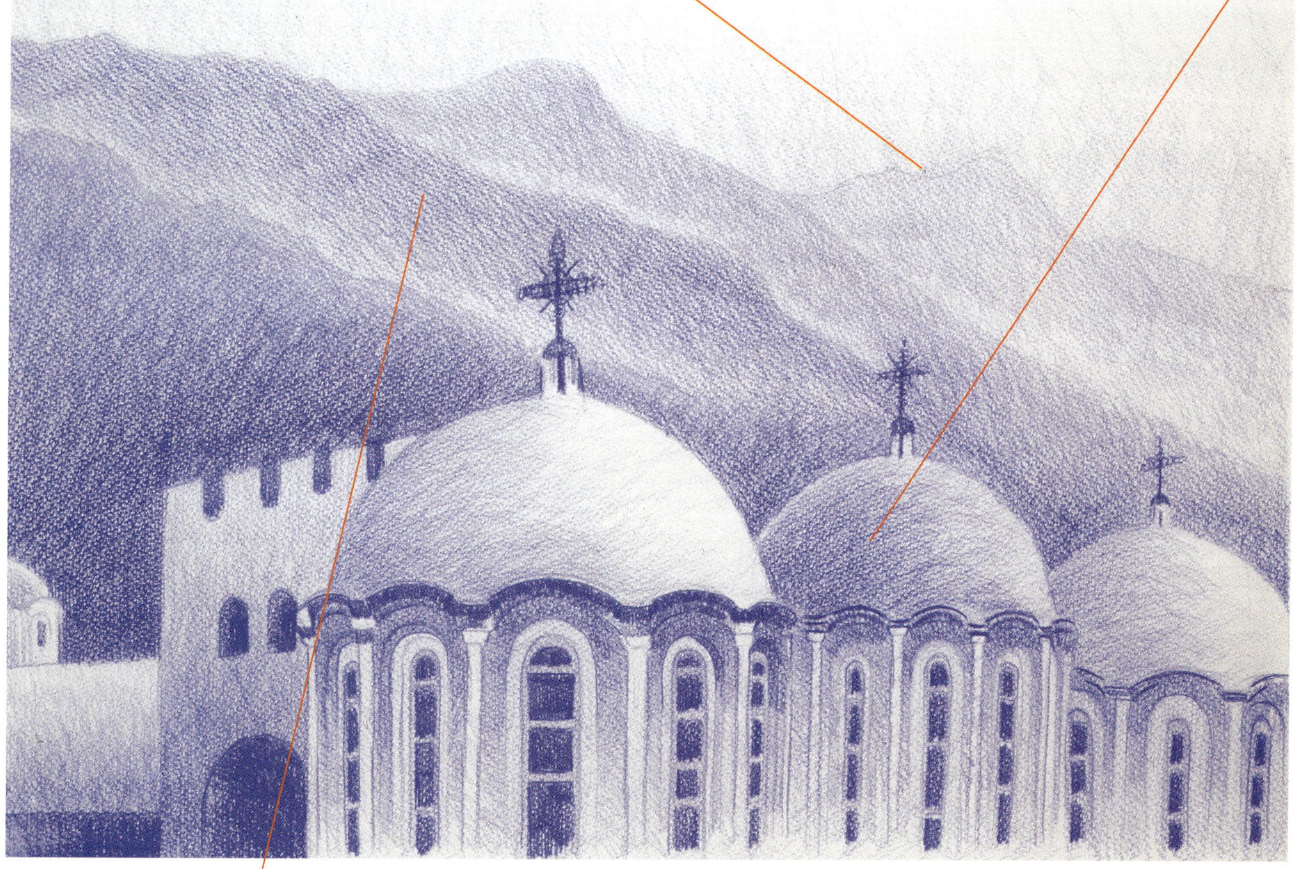

The last step of the drawing consists of detailing the architecture in the foreground, coloring the windows, drawing the crosses, and outlining the tonal effect of the columns. It is a matter of working the elements more with graded values than with pure lines. Drawn by Gabriel Martín.

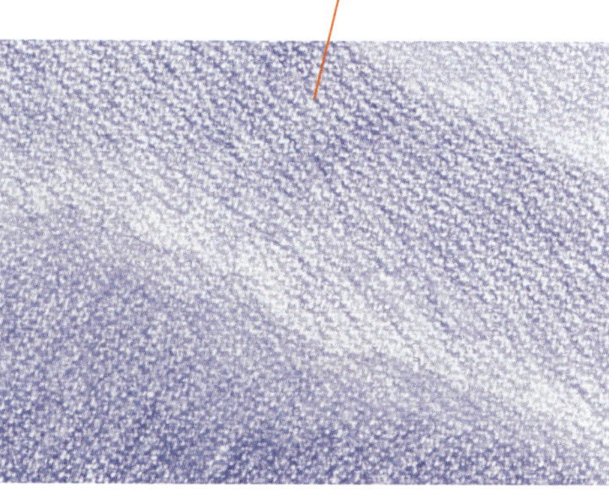

To illustrate the edges of the mountains, leave small, light graded areas that let the white of the paper show through, differentiating each plane.

THE EFFECT OF VOLUME. The two-dimensional representation of a three-dimensional model is initially an image in the brain; it is later defined on paper with a series of lines that indicate its silhouette and its main divisions. This is achieved by increasing the contrast between illuminated and shaded areas and combining them with a modeling effect that is more abrupt than usual.

13.1

PLANNING AND LINE DRAWINGS. Before you work with the shading, which is the aspect that creates the effect of three-dimensionality, make a line sketch of the model so that you can apply the shadows to a correctly constructed scheme.

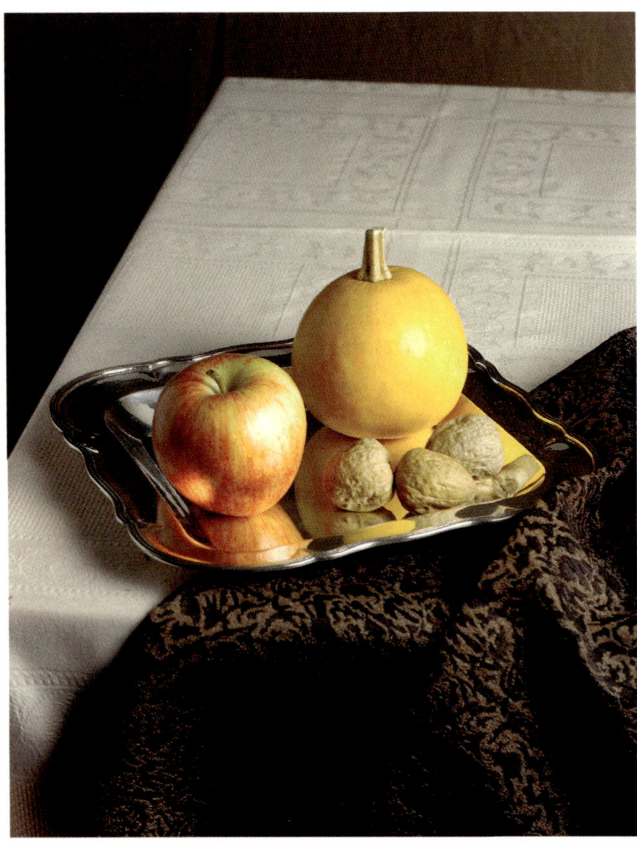

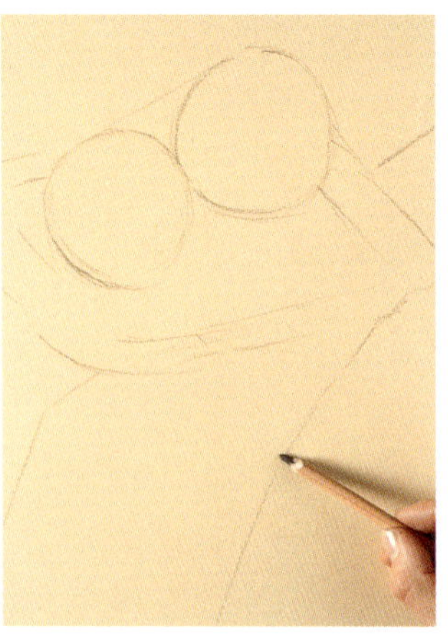

Make an initial sketch of the model with general, linear strokes using a sepia chalk pencil. Your hand should move across the paper with lightness and agility.

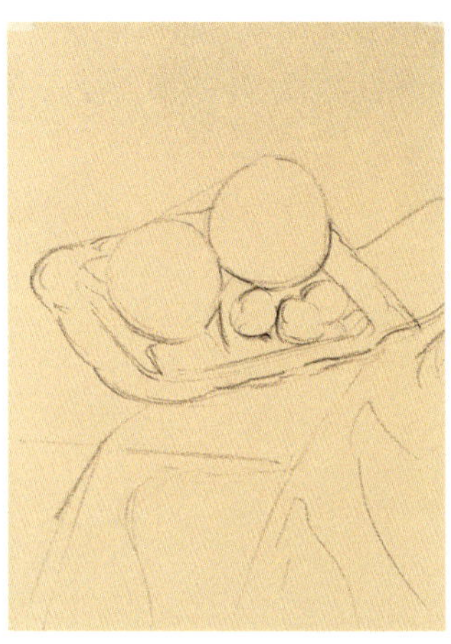

Synthesize the forms and the folds of the cloth, as well as the placement of fruit on the tray. These lines should be darker and more specific.

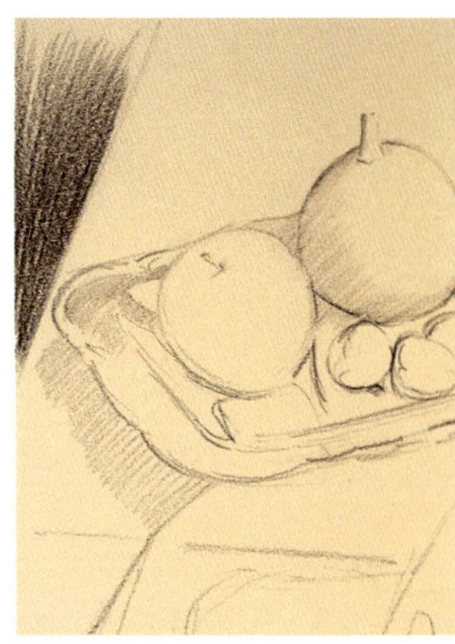

Once the drawing is completely worked out, add the first shading. The light source is to the right, so you should begin by drawing the shadows on the left side.

If you try working on a sheet of colored paper instead of a white one, you will find it easier to apply the tones because you will be able to work as well with white chalk as with sepia.

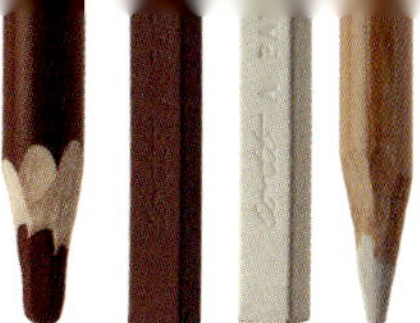

13.2

SHADING THE CLOTHS. Drawing the drapery constitutes a true exercise in seeing because of the complicated shading of its folds. The drapery's function is not just anecdotal; it is a formal counterpoint that helps harmonize and emphasize the still life, adding, if necessary, a note of contrast to enliven the composition.

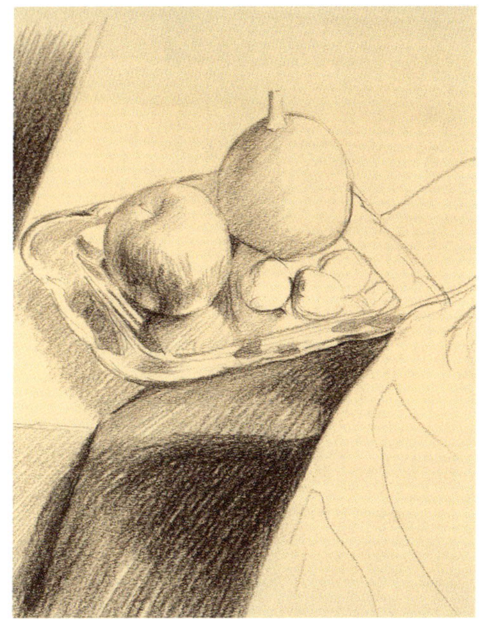

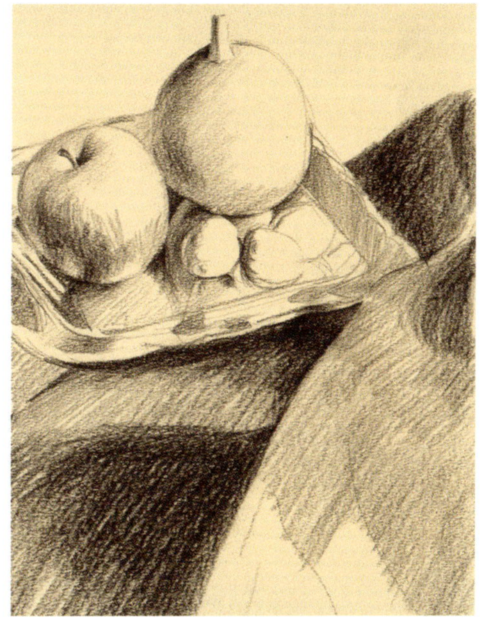

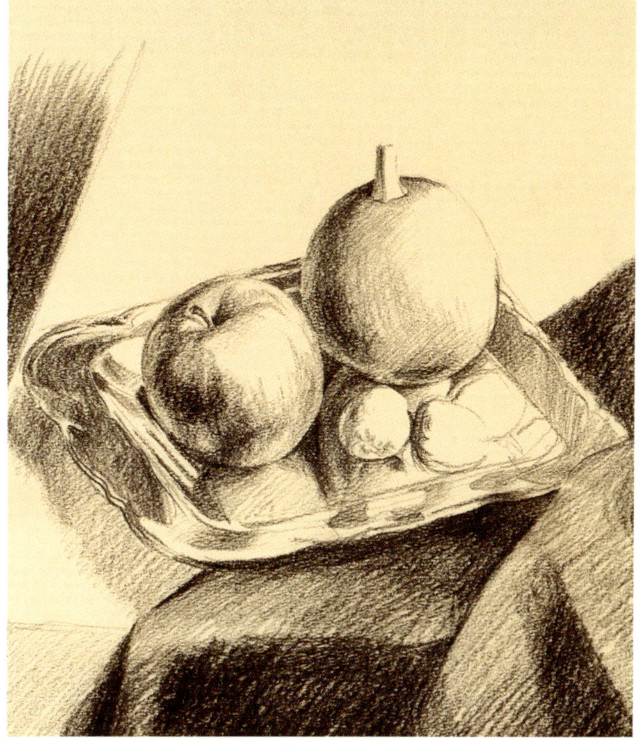

The first piece of cloth seems smooth, with hardly any wrinkles, but it indicates an important fold at the side of the table. Here, begin applying dark grays on the top part; the grays should become lighter as they approach the edge of the table. Draw a separating line there from which you again use dark shading that fades as it moves down the paper.

Do the same thing with the next piece, although this time you will follow a more irregular line. Using a dark sepia, outline the tray, making it lighter as you move away from it. The fold and the fall of the cloth are colored with a medium shading that lets the tone of the paper show through.

The folds are straight lines. Draw them by using the contrast between light and dark areas. From there, the tonal value fades. The key to drawing folds is to notice their structure and not forget the direction of the fabric: heavy curves and pleats that fall diagonally.

If you observe the drapery and folds of clothing in isolation, you can look at them as an abstract composition.

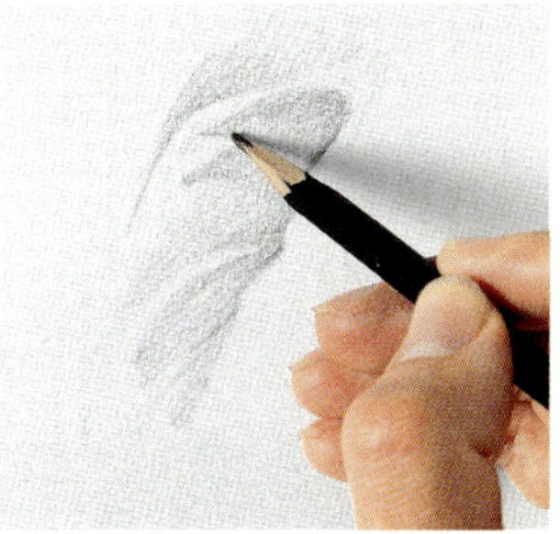

One practical exercise consists of making a sketch of whatever piece of cloth is at hand. This will show you that all fabrics have different folds and varied textures.

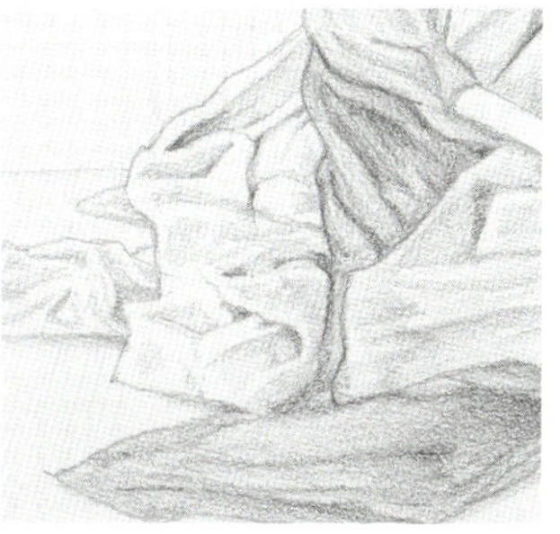

13.3

CONSTRUCTING VOLUME. Now you will try a study of light and shadow using a grouping of fruit. You will establish the different tones so that the forms are modeled beginning with a flat representation and finishing with a three-dimensional effect.

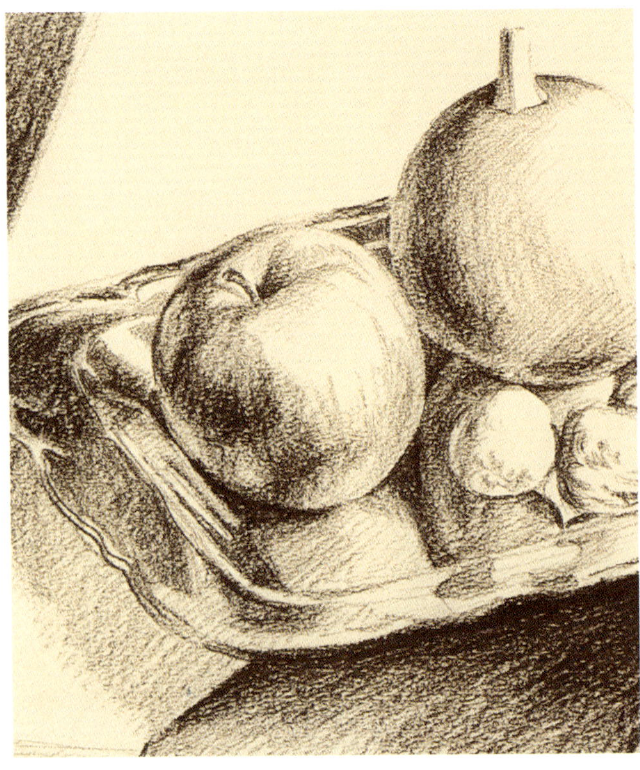

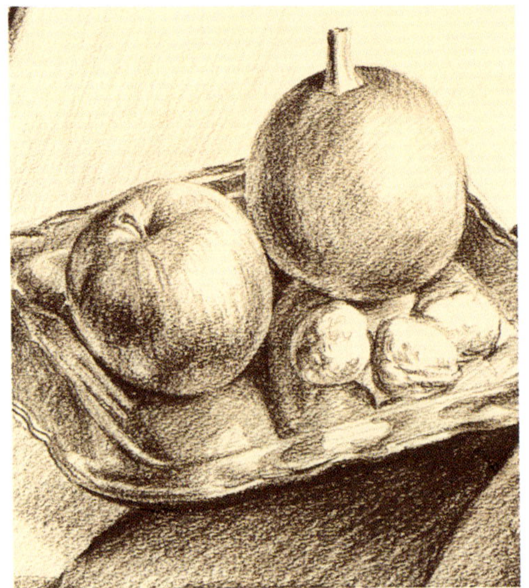

The best way to model fruit is by creating light gradations that move from the darkest area to the lightest that the paper allows. To avoid too many tonal jumps, work the apple and the squash very lightly with the sepia chalk, caressing the paper with the point of the chalk.

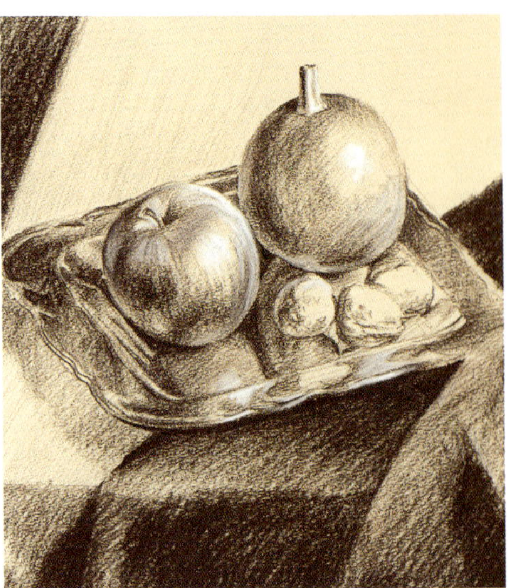

Add the highlights to the fruit with white chalk so that the contrasts between light and dark tones are maximized. Highlights can take the form of a reflected point on the squash or can be created with smooth transitions of tone that are integrated in the underlying shadows.

Darken the shading on the left side of the fruit with new applications of chalk. Darken the tray with graded strokes that leave open small areas where the color of the paper can be seen. Draw the reflection of the fruit on the metal tray. The reflection is always darker than the real model.

The direction in which you apply shading should not be random, but should follow the volume of the object. The application is circular in the case of a spherical object, curved on a curved object, and straight on a flat object.

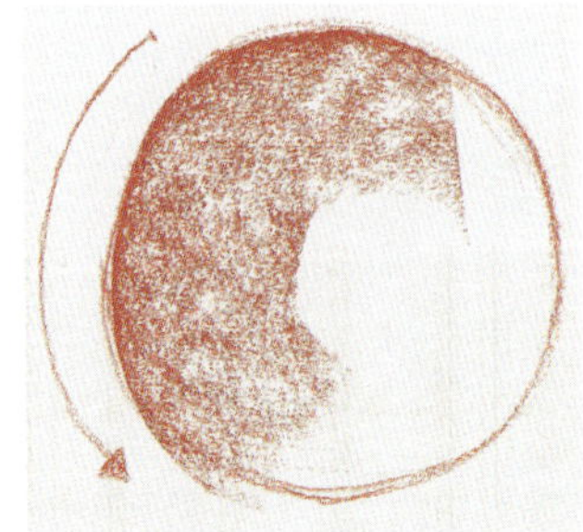

It is easy to create false contrasts, by adding highlights where on the model there is only shadow, so that the shape of the apple is not confusing and can be drawn with greater clarity.

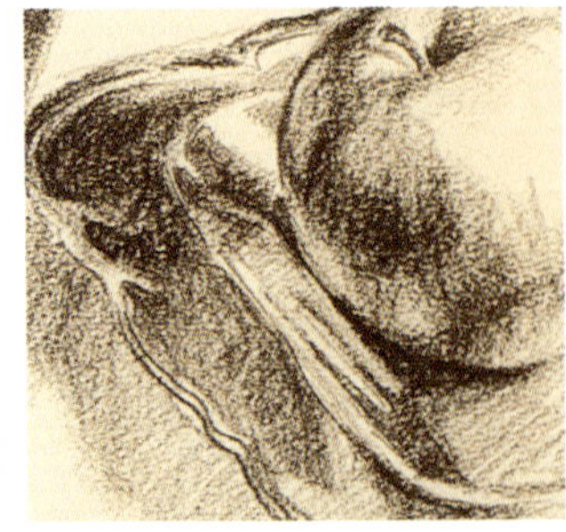

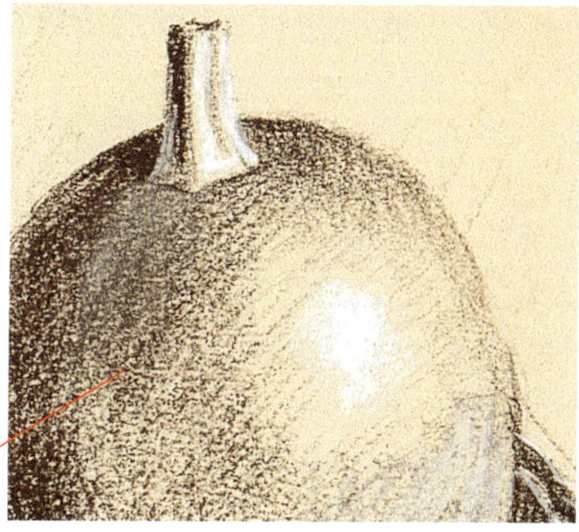

After the shading and the white highlights are finished, you can see how the artist created a successful value study of the subject, achieving a level of modeling that shows the objects in all their volume and relief. We can say that the artist models by imitating in two dimensions what the sculptor imitates in three. Drawn by Óscar Sanchís.

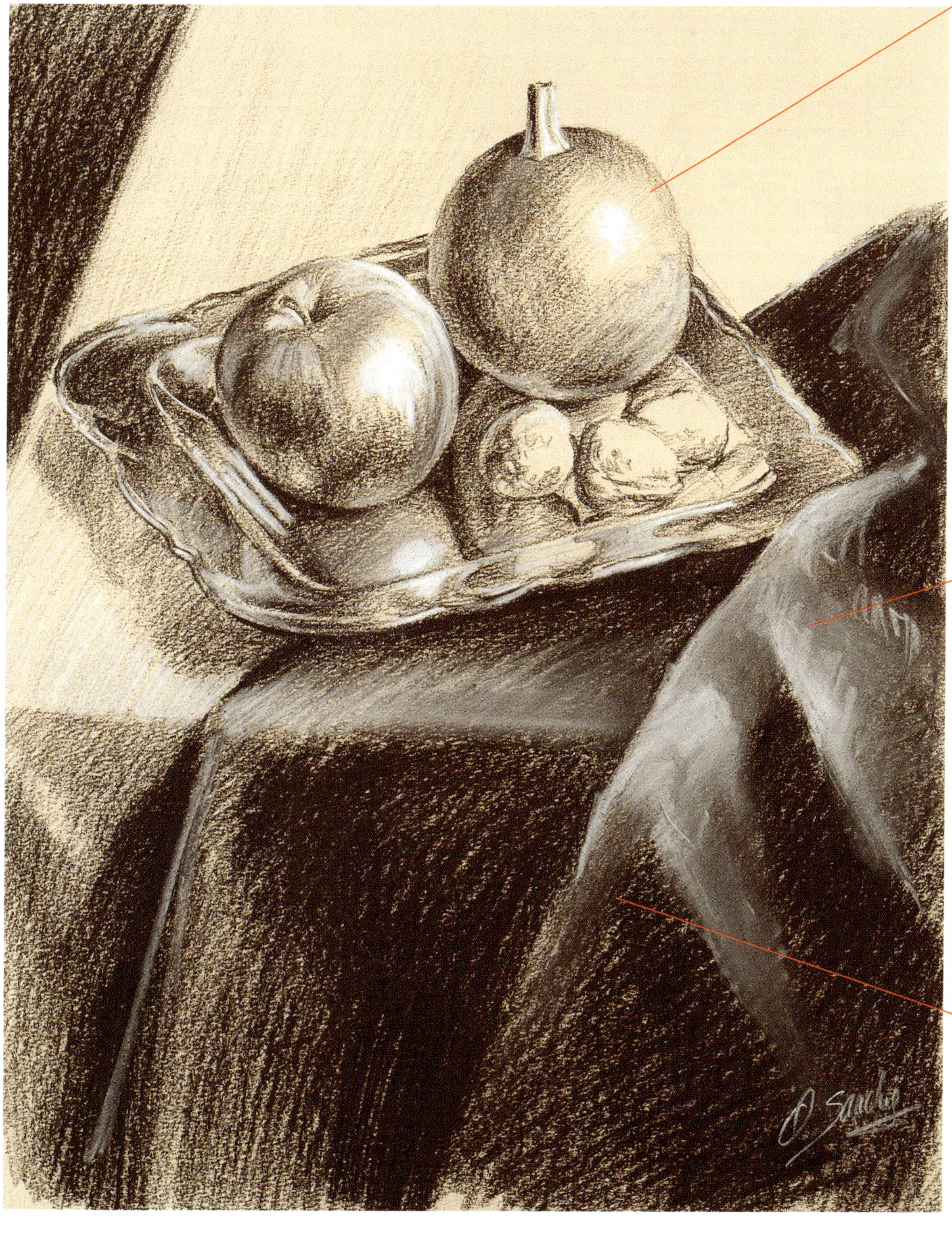

When you draw on colored paper it is important to experiment with the color that it adds. If you leave large spaces untouched, you allow the forms to be clearly perceived and offer a more linear finsh to the three-dimensional effect.

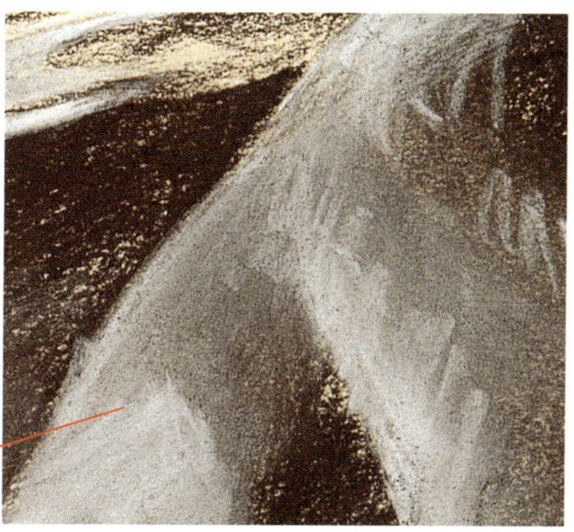

The applications of white chalk on the cloth appear blended and integrated with the shading. This way the transitions in tone are softer and contribute to the description of the delicate texture of the fabric.

The intention, density, and direction of the line varies according to the part of the cloth being drawn.

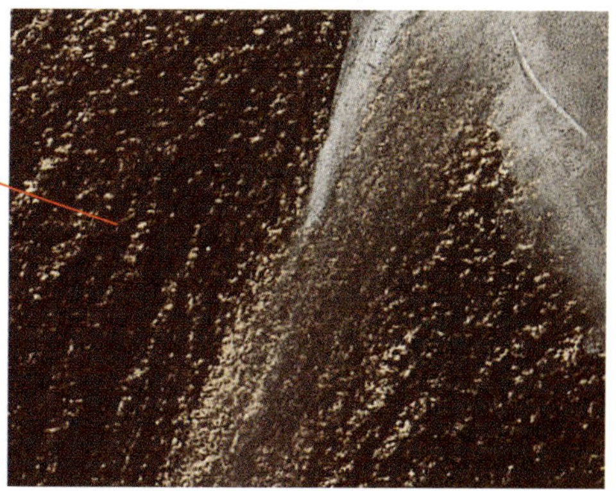

CONTOUR LINES. Lines should always explain the form of the object. If they are oriented in the same direction as the surface of the object, they will emphasize its volumetric effect.

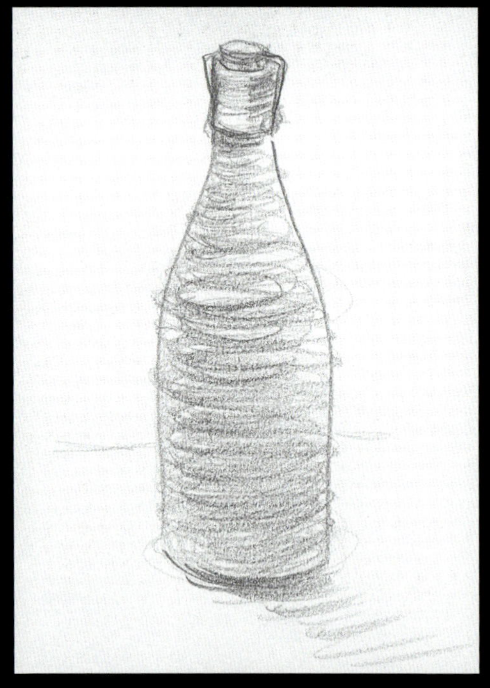

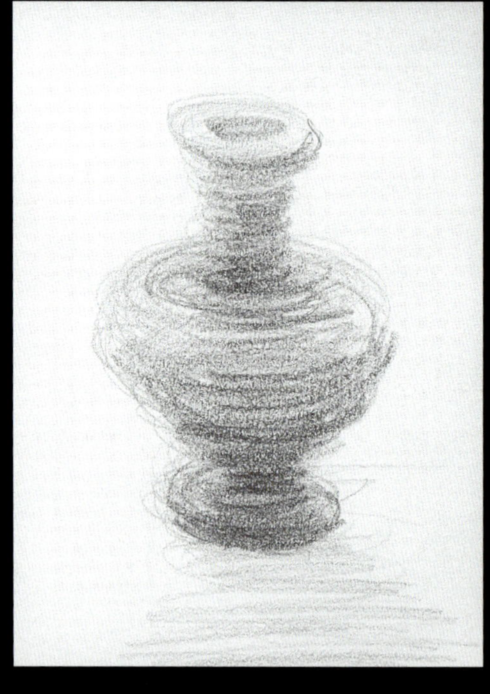

Apply shading in the form of spiral lines that wrap around the bottle. Simple shading with circular lines is enough to suggest the physicality of the object.

If you continue using contour lines to create several values you can create a softer effect around the silhouette of the object, adding, without really trying, a kinetic, spinning effect to the model.

THE DIRECTION OF THE SHADOW. In your drawing it is a good idea to emphasize the effects of light that you observe, and even to exaggerate them. You can also indicate the direction of the shadow.

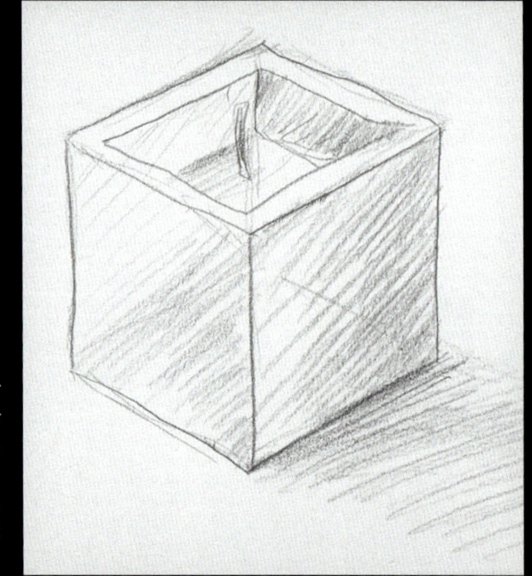

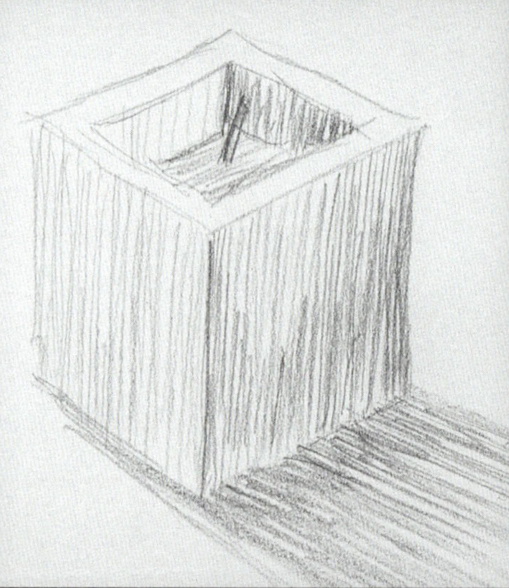

The shading should consist of straight lines on flat surfaces. If the projected shadow is going to be blurred, the shading itself, created with hardly any pressure on the pencil, should also look that way.

However, if you wish to give importance to the shadow projected by the object, giving it more strength and relevance, you should make the lines darker and emphasize their direction.

MODELING SPHERICAL FORMS. Shadows cast by objects, and those that describe a change of plane, especially when dealing with a rigid surface, usually have very defined outlines. On the other hand, spherical forms, soft materials, and textures with little relief project more subtle light and shadows.

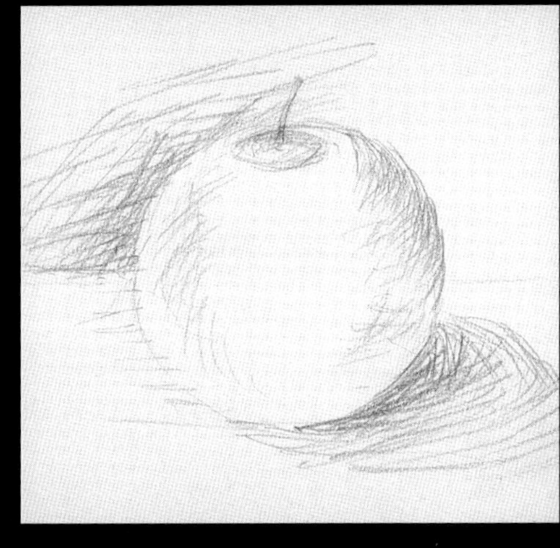

To shade a sphere, it is best to work with overlaid curved lines that help explain the spherical form of the model.

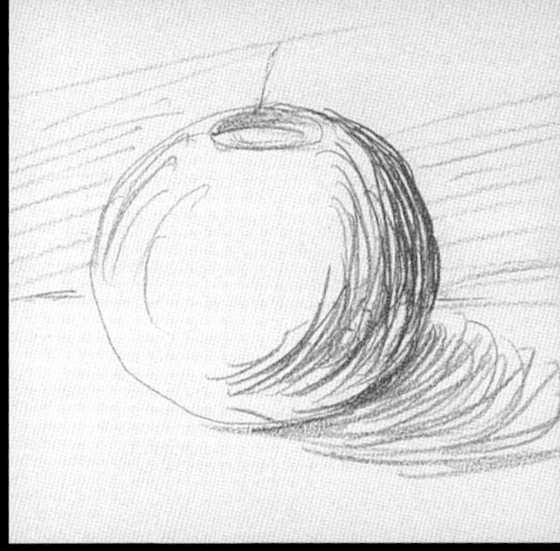

Line is very important in the graphic vocabulary of art because it defines volume, and, above all, because it establishes a sense of direction or movement, tension or reaction, and spatial rhythm or a feeling of repose.

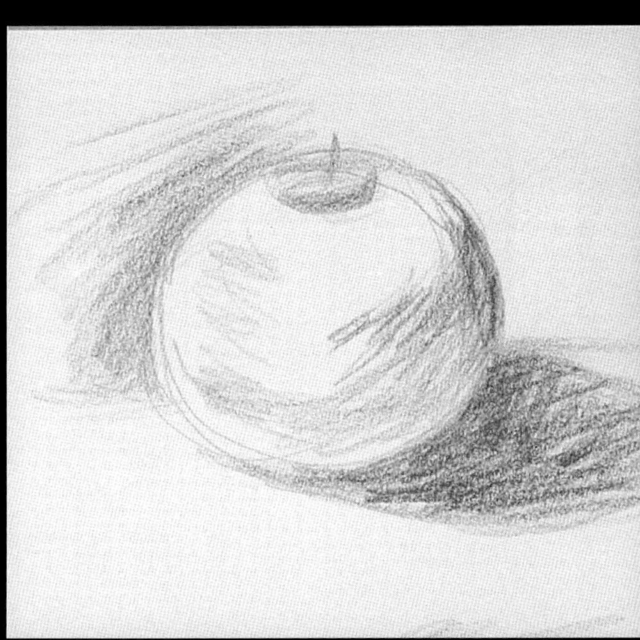

The pencil lines previously drawn for blended modeling do not fill the entire area to be shaded. The area where the final shading will be very light is not touched with the pencil; later blending will spread graphite to this part.

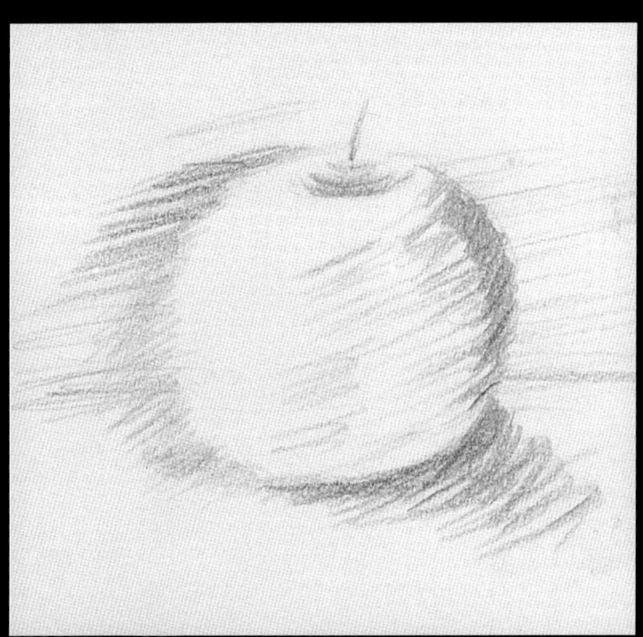

The effects of blending can also be created with light lines, made with very little pressure. No outlines are needed. Draw the form of the apple using the contrasting effect of line hatching.

Gradations are the best way to illustrate the volume of objects. Begin with very dark tones in the shaded area and gradually move toward white as you advance toward the lighter parts.

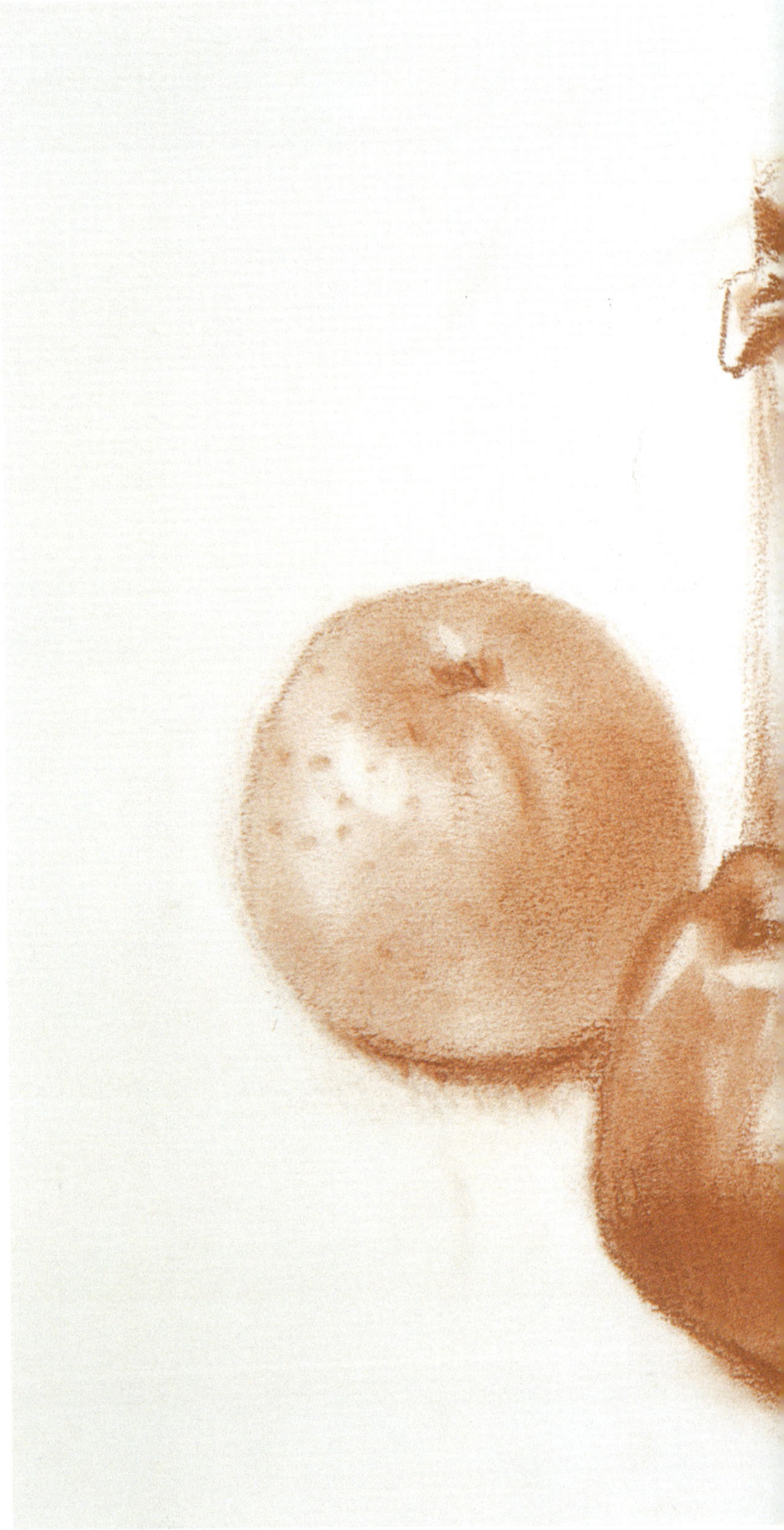

Make the initial applications of tone with the side of a sanguine crayon; this avoids the presence of lines and simplifies blending.

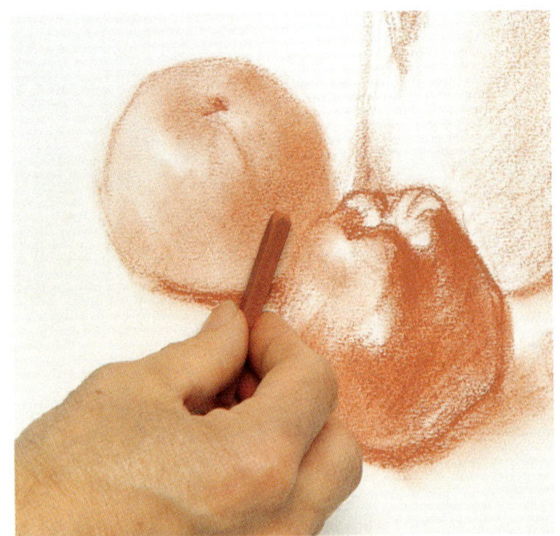

As you work with the tones, redraw the lines and the darkest areas using the point of the sanguine crayon.

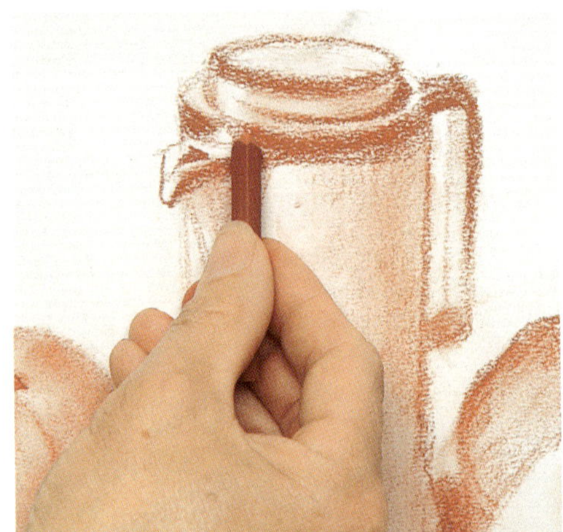

If you approach the drawing using hard, flat shadows, the graphic effect will be more striking, but without gradations the sense of volume will be reduced.

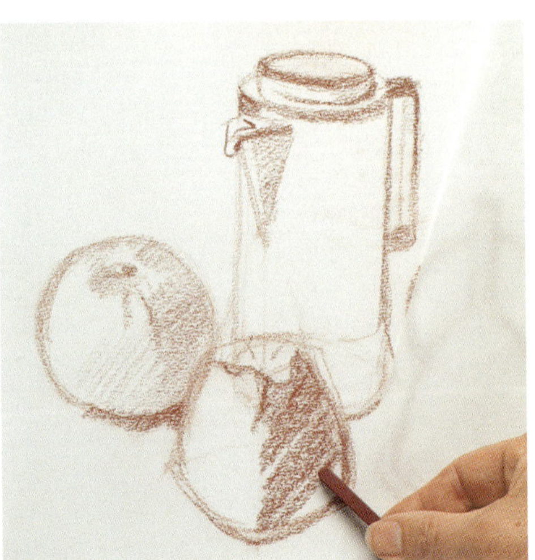

PRACTICING GRADATIONS. Graded values are a conventional method of describing form and volume. The quality of the effect depends on the tonal range that is used. The direct contrast of white and sanguine naturally has a greater impact than the gradual shading of white and sanguine to make reddish tones, although this second method better describes volume.

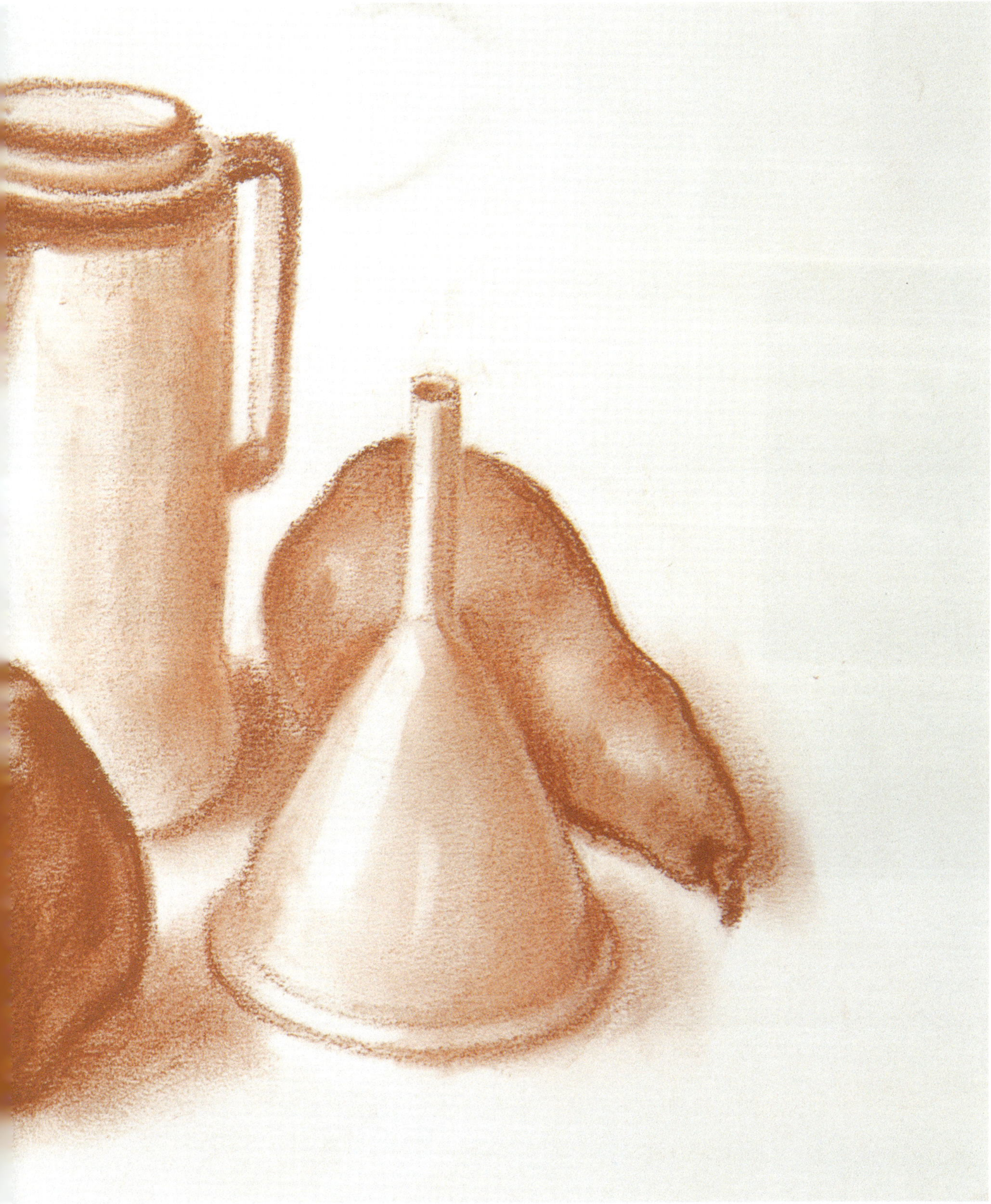

Here are two gradations that exemplify their application to drawing. The first was made by pressing hard on the paper with a crayon and blending very little. The second has been rubbed repeatedly with the fingertips.

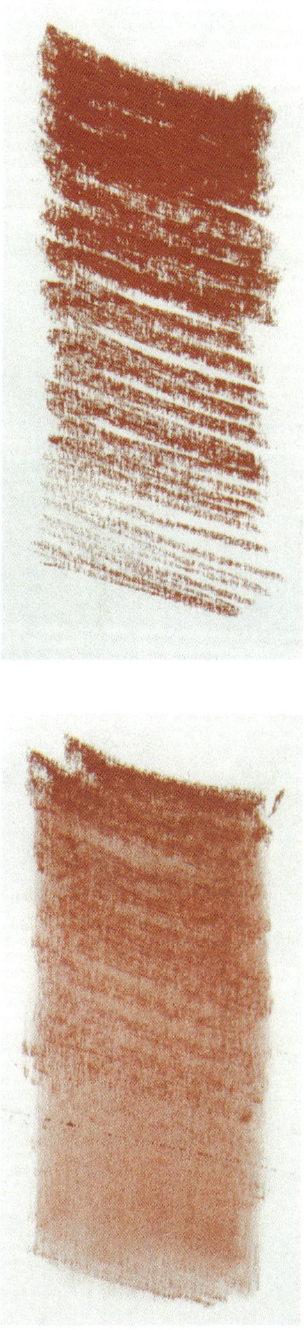

DETAILED CHIAROSCURO DRAWING. After all the work in the previous chapters of approximating the structures and proportions of objects, you will find it particularly pleasant to draw light and shadows. Drawings shaded using the chiaroscuro technique, that is, modeled with strong contrasts between the lighted and the shaded areas, is mainly done with vine charcoal and compressed charcoal because it is easy to correct errors and to achieve a wide scale of grays via the blending process.

14.1

COMBINING LINES. Seemingly complex still lifes can be made by combining distinct, loosely drawn charcoal lines. Pay close attention to the following exercise and see how easy it is to learn this technique.

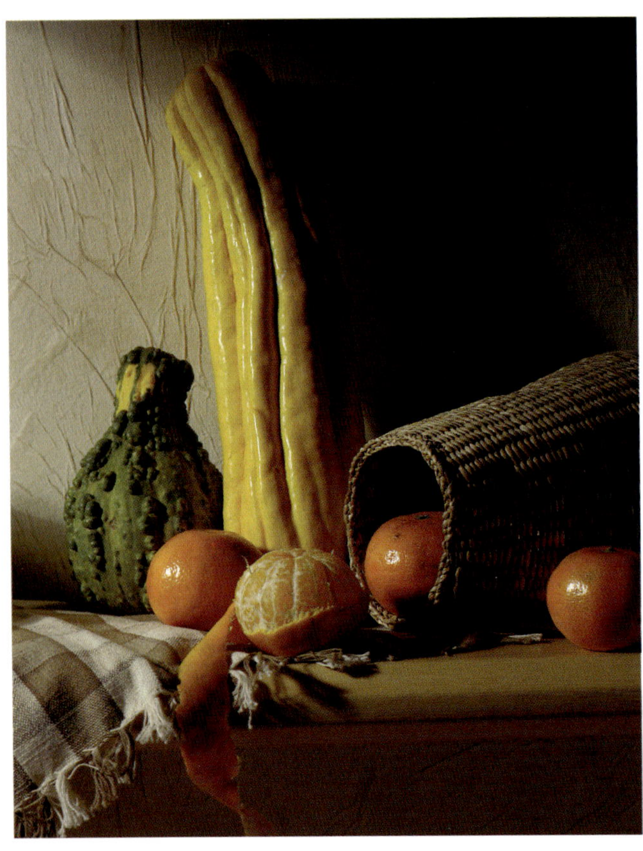

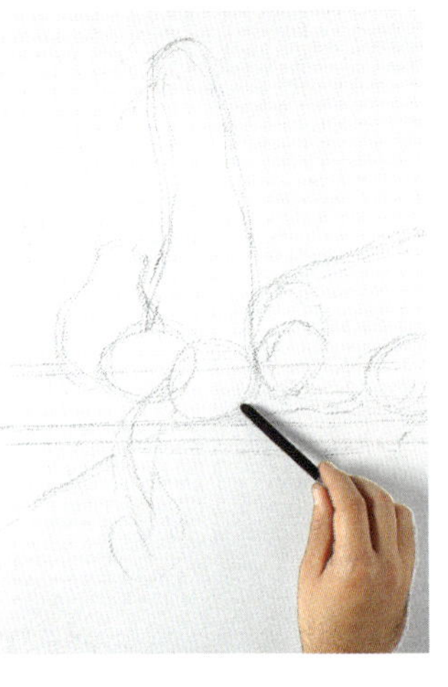

This exercise does not require you to draw very precise forms. Barely touch the surface of the paper with the point of a long vine charcoal stick to make searching and roughly approximate lines. This technique requires strict control of the relationships and proportions among elements rather than great accuracy.

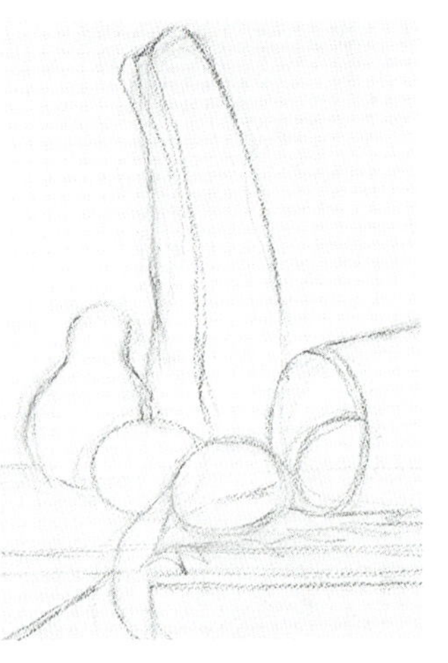

Once you have sufficiently indicated the layout of the main lines, you can tighten up the forms in the still life. You will use a new line, a little darker than before, to outline the model. Without the previous sketch the elements of the model would not be correctly placed.

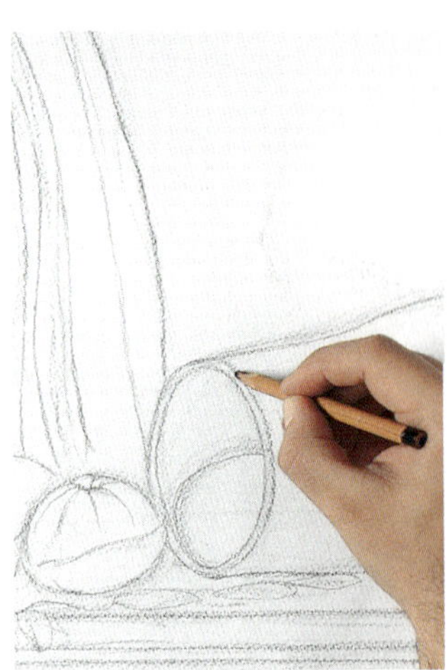

After some erasing that still leaves the charcoal lines visible, you can resolve the last stage of the drawing. Using a soft compressed charcoal pencil with a sharp point, very carefully draw the exact shape and form of each object. This drawing will serve as a guide for the first stages of shading.

When working on a sketch with vine charcoal, remember to use a cotton rag for erasing.

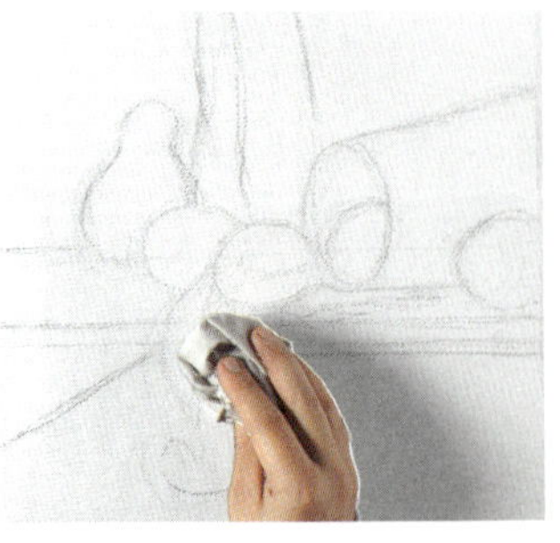

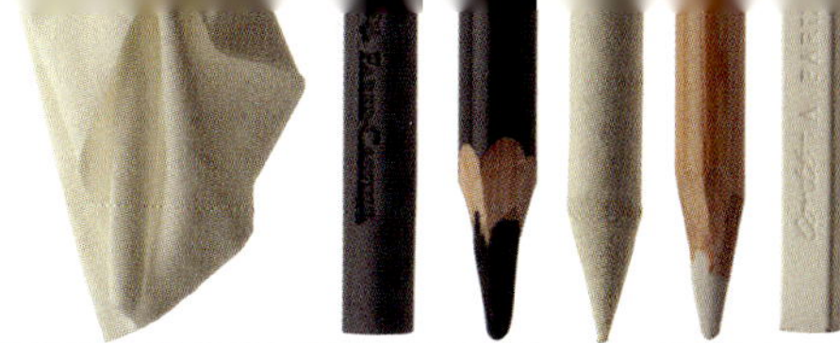

14.2

THE BASE FOR SHADING. The result of the following stage should be a drawing with an initial shaded base that can be used as a point of departure for later effects, correlation, and improvements. The tones will be very flat, monotonous, and without modeling.

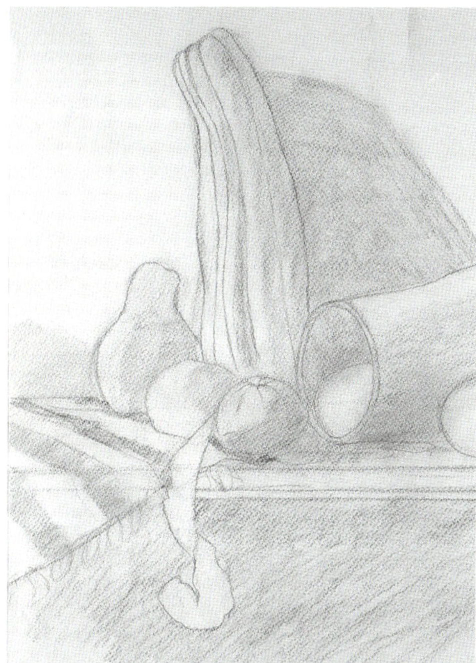

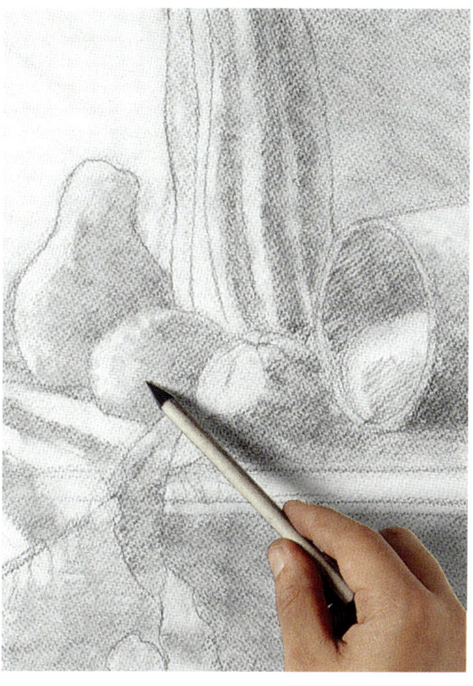

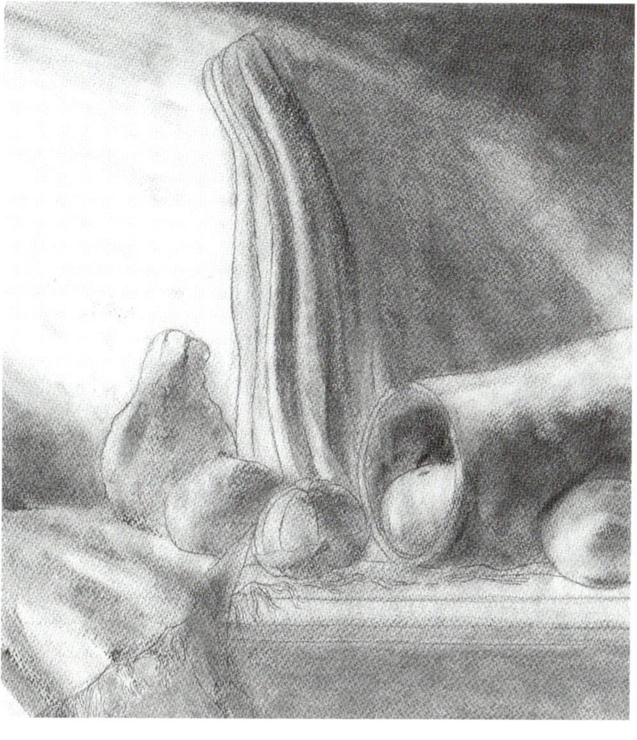

Lightly holding the charcoal stick, mark the darkest parts of the drawing with its point. When applied softly, the shading is quite light but understandable enough. The gray should be a monotone, with no gradations or differences.

The effect of the shading continues to be light. The process of darkening is slow and progressive. As you apply each new layer of charcoal, rub it with a blending stick. Using tones with slight differences of value tends to produce soft, trivial, and austere effects.

Now you will focus on darkening the shadows and contouring the tones. Use the side of a piece of vine charcoal to carefully trace the forms of the shadows, taking care to follow the outlines of the elements and maintain the proper proportions among them without worrying about the details.

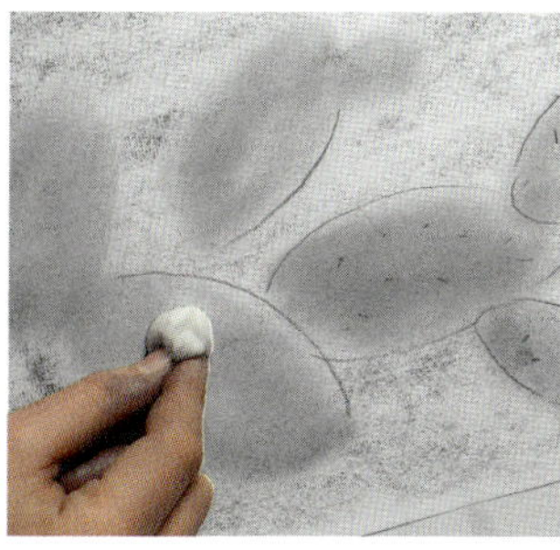

Apply the shading with moderation in the beginning and try blending it in different ways: with your fingers, with a cotton ball, and with a piece of cloth or paper.

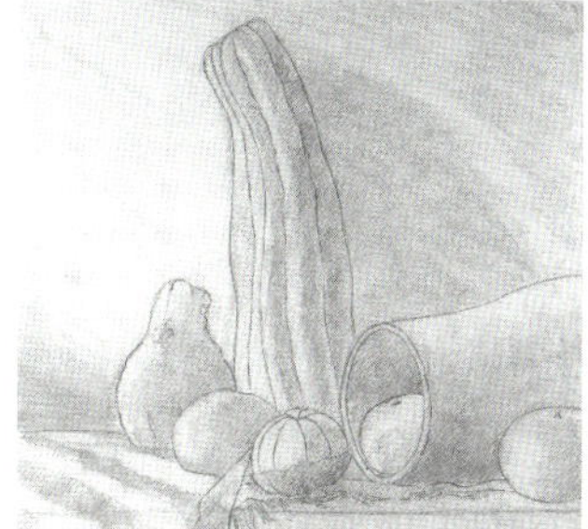

As you shade you can redraw the elements with the compressed charcoal pencil to avoid losing the preliminary drawing. Work very lightly, applying minimal pressure.

14.3

THE CHIAROSCURO EFFECT: REFINING THE SHADING. If you have carefully distributed the light and shadows, the drawing will be at a very advanced stage. All that is left is to increase the contrasts to create a chiaroscuro effect and refine any area that requires it.

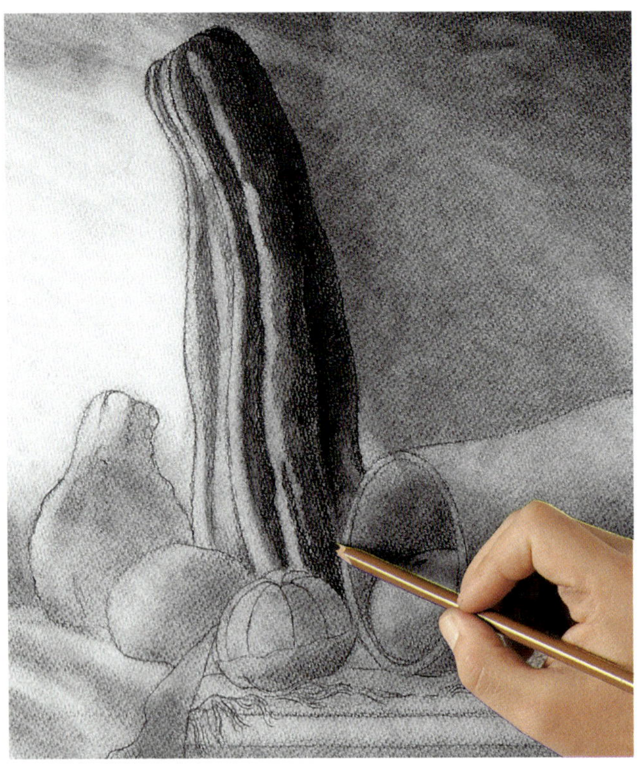

Now, shade with the compressed charcoal stick and pencil. Both make dark blacks that emphasize the chiaroscuro effect. You will have a stronger sense of volume as a result of the greater contrast between light and dark areas. Begin working on the squash, emphasizing its characteristic striated surface.

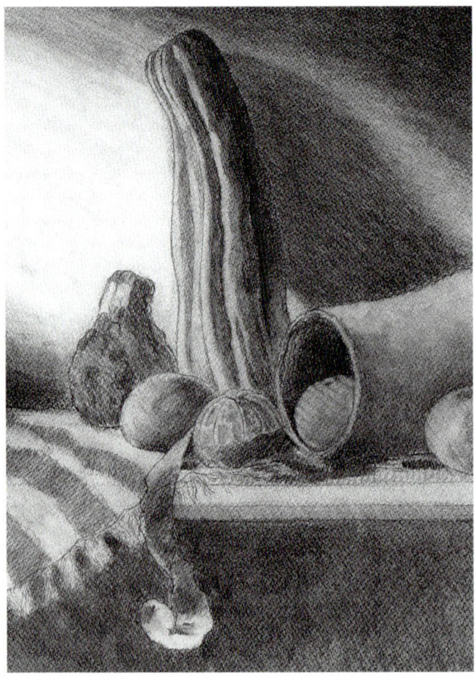

Darken the background with soft gray tones using a stick of compressed charcoal. Work the shadows that outline the elements with their contrast using the compressed charcoal pencil to avoid drawing over the shapes of the objects.

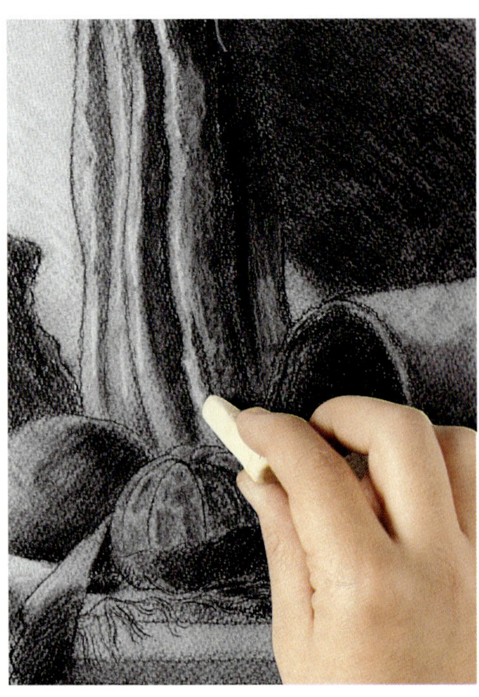

The final touches consist of making highlights with the eraser and resolving the texture of the napkin. Draw the reflections on the surfaces of the fruits and vegetables with a stick of white chalk. If the area you are working on requires more detail you can use a well-sharpened white chalk pencil.

It is typical to incorporate small amounts of white chalk in the shaded areas. Used in this way, they do not act as highlights, but instead help to lighten a black that is too dark.

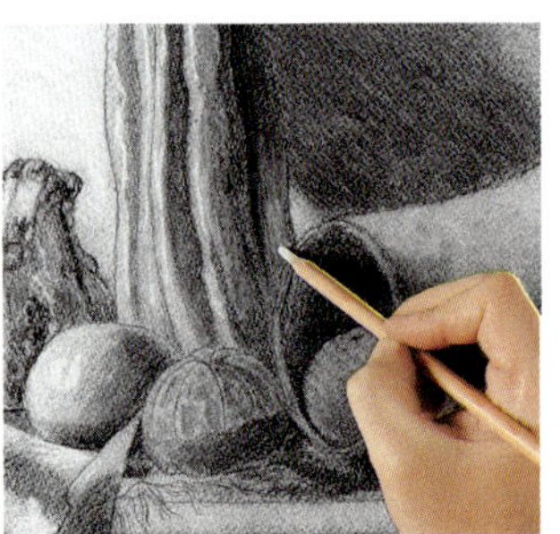

Charcoal pencils can be soft, medium, or hard. If little pressure is applied to them they function like normal pencils.

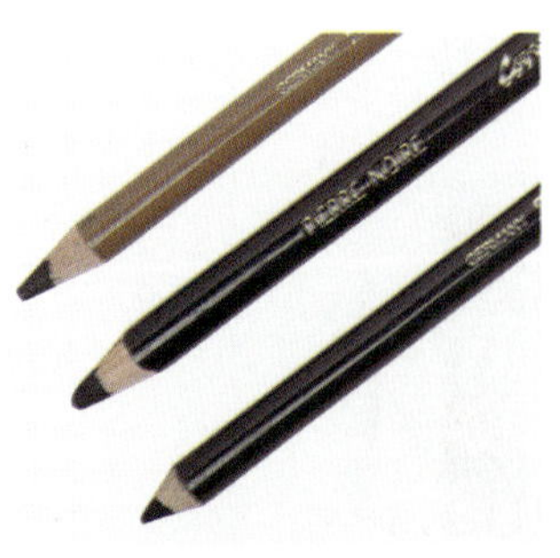

The set of values in a chiaroscuro drawing is referred to as a range. A range can be light or dark. Ranges can also reveal the contrast between extreme values, those nearest to the lightest tones or absolute black; these are referred to as ranges of greater or lesser contrast. Drawn by Gabriel Martín.

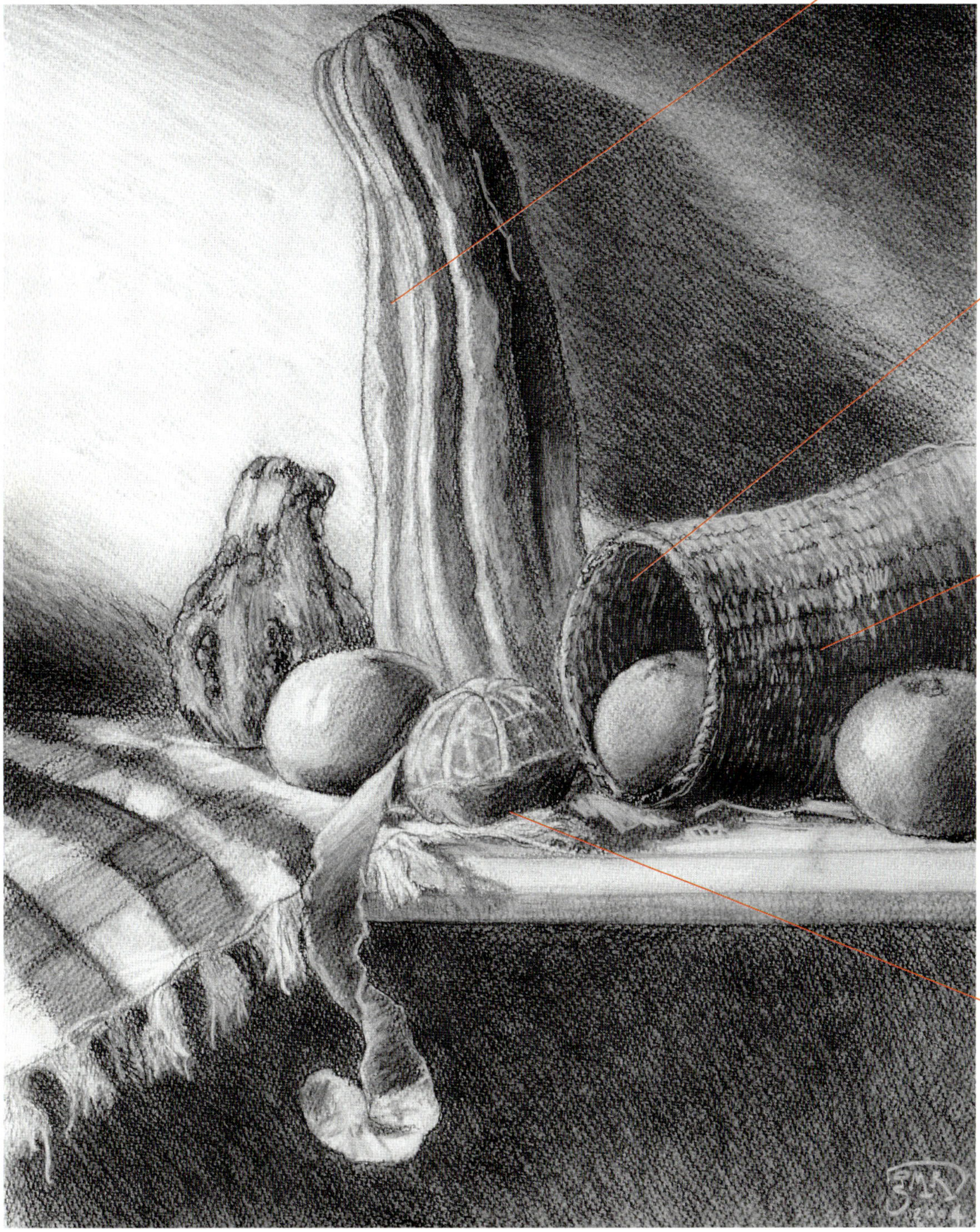

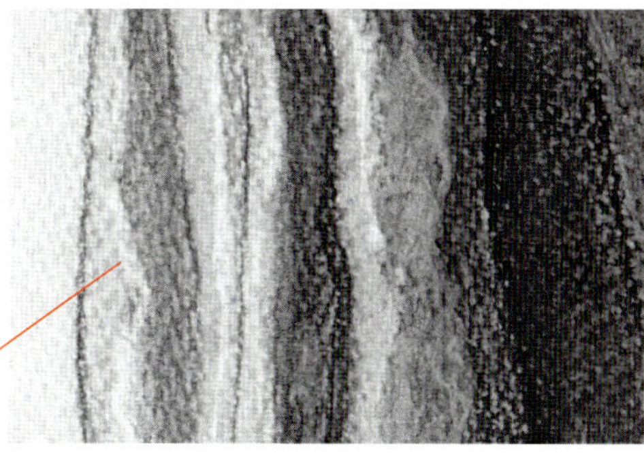

The light areas on the squash were made with a rubber eraser. The highlight effect created in this way is evident.

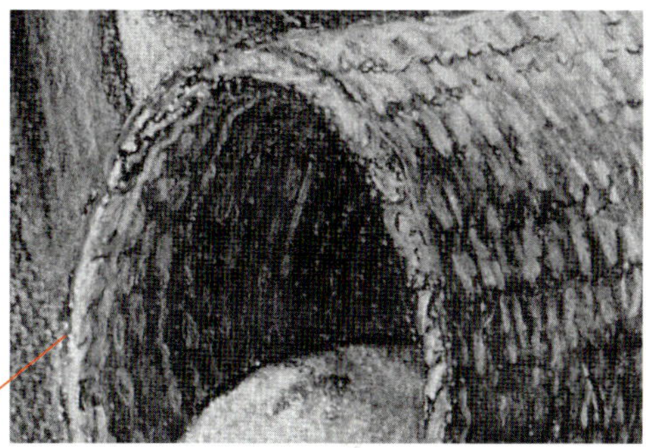

Strong tonal contrasts define the forms of the tones and reveal the relief on the object.

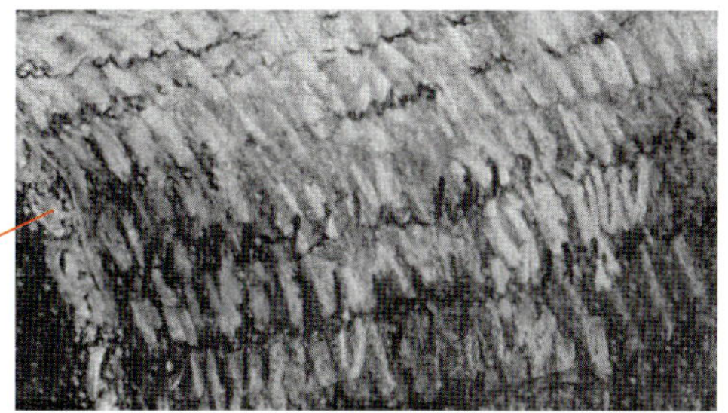

To draw the texture of the wicker basket, first apply the graded shading to the basket. Then sketch the weave over the shading with the white chalk pencil.

Create the texture of the orange by drawing lines with the rubber eraser over the previously shaded surface.

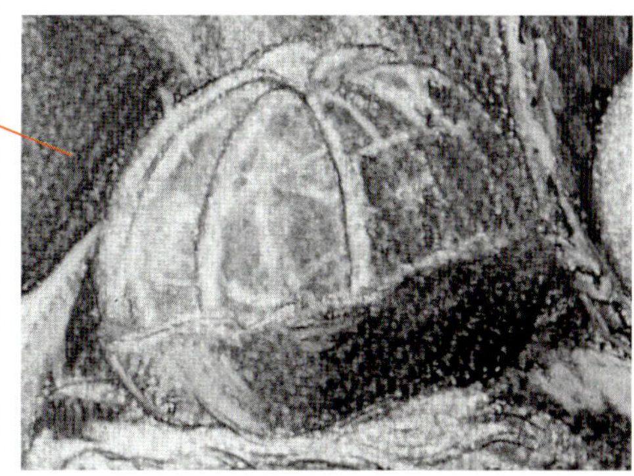

A SUBSTANTIAL DIFFERENCE IN TONE. The basis of any contrast is the evident difference between two tonal areas. Such areas should have clear edges without gradations, rubbing, or blending. The greater the difference in tones, the greater the contrast.

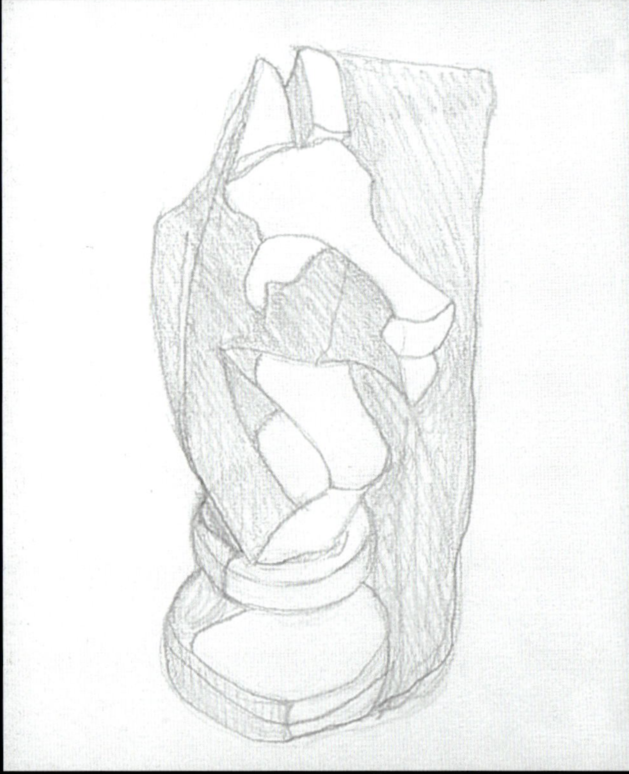

The effect of contrast on a model is achieved by clearly differentiating two areas with different tones. If the shading is light the contrast will be pleasing and not very abrupt.

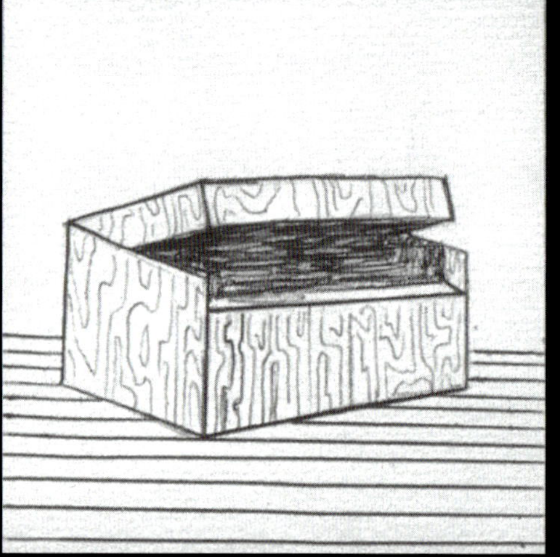

Contrast is not only created by shading. The direction of hatch lines is enough to differentiate two tonal areas. In this case, the horizontal lines of the table contrast with the vertical lines of the box.

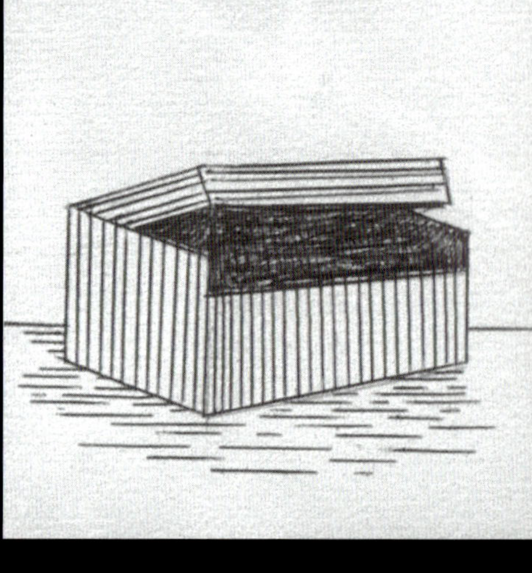

Close hatch lines give the box a general tone that contrasts with the white of the background. On the table a few horizontal lines are enough to create contrast as well.

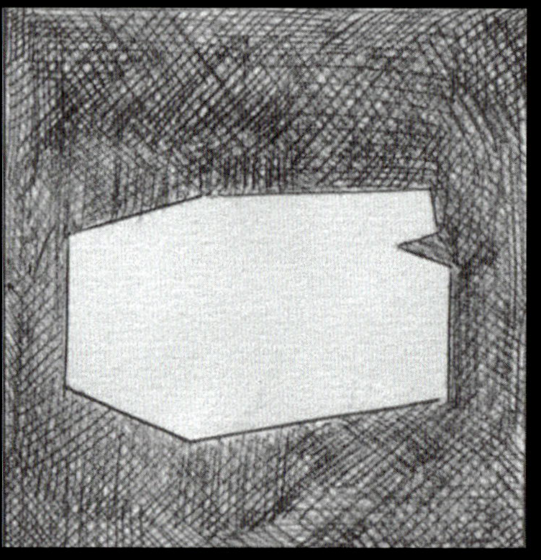

A light, intensely illuminated object creates the most contrast when it is on a completely dark background. In this case the outline is clearly visible.

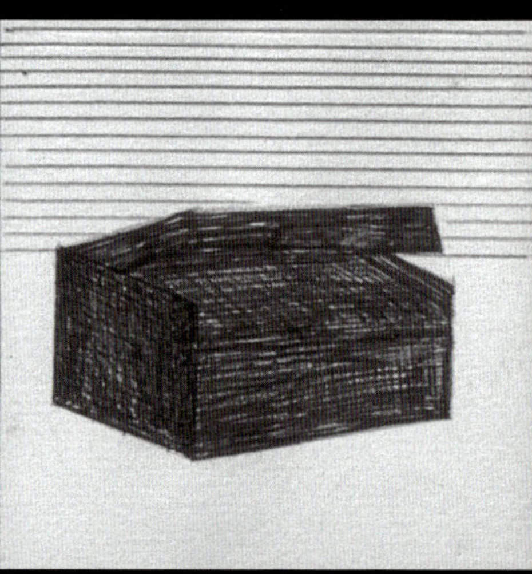

The same thing happens when a dark object is placed on a light background.

CONTRAST. The representation of contrasting light will help you define and clarify the models in your drawings. In fact, it is essential that you learn to explore, distort, and exaggerate the effects of contrast in your drawings to better identify objects or create a greater separation between planes.

THE SHADOW SURROUNDS THE OBJECT. When an object does not stand out enough from the background, shading is often applied around it to make it more visible. Many times this shading does not correspond to the real model; it is a technique that the artist uses to create greater contrast.

To emphasize an object it is not necessary to make its outline heavier; it is enough to darken the shadow around it.

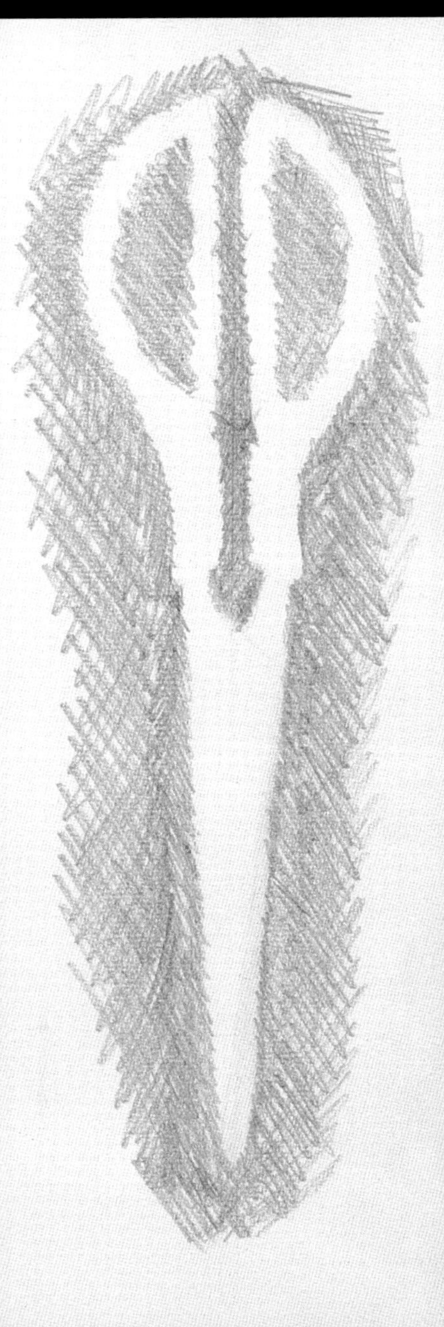

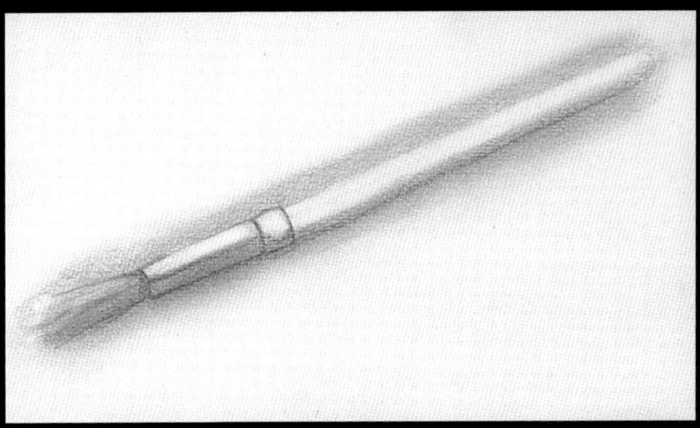

Darkening the area around an object to make it stand out from the background even more is a very common technique used by artists.

Working on a flat, medium-tone background allows you to experiment with the whites while darkening the shadows of the object so that its silhouette is drawn by the contrast.

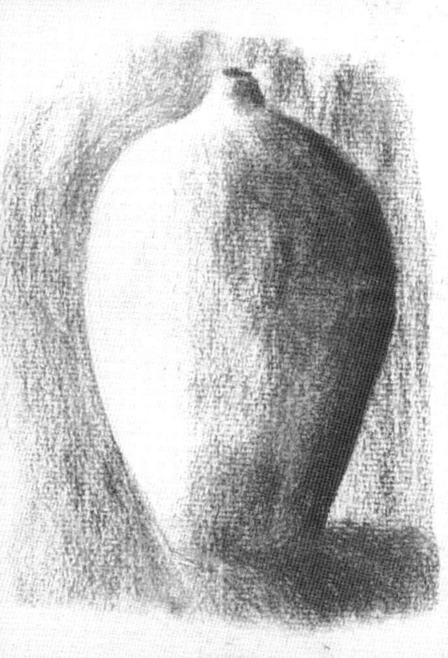

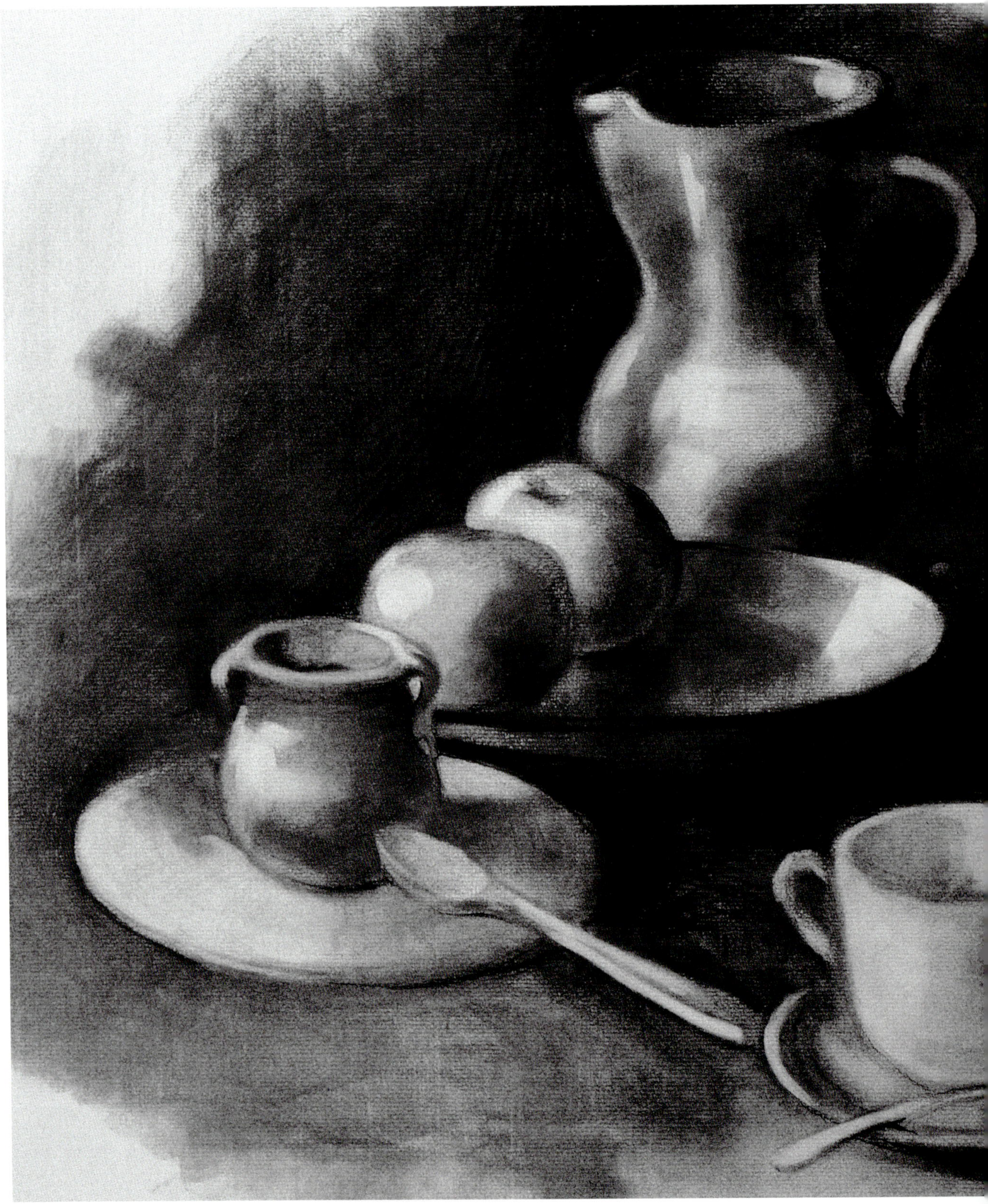

In chiaroscuro, it is not enough to shade and model. The outlines should be clear and defined by changes in tone. Darker shadows heighten the modeling effect.

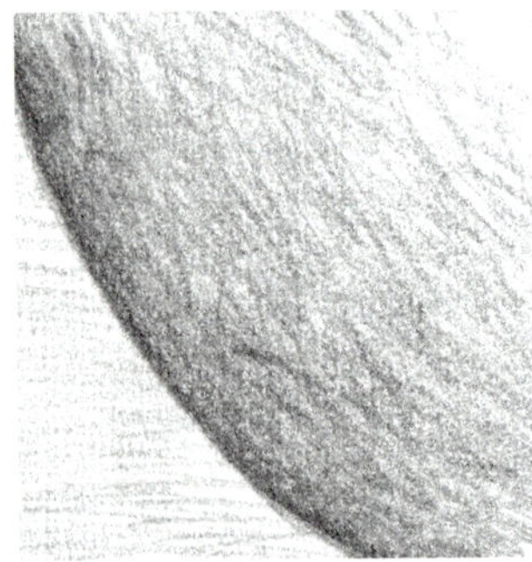

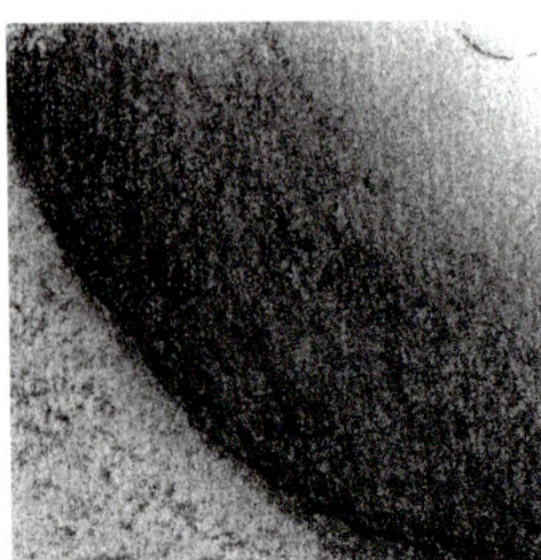

THE EFFECTS OF CHIAROSCURO. A careful analysis of the effects of light and shadow will allow you to get closer still to the elements that will impart realism and volumetric effects to your drawing. Chiaroscuro is the privileged territory of drawing materials like charcoal, chalk, and sanguine, which are considered unstable media, but which let you closely approximate the model by accentuating its volume.

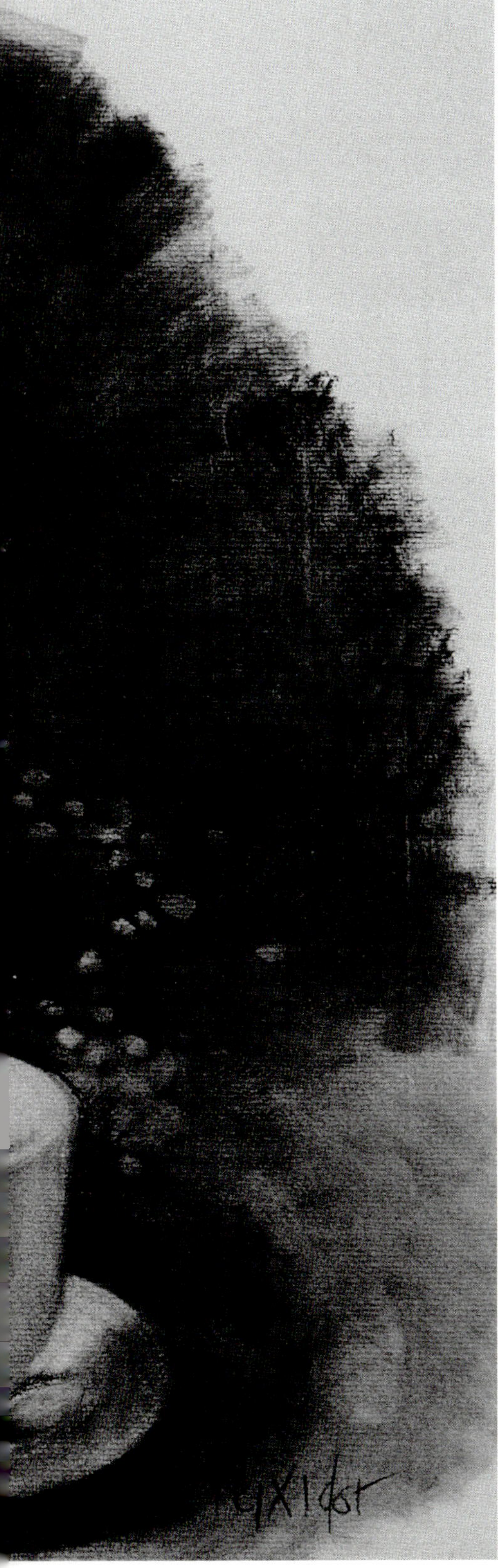

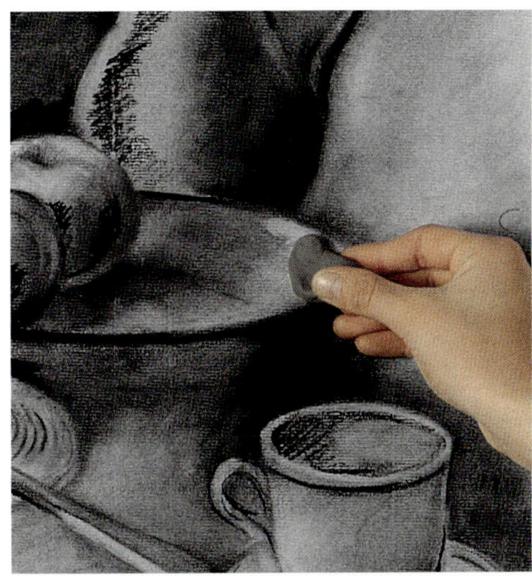

The rubber eraser is used like a pencil to make lines that become very luminous and contrasting white strokes.

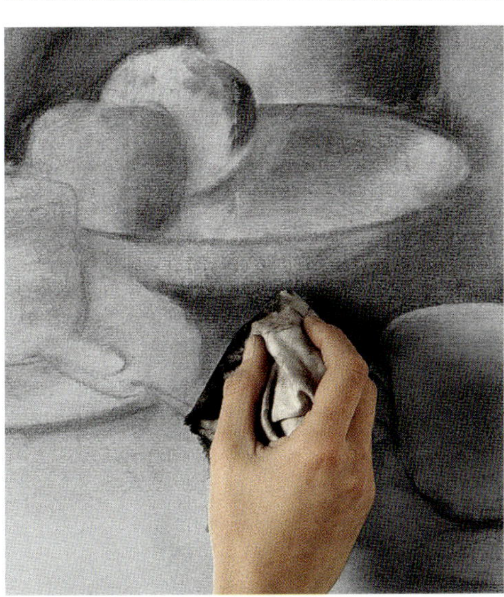

Rubbing with a cotton rag removes jumps in tone in the intermediate shading.

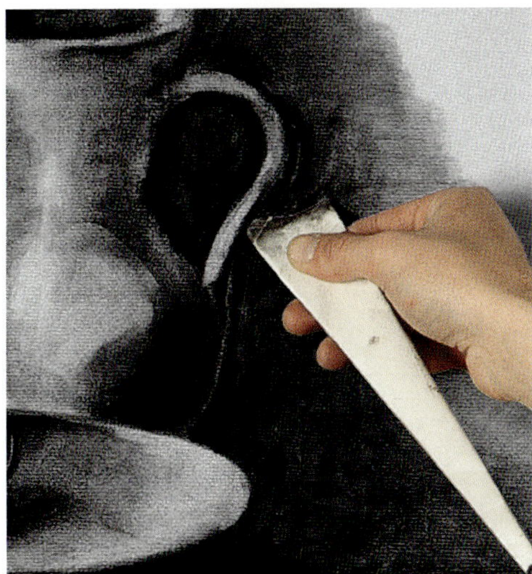

The most precise outlines can be made with a homemade blending tool: a sheet of paper rolled into a flattened cone like a spatula. Working with the wide edge you can do some very expressive blending, with effects similar to those created with a brush.

Blending is essential to heighten the effect of chiaroscuro when working with compressed charcoal or chalk. Notice in these two gradations how rubbing B with a blending stick causes its tones to become darker and denser than those of A.

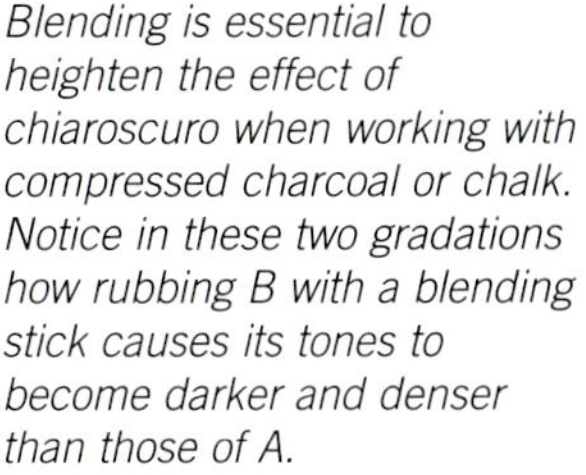

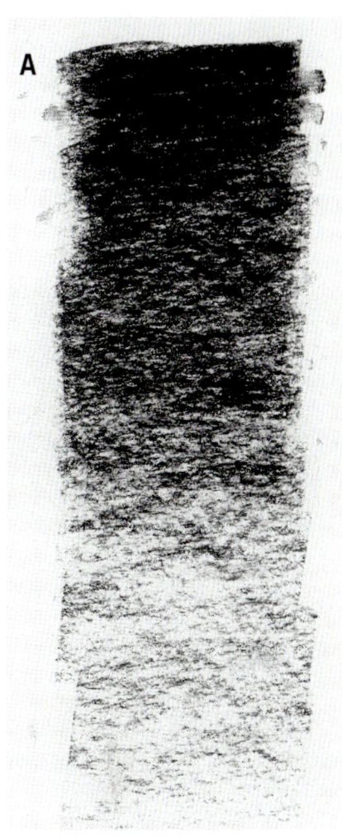

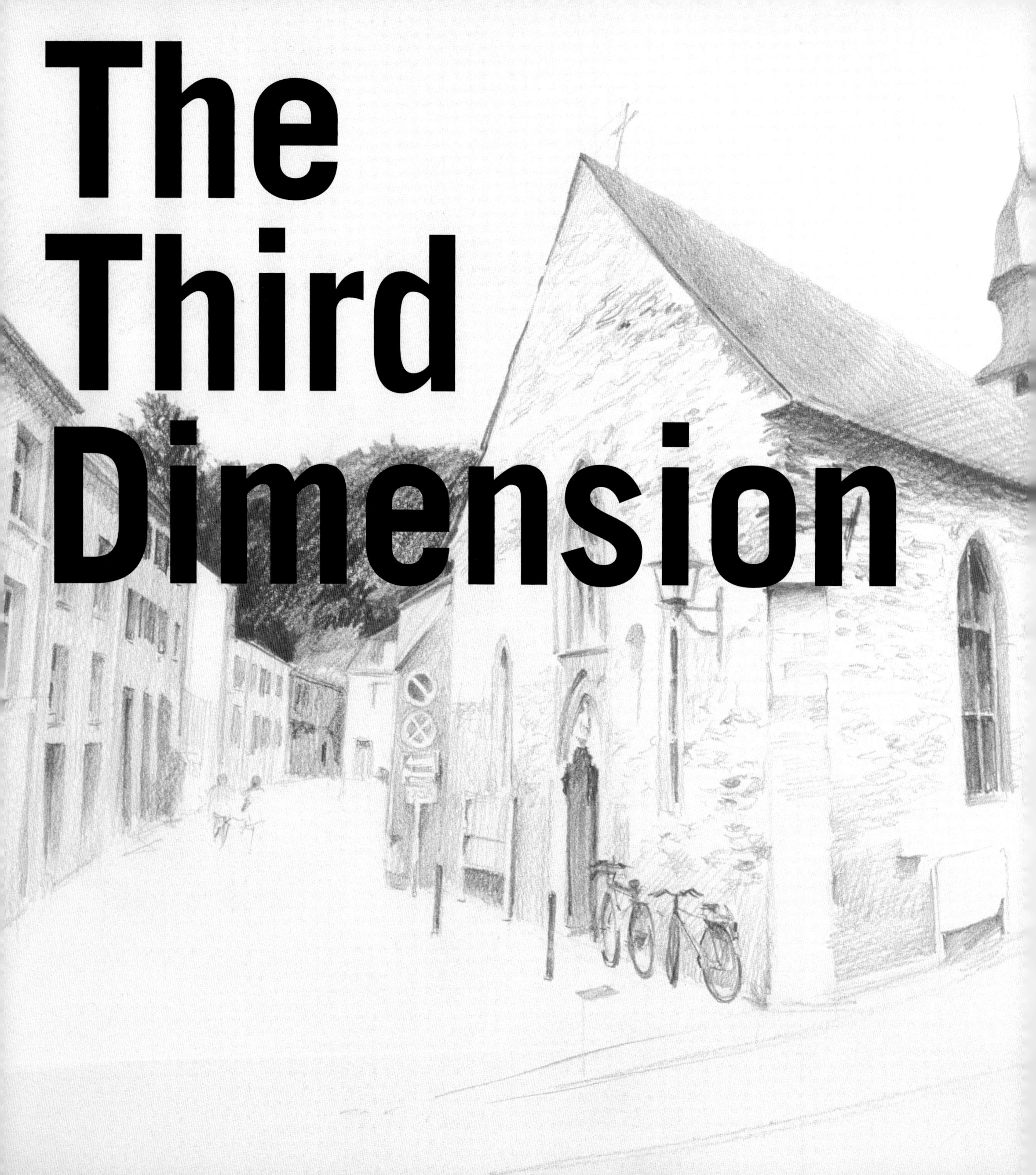

The Third Dimension

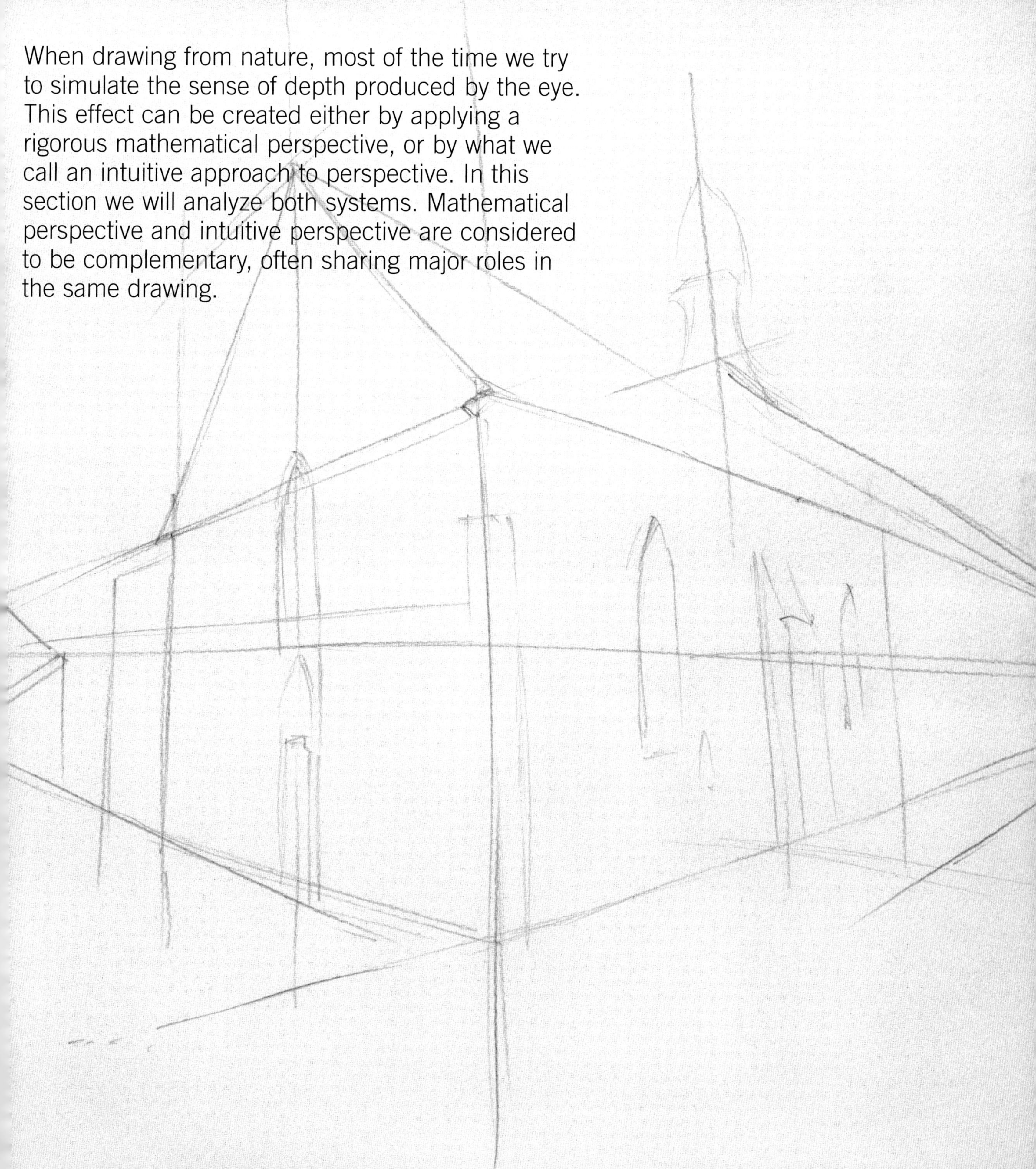

When drawing from nature, most of the time we try
to simulate the sense of depth produced by the eye.
This effect can be created either by applying a
rigorous mathematical perspective, or by what we
call an intuitive approach to perspective. In this
section we will analyze both systems. Mathematical
perspective and intuitive perspective are considered
to be complementary, often sharing major roles in
the same drawing.

DRAWING DEPTH. Generally speaking, there are a number of visual elements that create space: Details in the foreground are larger and better defined than those in the background; at the same time, colors are brighter and more saturated. Distant objects, on the other hand, seem colorless and blurry due to the atmosphere between us and them.

15.1

THE LINES OF THE LANDSCAPE. As always, the initial layout of the drawing plays a crucial role in the development of the landscape. The different planes that are going to be developed need to be completely defined; you must know the graphic role of each one of the lines that mark it.

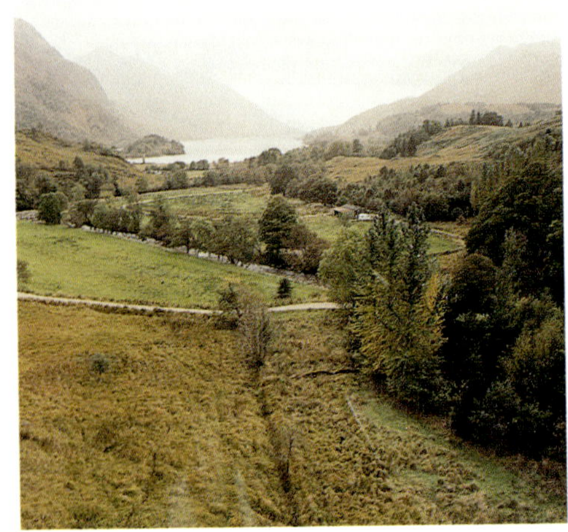

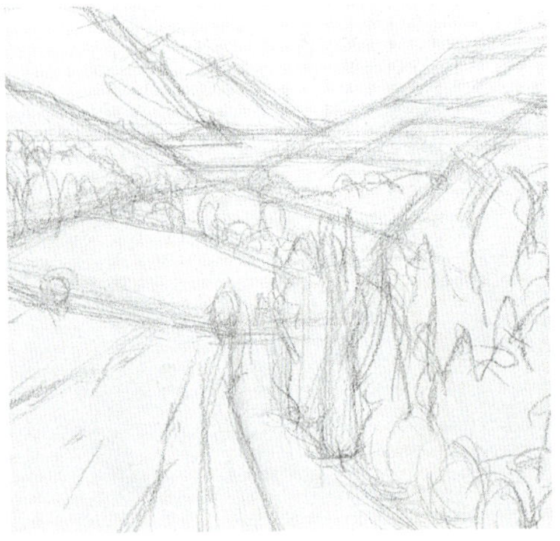

Sketch the general elements in the initial layout, which indicates each area of the landscape. This first sketch is made with the point of the charcoal, held at somewhat of an angle.

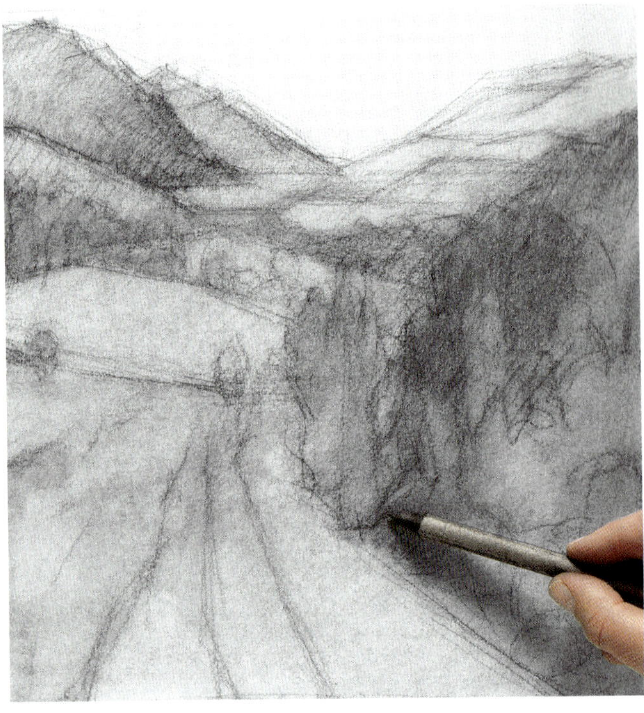

Shade the vegetation in the foreground and middle ground with the charcoal stick, later rubbing the areas with a blending stick. Leave the fields lighter. It is important to study the lighting of each area so that the landscape will have the realism that is needed.

The initial sketch must be well laid out, even if that means forcing some lines to move toward the horizon so that the lines that indicate the perspective create a balanced drawing.

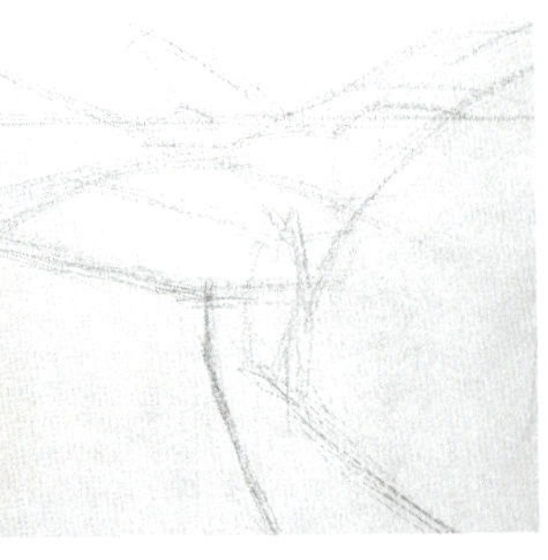

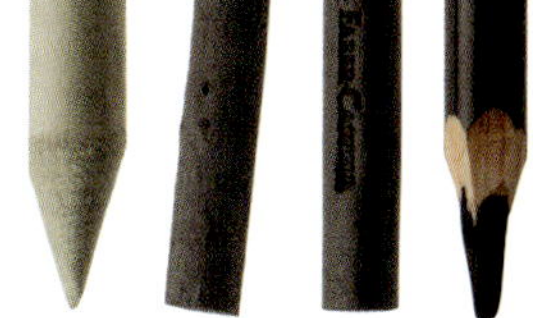

15.2

ATMOSPHERIC AND DEPTH EFFECTS. You must work the background with very light shadows and outlines to create a sense of distance. The foreground, on the other hand, should seem more detailed, showing the textures of the vegetation with very intense blacks.

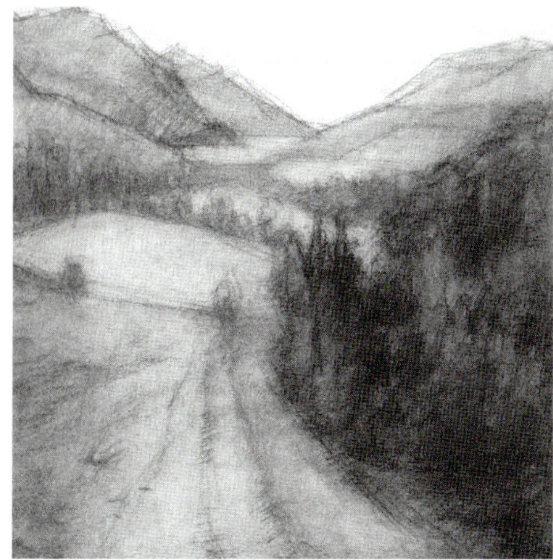

Now, increase the densest shadows of the landscape. Darken the farthest shadows with the charcoal without overworking the group of distant mountains, which should be very light gray with light outlines.

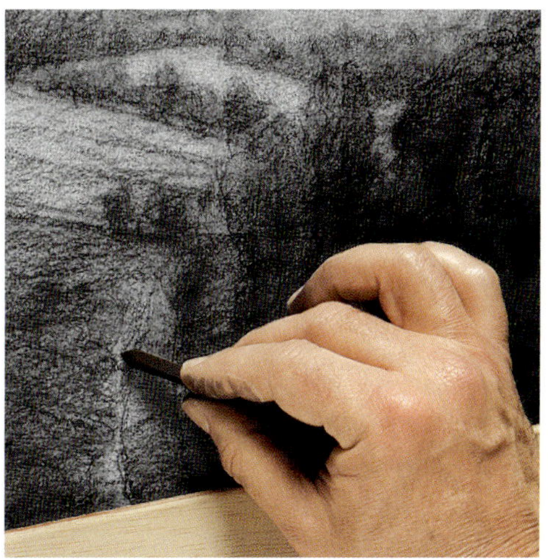

Now is the time to use a stick of compressed charcoal to draw a much more defined separation between the foreground and the rest of the landscape. Compressed charcoal is not easily erased, so you should test the intensity of the tone before you draw the dark areas of the vegetation.

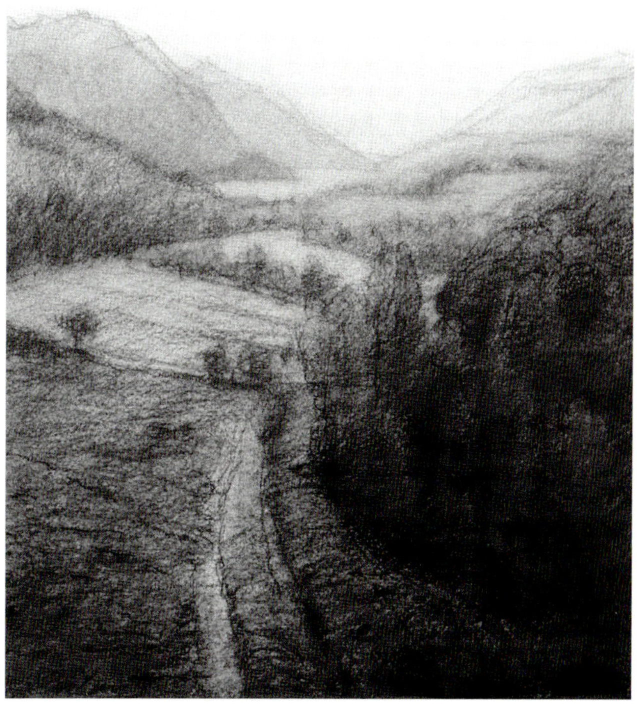

Apply the densest shadows and the texture of the tree leaves in the lower part of the drawing with a charcoal stick and a compressed charcoal pencil. The shadows you made with the vine charcoal, which before were the darkest tones in this area, are now the middle tone areas. Drawing by Carlant.

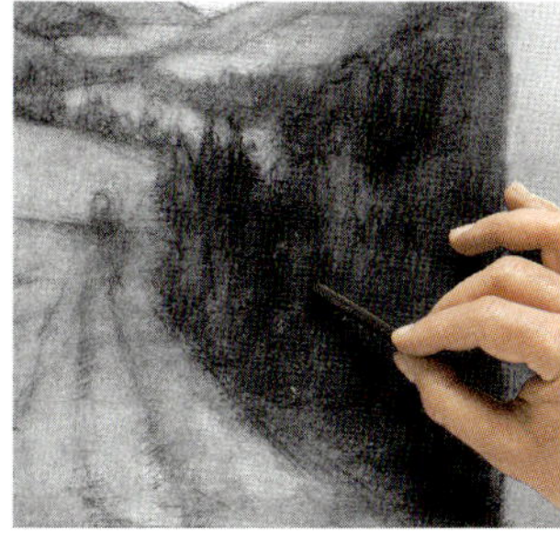

It is a good idea to draw with the point of the vine charcoal when shading the foreground. It is also important to combine tonal areas with some lines to help describe the texture of the trees.

MODEL AND BACKGROUND IN A STILL LIFE. The perspective effects in a landscape translate very well to a small format, such as a still life, as long as the elements that describe the space and distance are carefully chosen. These visual clues can be very simple: The nearest objects will have darker tones and more details than those located in the middle ground, which will be more sketchy and blended. This exercise is done with dark blue, light blue, and white sticks of chalk, along with a blending stick.

16.1

DRAWING THE FRAMEWORK. The initial guidelines create a framework upon which the precise forms of the model can be built. To work this way you must become accustomed to looking analytically and understand that basic lines will be the keys to the final drawing.

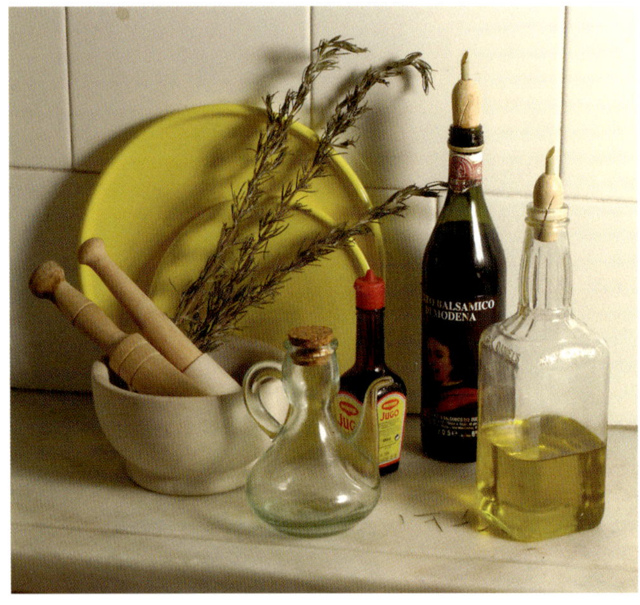

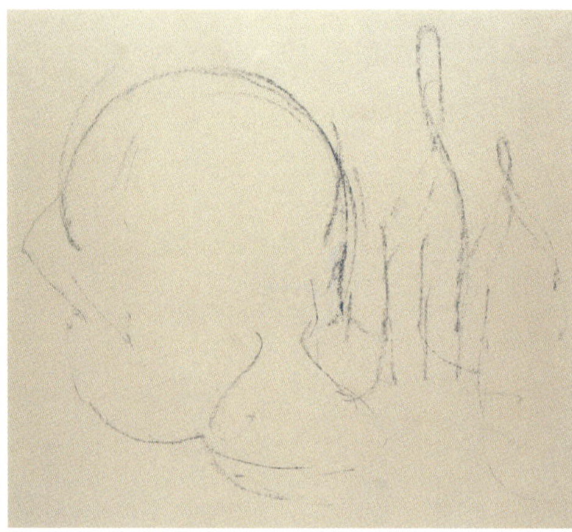

When you wish to make a very realistic drawing, it is a good idea to begin with some light guidelines to help locate the objects correctly and to achieve acceptable shapes and sizes.

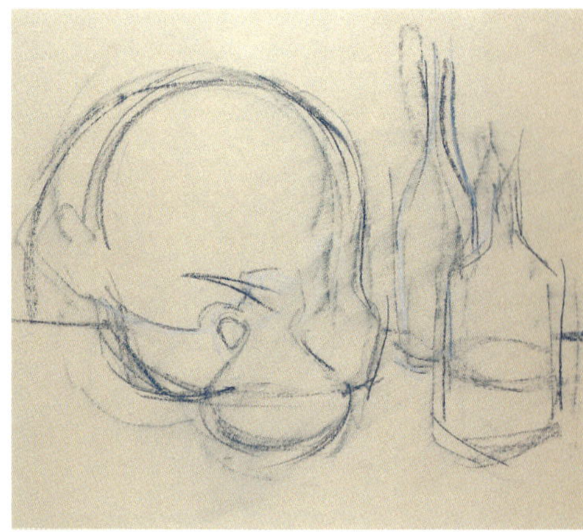

Draw the shapes precisely with dark blue chalk, indicating the outlines of the objects without making them too finished. It is a good idea to use the flat side of the stick when drawing these structured lines. Any corrections should be made in this first stage.

Apply first shading with the blending stick, blurring the outlines of the farthest objects and coloring the background with a very faint blue.

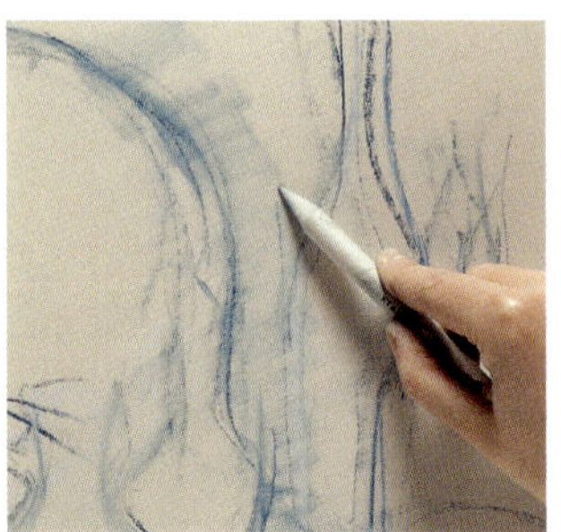

If you draw the structural lines with the flat side of the stick, these straight lines will be narrow, strong, and easy to correct.

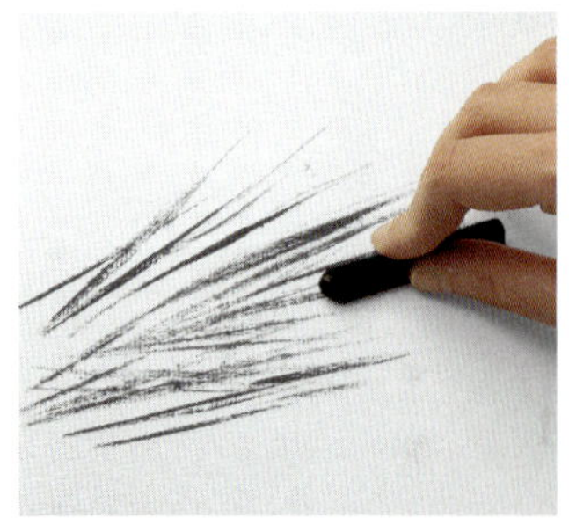

16.2

GENERAL TONES. When the drawing is completely laid out, begin to apply the first shading, creating a study of the depths of the different planes. This second stage of the drawing will be done with the flat side of the chalk, so corrections can be made more easily.

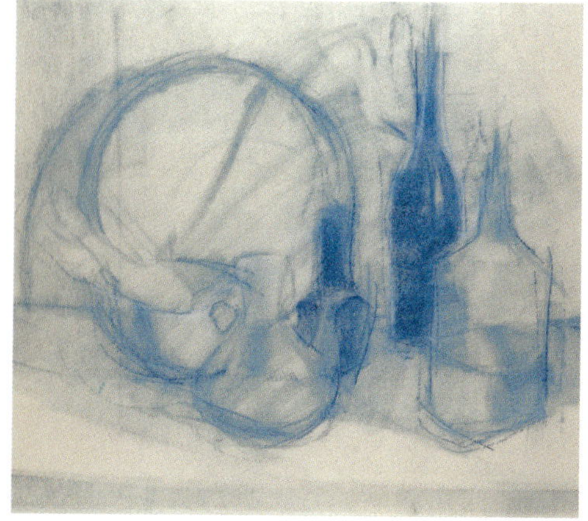

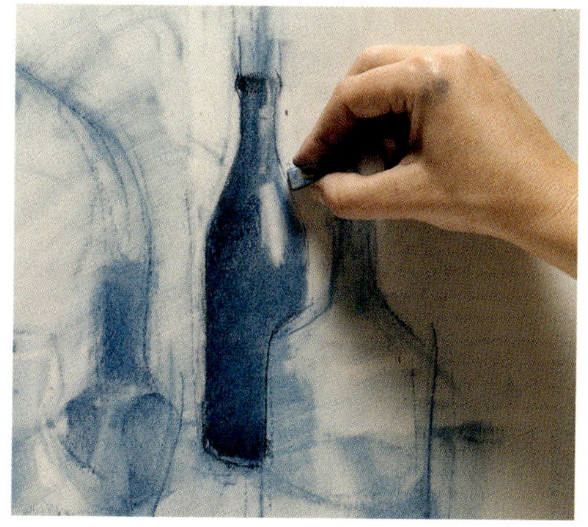

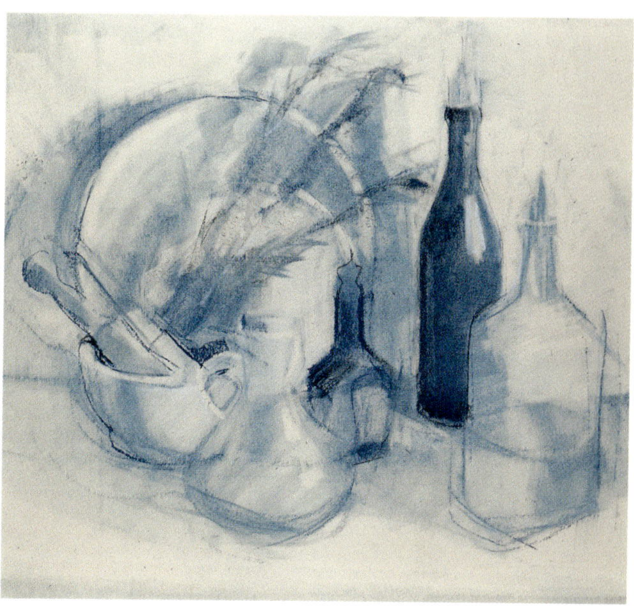

Apply light shading to the paper with the flat side of the blue chalk stick. Work with quick, wide strokes so the shading will be even without filling in the texture of the paper. After you apply the color, blend the drawing by lightly wiping it with your hand.

Color the bottle on the right by mixing the light blue and dark blue chalks to make a clear gradation. Apply enough pressure to the stick to completely cover the area, filling the texture of the paper. Next, you can retouch the outline of the bottle and create highlights on its surface with the eraser.

When you create the values of the volumes in unison, if you darken one object too much the previous light tones can seem too light. To correct this, increase the tones and contrast to balance the grouping.

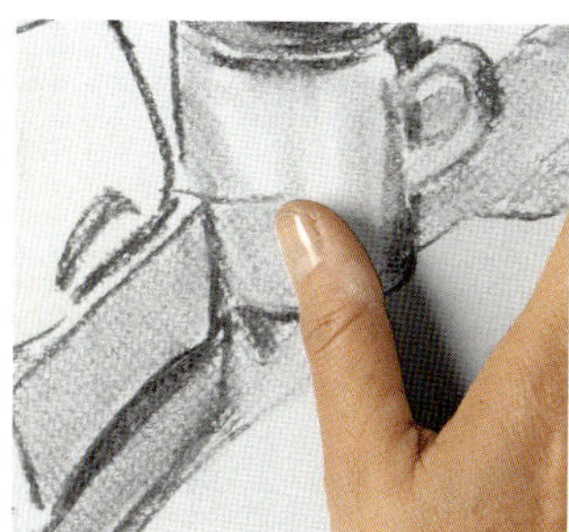

The blending stick lets you blur a line and make a graded shadow on the paper; however, in some cases it is much simpler to blend with your finger.

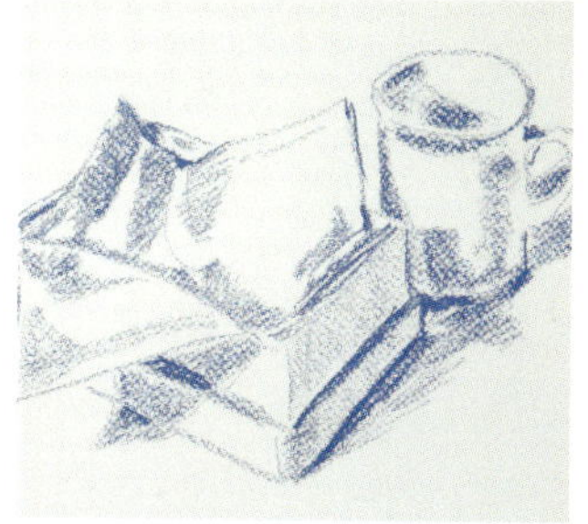

When drawing with chalk you should carefully control the pressure of the stick on the paper, because the lightest tones are created by making very light strokes with the flat side of the stick.

16.3

DIFFERENTIATING PLANES. Once the primary values have been completely developed, you can begin to finalize the planes, leaving the farthest ones sketchy while detailing and outlining the nearest one.

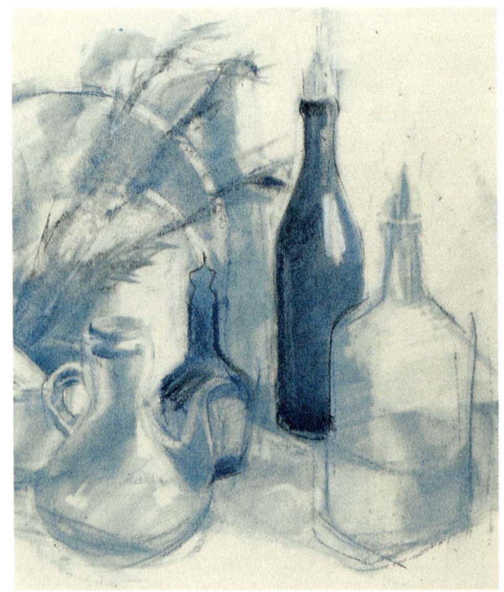

The finish of the objects in the background is vague, diffuse, and without great tonal contrast. The modeling does not look heavy, but rather appears light and atmospheric, thanks to the attractive tonal values made with the chalk.

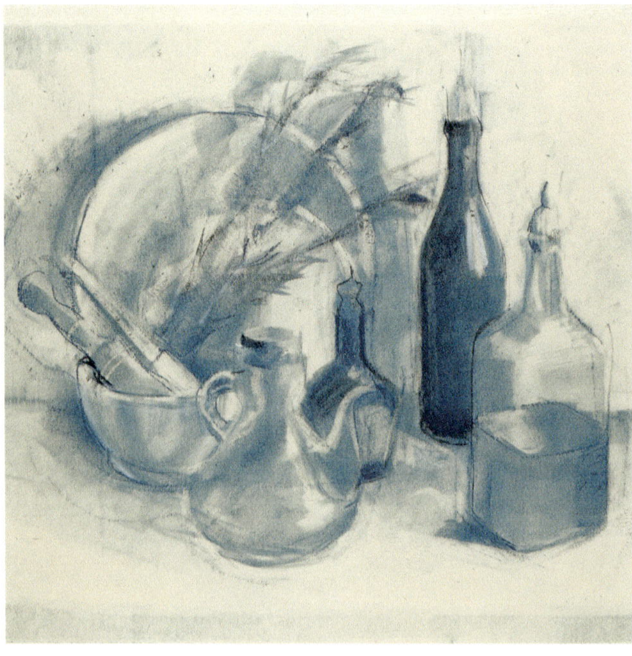

With the background resolved, lightly increase the contrast of the objects in the middle ground and highlight those in the foreground. As you shade the glass objects, rub the surface of the paper with your fingers to model the form and create the illusion of volume.

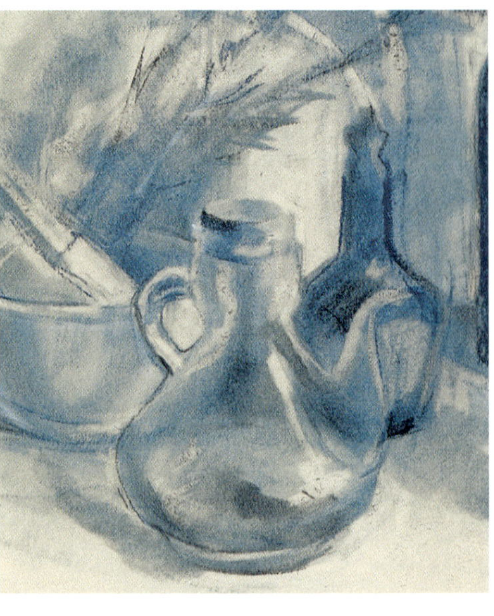

Create highlights on the glass objects in the foreground with the eraser. The darkest shadows on them separate the different planes of the drawing even more, while giving the objects a more substantial feeling.

It is normal for the color to extend past the edges of the objects during blending. In such cases the chalk should be removed and a new outline created with an eraser.

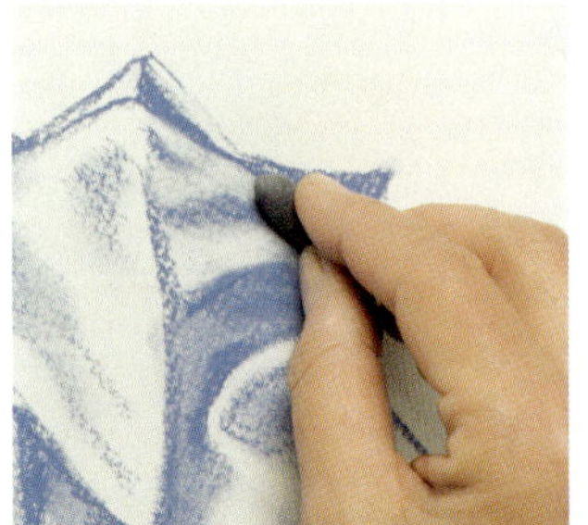

Draw the outlines of objects in the foreground with the point of the chalk stick, controlling the pressure and direction of the line.

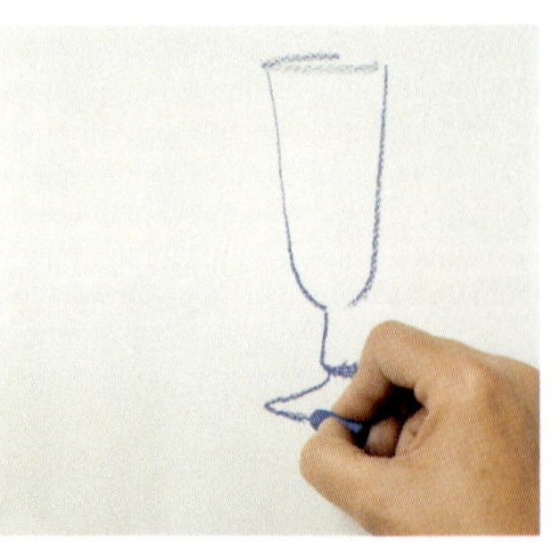

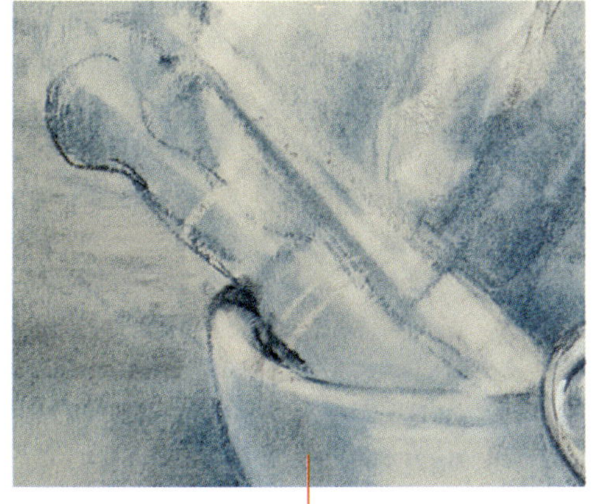

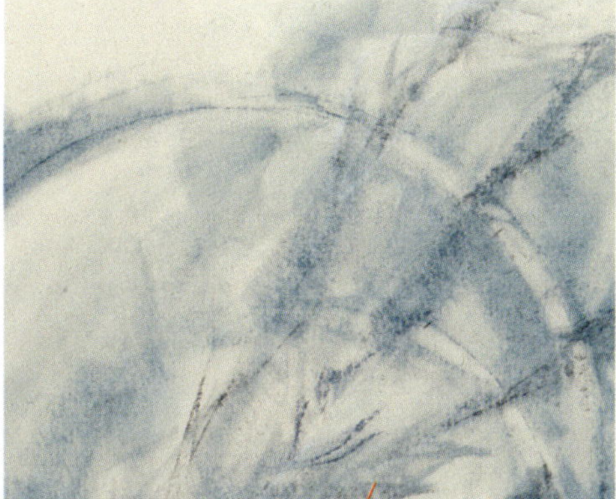

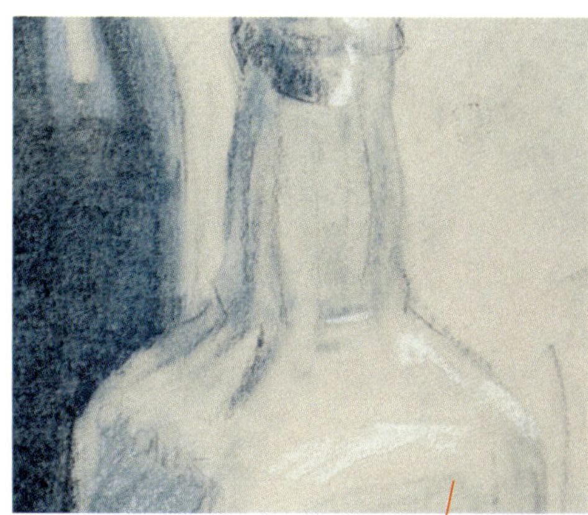

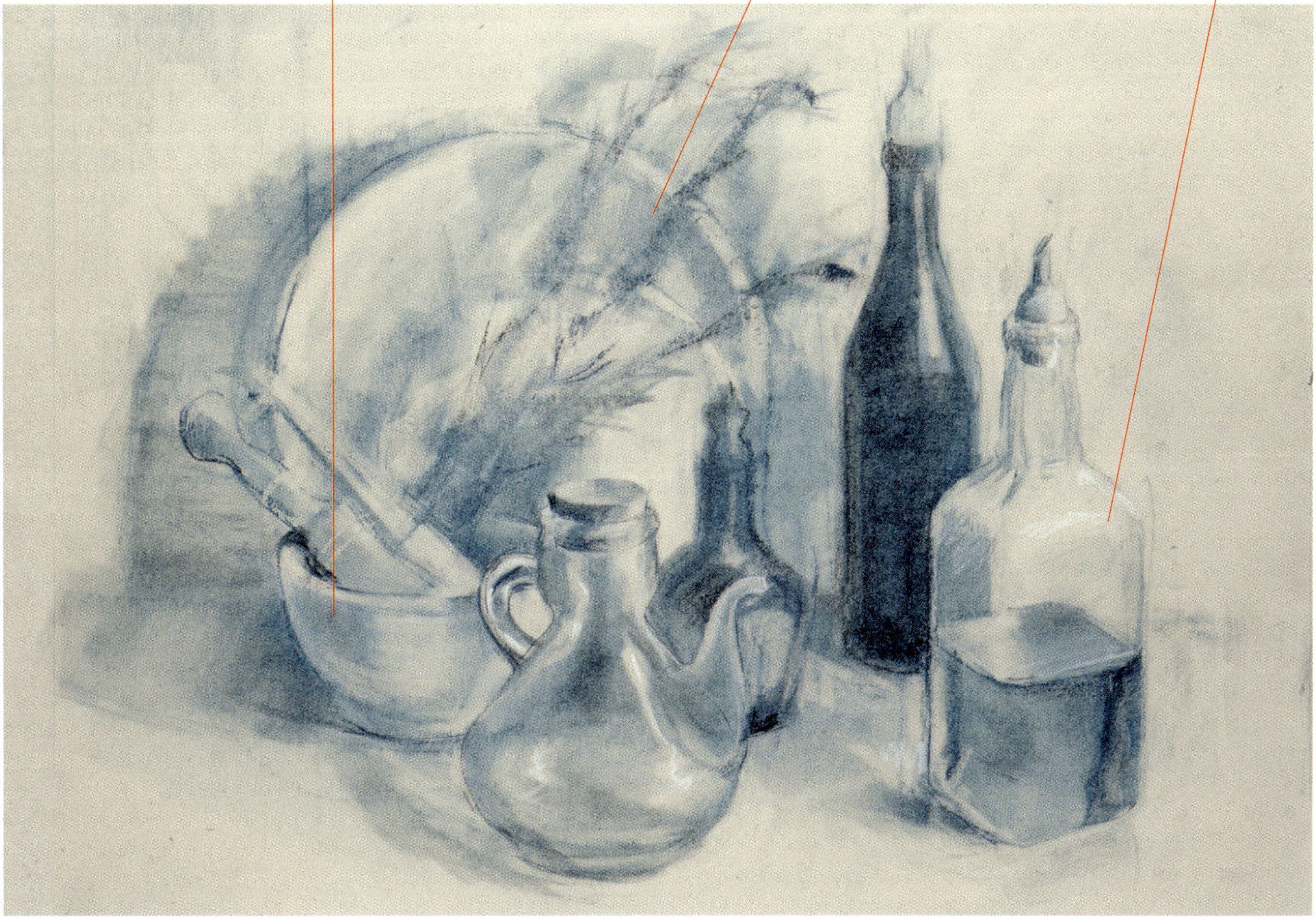

You can see from the finished drawing that creating the impression of space on a two-dimensional surface is a matter of focusing. The objects in the foreground seem more defined and focused, while those that are located just behind them have lighter colors and blurred outlines. Drawn by Mercedes Gaspar.

FADING THE GROUNDS. There are several techniques for illustrating the third dimension in a drawing by using contrast on the nearest planes and fading the farthest ones. The sense of depth is an optical illusion created by representing the water vapor contained in the atmosphere.

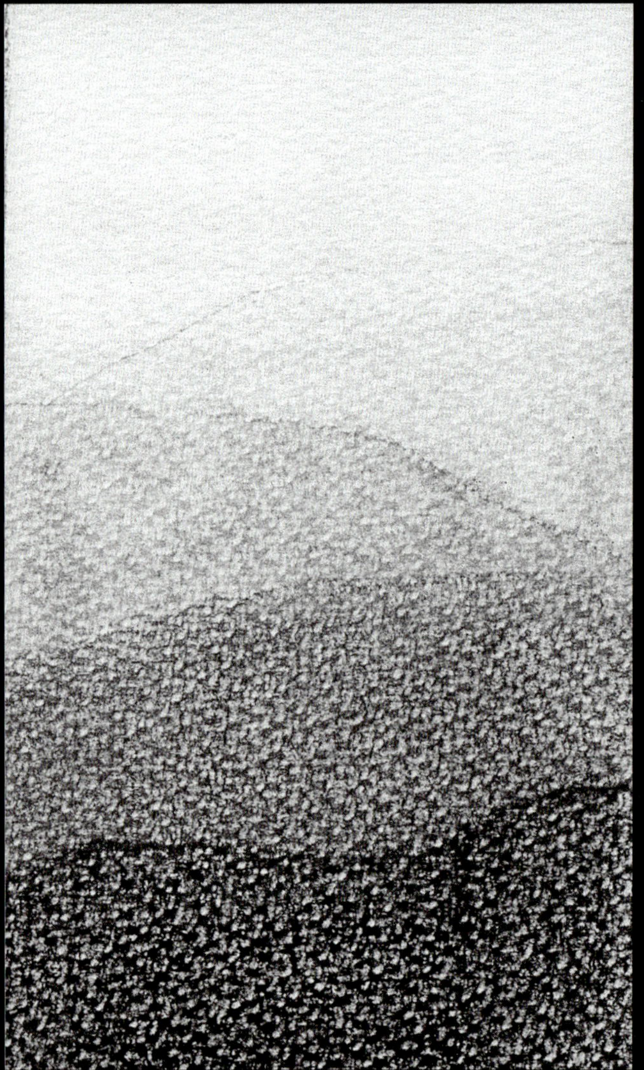

To create the effect of the atmosphere, lighten the farthest mountains and rub them with a blending stick. Remember that when you look at a plane near you, your eyes put the farthest plane out of focus.

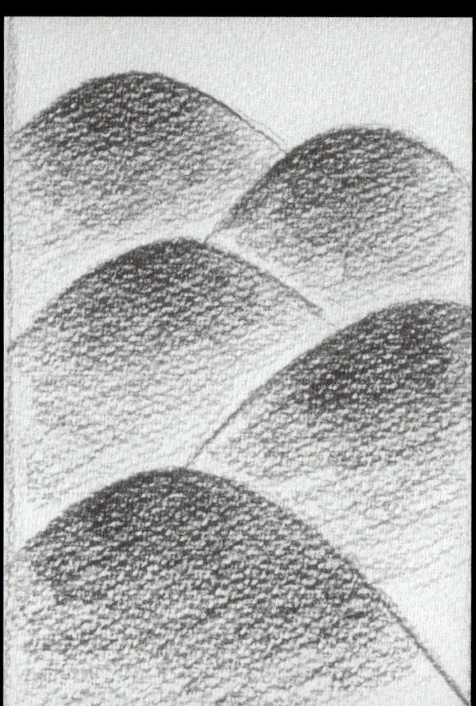

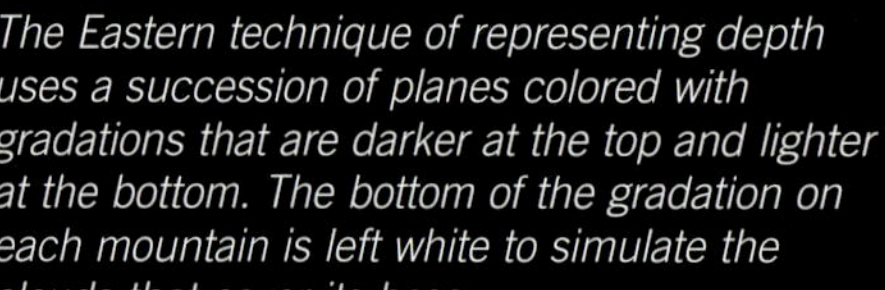

The Eastern technique of representing depth uses a succession of planes colored with gradations that are darker at the top and lighter at the bottom. The bottom of the gradation on each mountain is left white to simulate the clouds that cover its base.

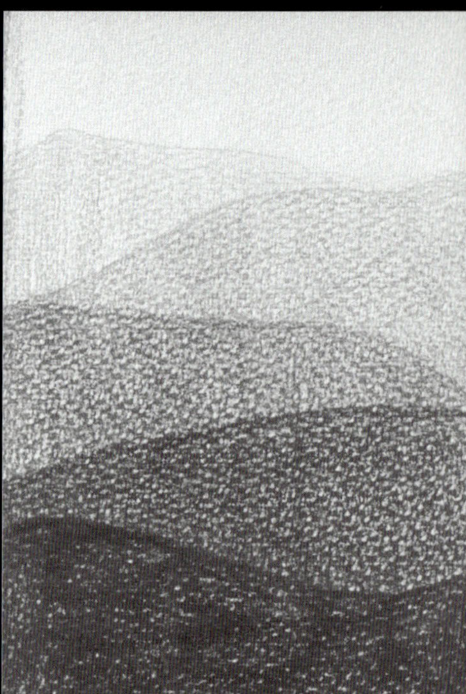

The Coulisse effect is one of the techniques most commonly used for drawing a succession of planes. Each plane is drawn with a uniform tone, which is lighter for each successively receding plane.

DIFFERENT PLANES. Our eyes are accustomed to defining visual space in terms of foreground, middle ground, and background or distance. By using perspective and atmospheric techniques, it is possible to represent depth and differentiate each of the planes in a drawing. In the remainder of this book, we will study the most common techniques used by professional artists.

DEPTH IN THE COMPOSITION. The effect of depth is not created solely by fading the receding planes. Framing and altering the composition of the picture to reinforce the sense of perspective also contribute to this effect.

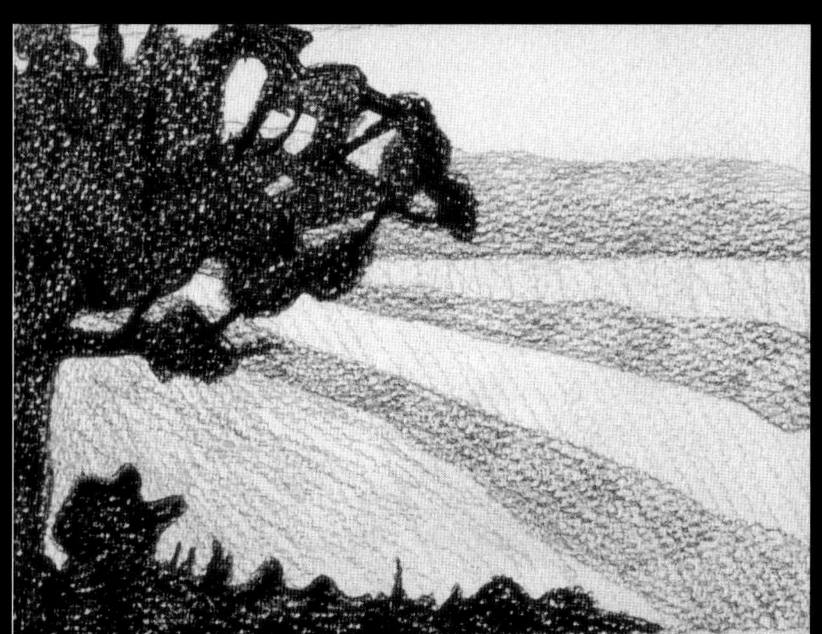

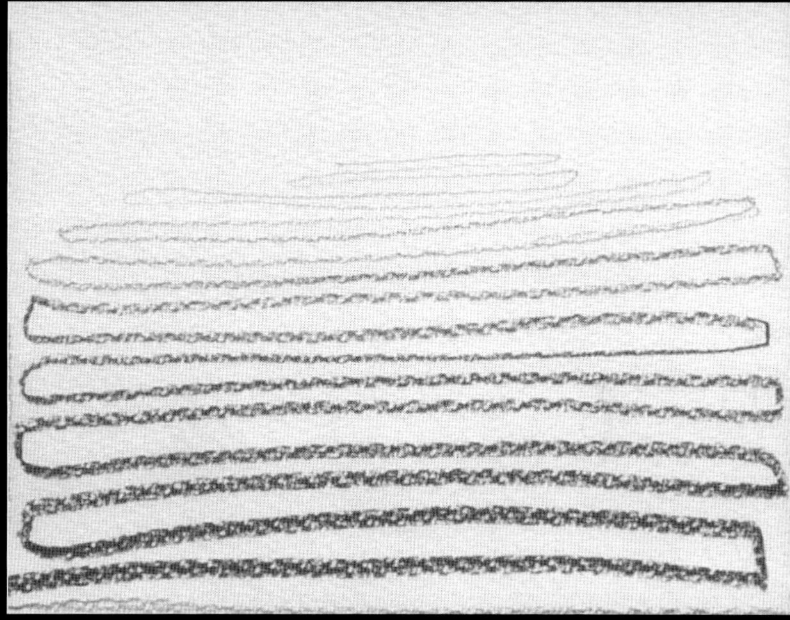

If you cause the foreground to stand out with an abrupt change in light, that is, a strong contrast against the background, you can create a feeling of depth in the drawing.

The weight of the line is important for communicating distance in a drawing. Notice how in this experiment, created with a decreasing zigzag line, the widest and darkest line seems closer than the thinnest, lightest one, which seems to be moving away from the viewer.

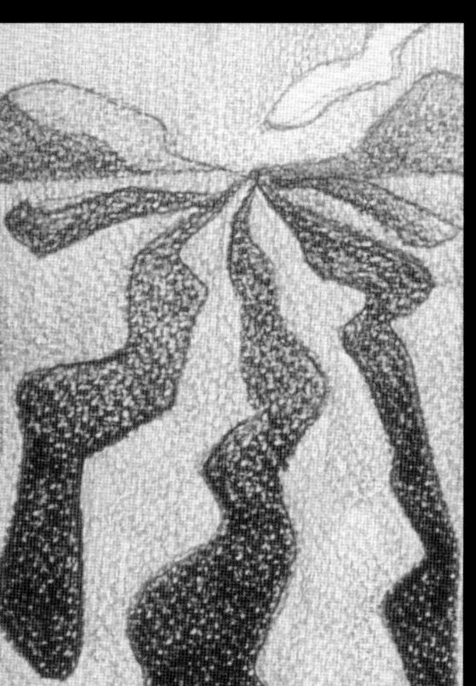

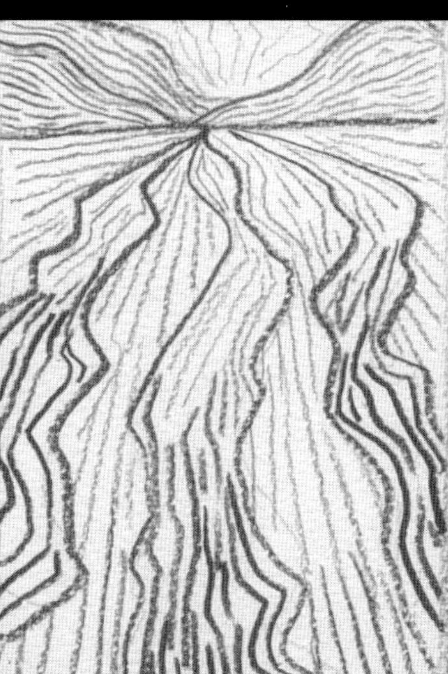

When composing a landscape you can modify the masses so they converge at a point on the horizon. This convergence leads the eye of the viewer to the picture's background.

Just as the composition can increase the feeling of depth, so can controlling the direction of the lines so that they converge in the same place on the horizon line.

ATMOSPHERIC PERSPECTIVE. An important factor in drawing landscapes is the representation of the third dimension using light, shadow, and blending techniques; the feeling of distance is created by reproducing the effects of the atmosphere. This is an optical illusion caused by water vapor and dust particles in the air, which lighten the colors and soften the edges of the forms in the distance.

17.1

DRAWING THE ATMOSPHERE. The farther away the plane, the more it fades; distant landscape has duller colors and blurry forms. Therefore, you should begin by drawing the atmosphere, which is the farthest planes, and then work toward the foreground.

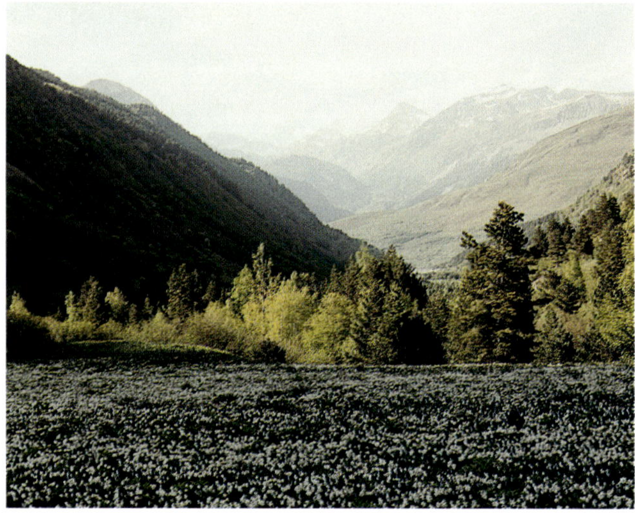

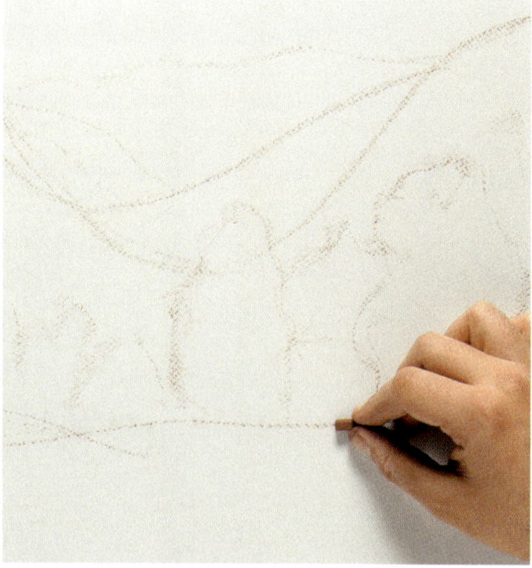

Begin this compositional study by indicating the main areas of the picture, starting with the mountains and ending with the sketch of the trees in the foreground. Work with the flat edge of a piece of sanguine crayon, applying a very fine line that you can easily erase in case of error.

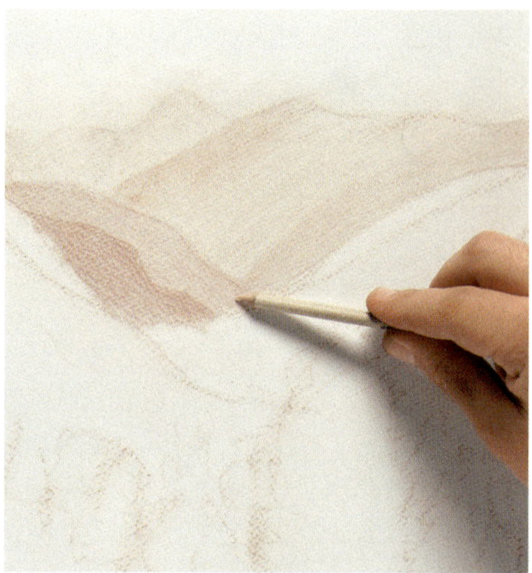

Using a good combination of light shading, made by lightly coloring with the edge of a sanguine crayon and rubbing it with a blending stick, it is easy to create the atmospheric effect of the mountains in the background. As you can see, the preliminary shading is barely visible against the white of the paper.

If you do not feel confident with a sanguine crayon, make the preliminary drawing with a sanguine pencil; this will allow you to rest your hand on the paper to draw better lines.

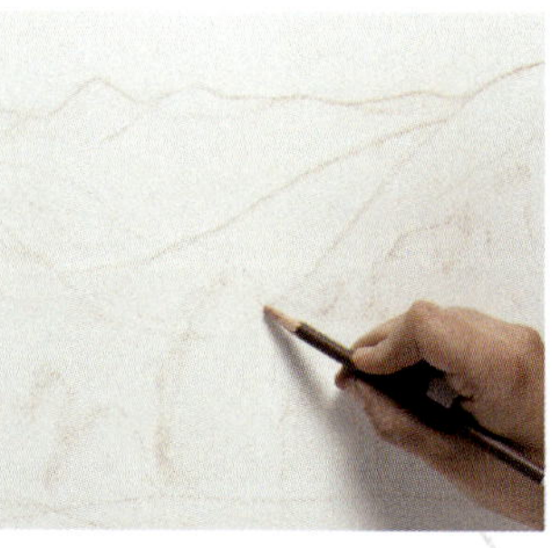

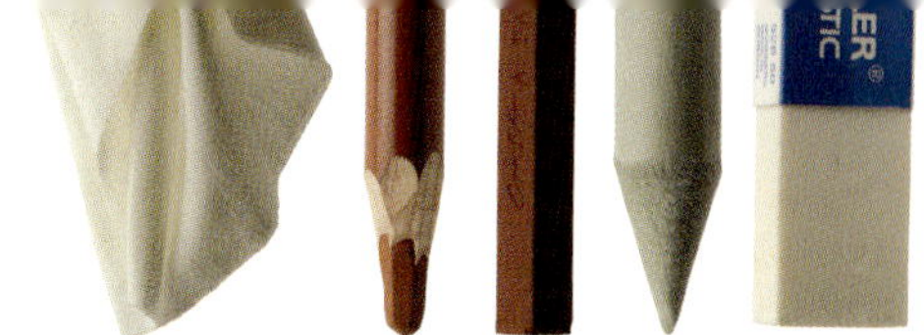

17.2

BUILDING THE TONES. In this drawing, the darkest tones should be applied progressively. Light tones in the distance will be darkened as you shade the nearer planes, as if you were working with a scale of tonal values.

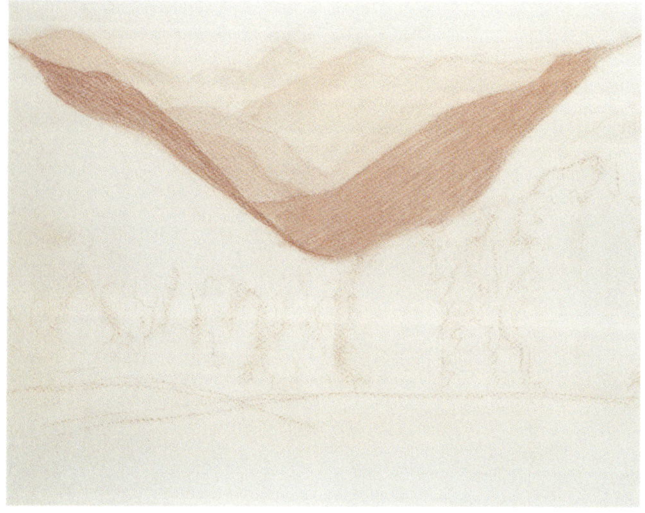

As you move down the surface of the paper, apply the intermediate tones. Each new plane should be resolved with a slightly darker shading than the previous one. It is better to fall short in the intensity of the shading, which you can adjust at the end by darkening it as much as needed with a sanguine crayon.

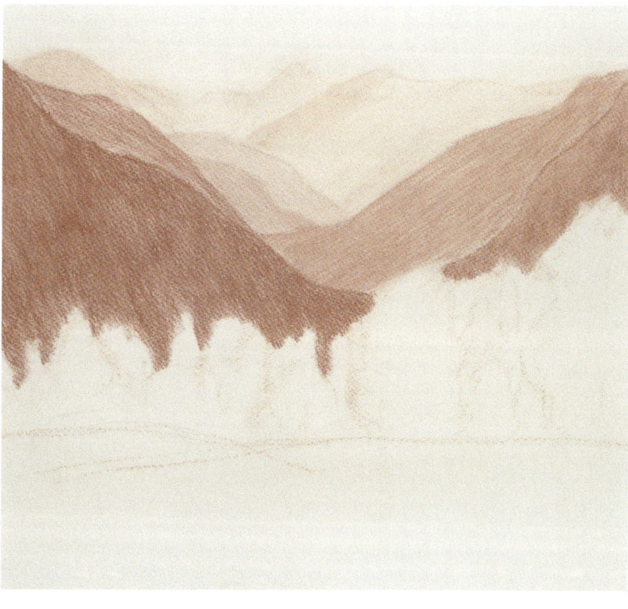

At this point you have resolved the overlaying of the mountains. The drawing is a gradation, so that the eye of the viewer is drawn into the picture by the subtle variations of tone that suggest an infinite space.

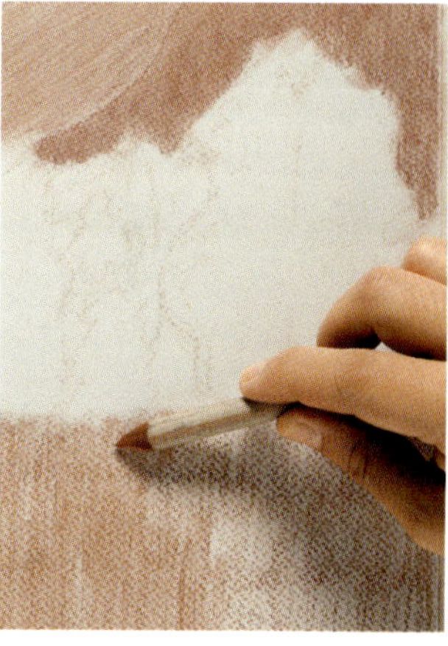

Leaving the space for the vegetation blank, color the large meadow of grass in the lower part of the picture. First, using the point of the sanguine crayon, cover the field with a uniform color; then unify the shading by simply rubbing it with a blending stick.

The atmospheric effect can be conceptualized as a picture covered with a gradation that becomes lighter as it moves up the paper.

17.3

THE TEXTURE OF THE VEGETATION. The texture of the vegetation should not be a mere copy of reality, but should also provide a way of distinguishing a foreground from a less detailed background. Furthermore, the value of the texture becomes a vehicle for dramatizing the forms of the landscape.

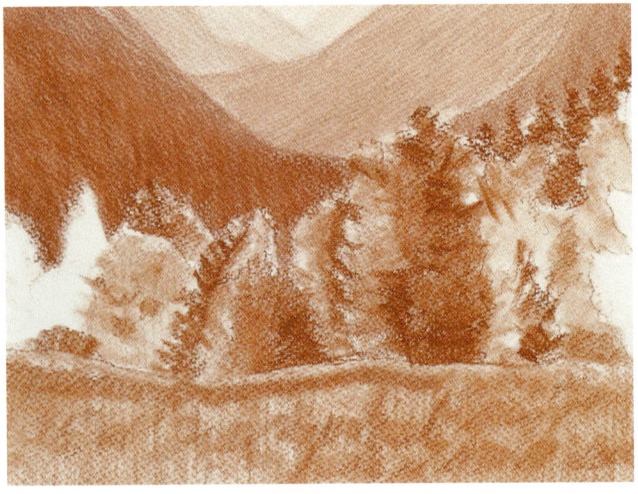

Adding a sense of texture to the group of trees in the foreground makes them appear closer, creating a greater sense of depth in the background.

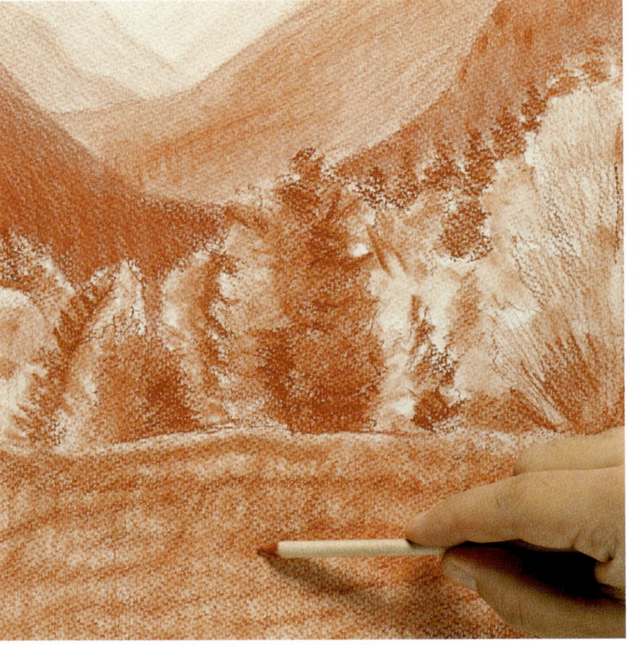

Continue working the texture of the trees and the grass meadow with a blending stick charged with sanguine. Combine the blended color with lines that simulate the branches in the tops of the trees. The grass is not just lines; it is composed of areas of light and areas of shadow.

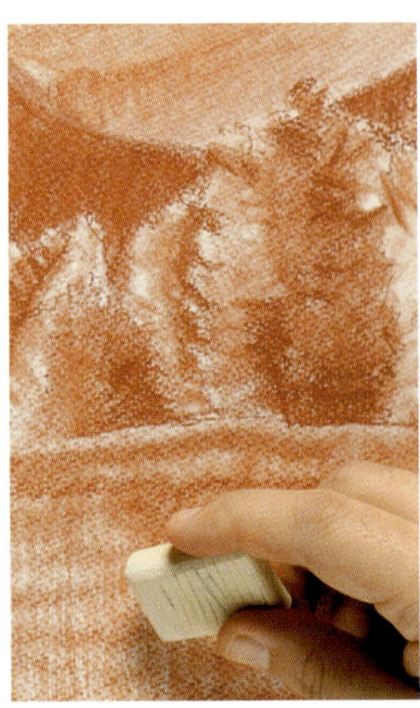

To suggest clumps of grass, make short vertical strokes with a rubber eraser. When they are seen against the darker, more shaded background, the white areas indicate the shapes of the bunches of grass. This line work defines the texture of the grass in a general way.

Use tonal contrasts to control the light in the foreground. The darker the tone that surrounds the tree, the more luminous it will seem.

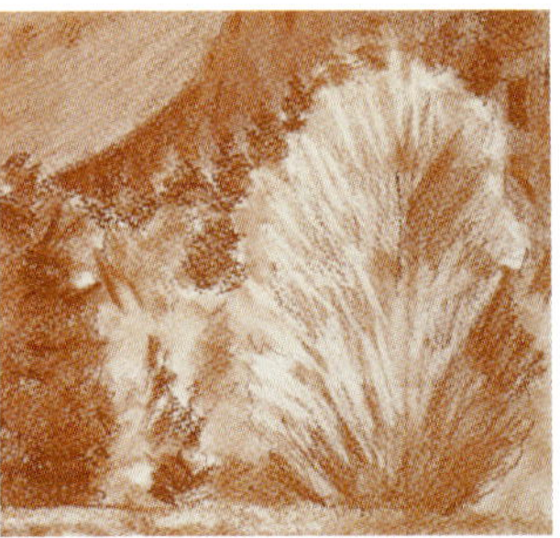

Do not apply texture effects to the rest of the vegetation in the landscape; only use them in the foreground. Otherwise, the illusion of depth will be reduced.

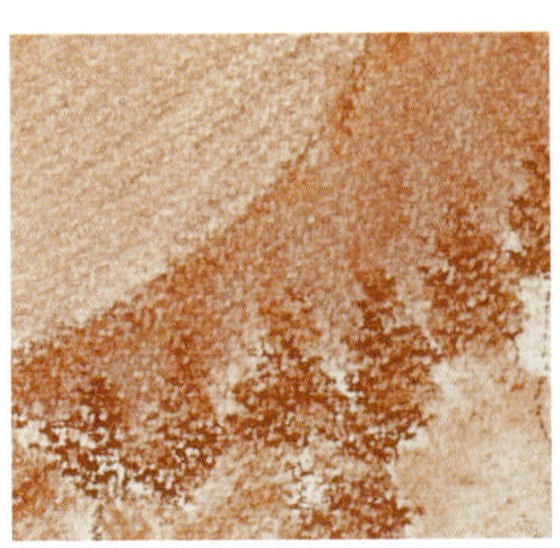

The contrast between the dark background and the lighted trees in the foreground is important for the definition of the vegetation and keeps it from looking like part of the background.

Light variations of tone and subtle erasing contribute to making the irregularity of the grassy meadow stand out.

Resolve the most distant trees with very small conical lines in horizontal groups.

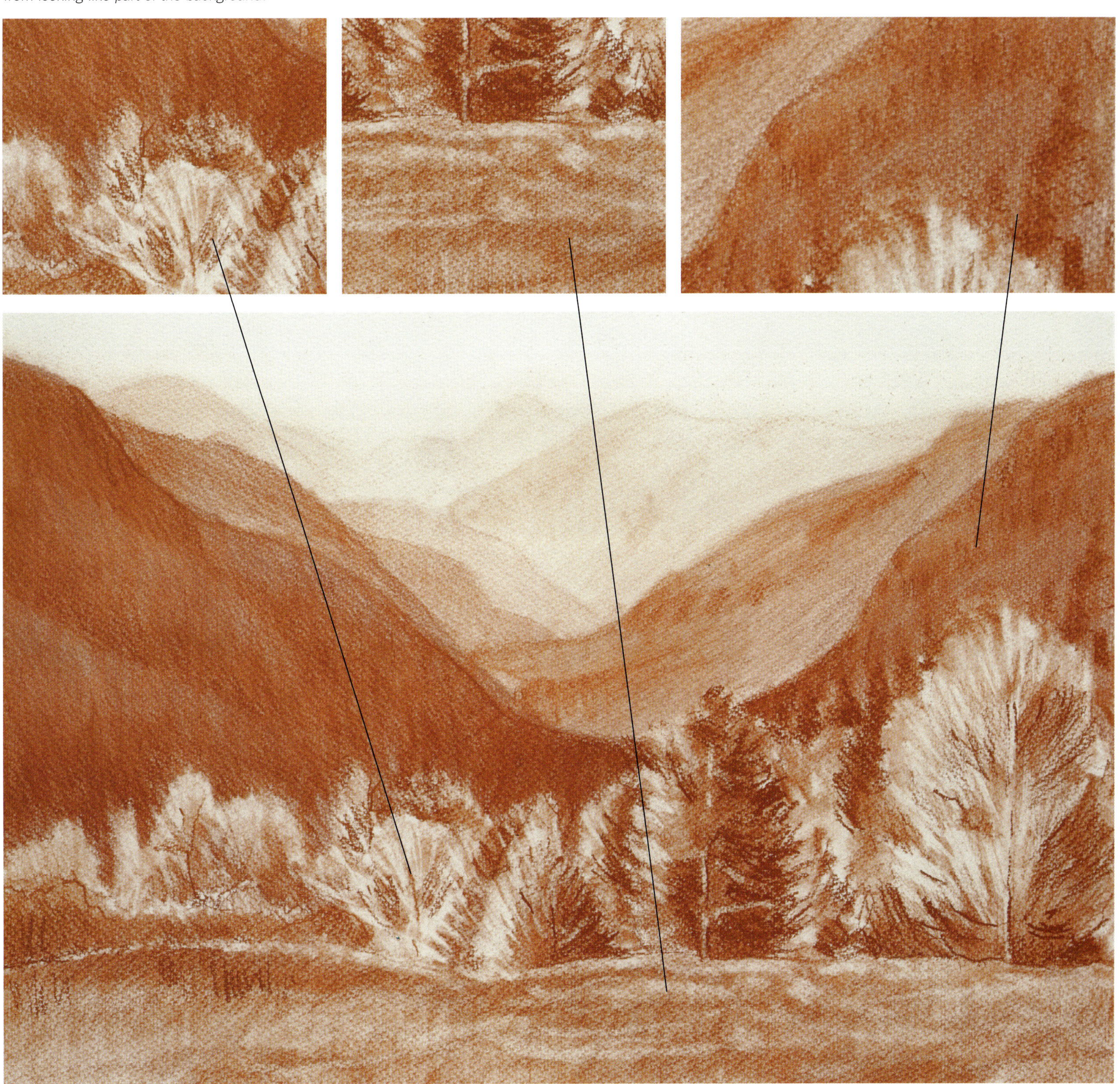

To finish the drawing, continue emphasizing the contrasts and the texture of the vegetation in each area of the picture, such as the grass meadow and the trees. Draw new branches with the point of the sanguine pencil; draw groups of leaves with a corner of the rubber eraser. Drawn by Gabriel Martín.

URBAN LANDSCAPE IN PERSPECTIVE. The laws of perspective are a systematization of mechanical vision; they come into play when the work must be an exact transcription of nature. Knowledge of the basic rules of perspective is very helpful when making drawings of urban landscapes, although it is not an absolute requirement.

18.1

FIRST LINES OF OBLIQUE PERSPECTIVE. Oblique perspective is characterized by having two vanishing points and by the fact that vertical lines are the only ones that are always parallel to each other. This perspective is the most useful kind for drawing buildings.

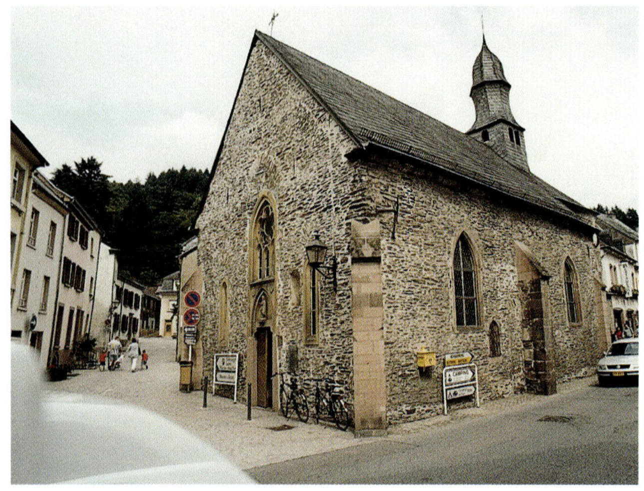

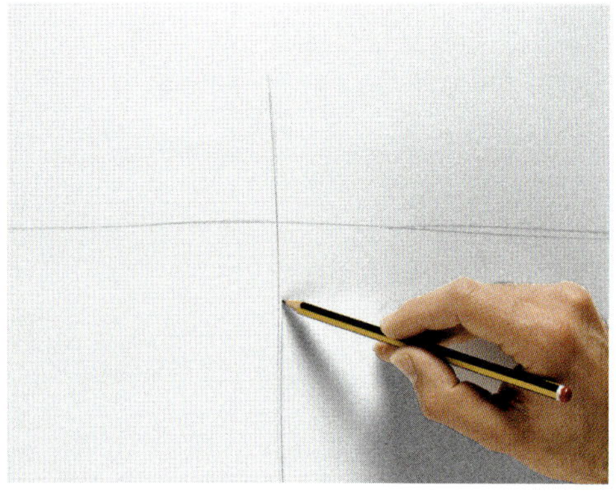

The first step in a perspective drawing is locating the horizon line. This is an imaginary line that lies at the height of our eyes. Draw a perpendicular vertical line across it to represent the corner of the building that you are going to draw.

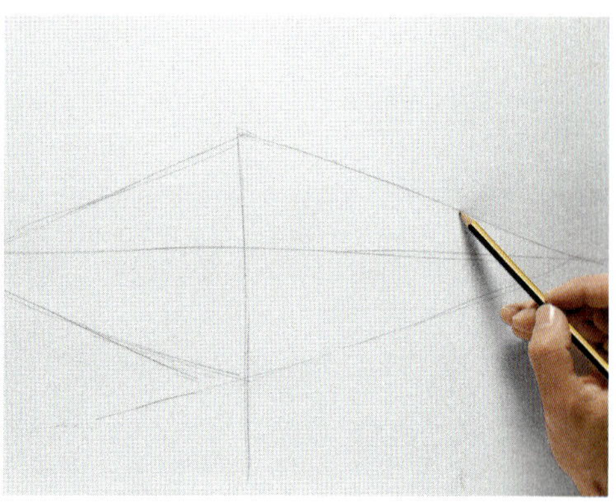

When you stand in front of the corner of a building, two groups of diagonal lines converge at two vanishing points, one at the left of the horizon and one at the right. It is a two-point perspective.

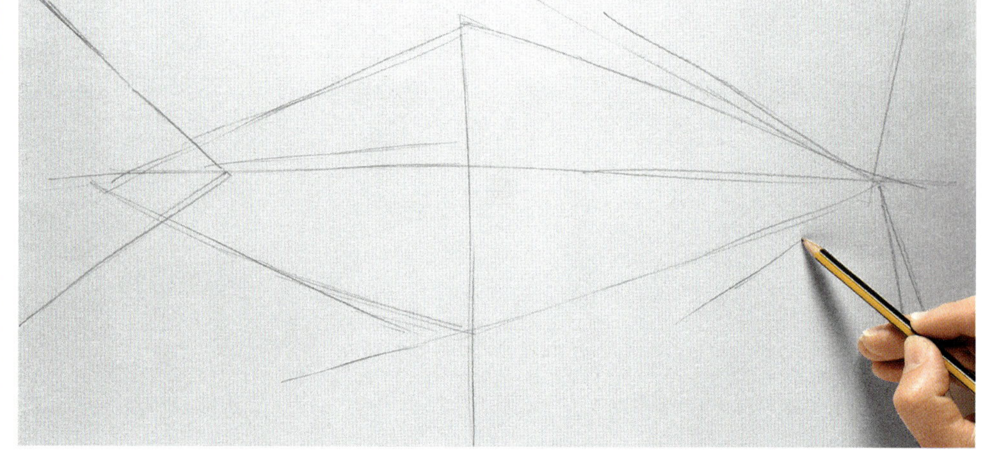

To finish the initial sketch, project the perspective of the façades of the neighboring houses. Indicate a single point at each side of the paper and from these points project two diagonal lines. Their angles will vary depending on the view that you have of the façades.

Horizon and eye level are basic elements of perspective drawing. The apparent separation between the earth and the sky is called the *horizon line*. It is equivalent to the height of your eyes from ground level.

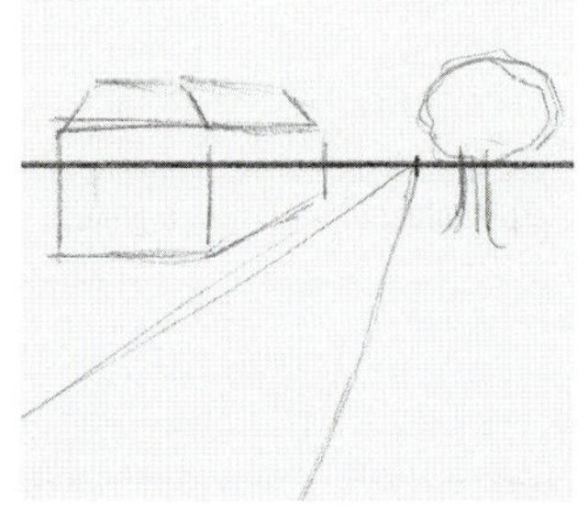

Some artists systematically avoid drawing front views of buildings because they can seem flat and lacking in interest; they prefer an oblique point of view because it creates a strong relief with angles and planes.

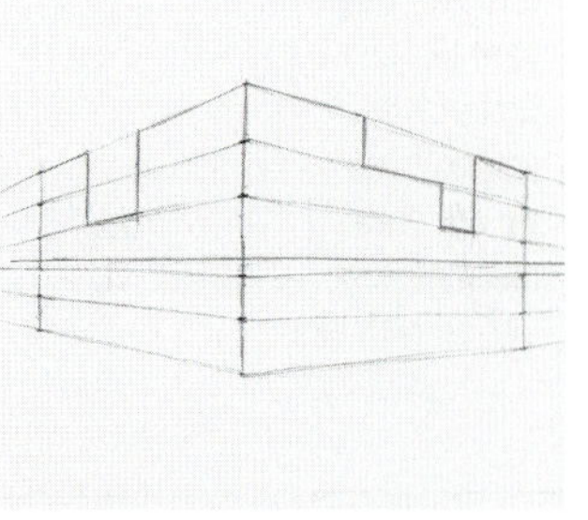

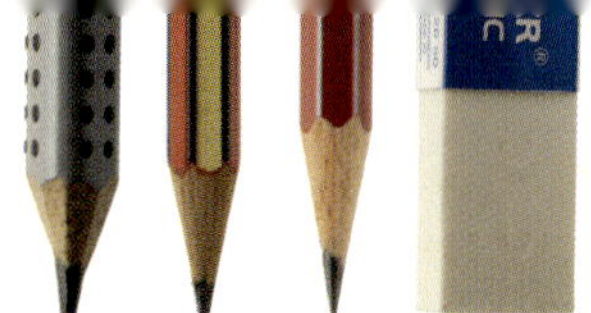

18.2

STRUCTURED LINES. The first lines should be the most structured ones of the drawing; therefore, you need to search out the fundamental lines. This requires you to pay careful attention to the lines and their angles. If this stage of the drawing is correctly resolved, the definitive drawing of the forms will be very simple.

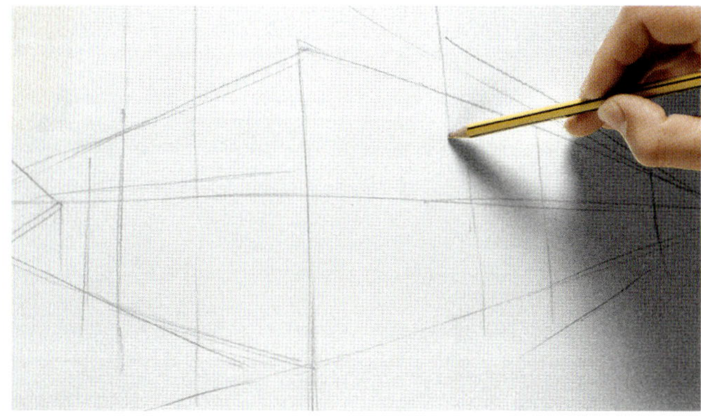

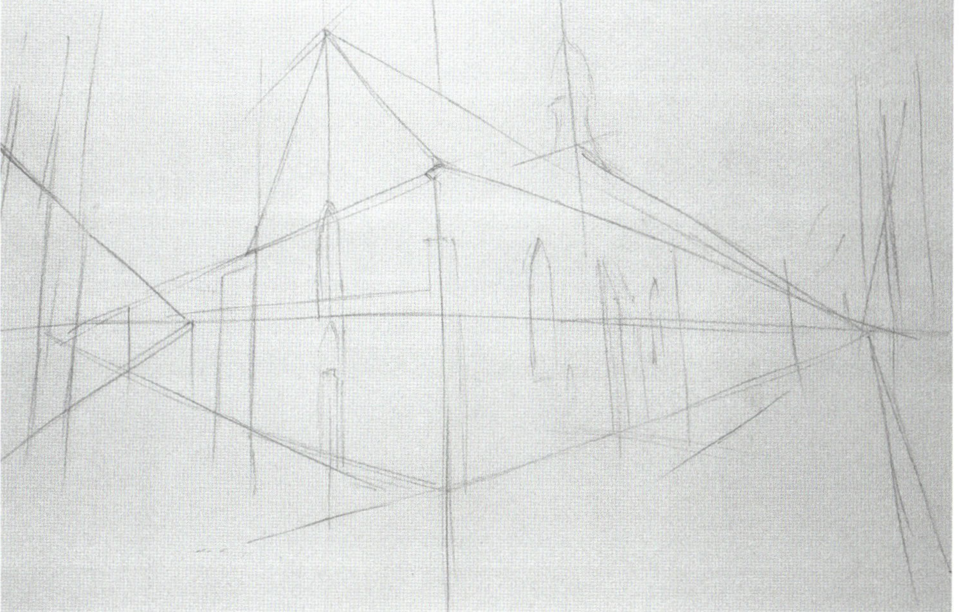

Once the lines of perspective have been established, you have a base on which to begin projecting the vertical lines that define the edges of each façade. Begin by projecting the edges of the central building and the divisions of the façades of the row of houses. Then divide the two walls of the church into two equal parts and draw straight, parallel lines.

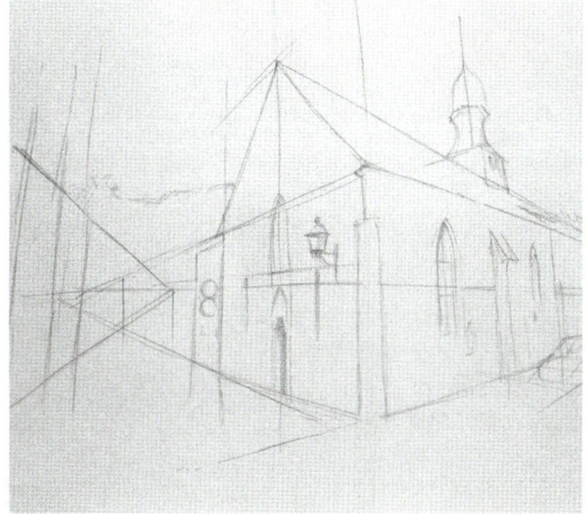

The previous division of the church's walls into two parts will help you locate the peak of the slanted roof and the point of the small bell tower. Draw the angle of the roof from the point where the diagonal perspective lines of the two straight lines intersect. New measurements allow you to locate the windows and the door of the building.

The secret of reaching this level of development is to always work with sure and accurate lines and to constantly measure distances.
Once the structure of the scene is finished, carefully draw the forms. Although they are still sketchy, you can distinguish the bell tower, the openings in the walls, a street lamp, and the buttresses of the church walls.

It is not necessary to press too hard on the pencil during these first stages. If you do so, the pressure you apply to the surface we are drawing on will create resistance, impeding a quick and smooth line.

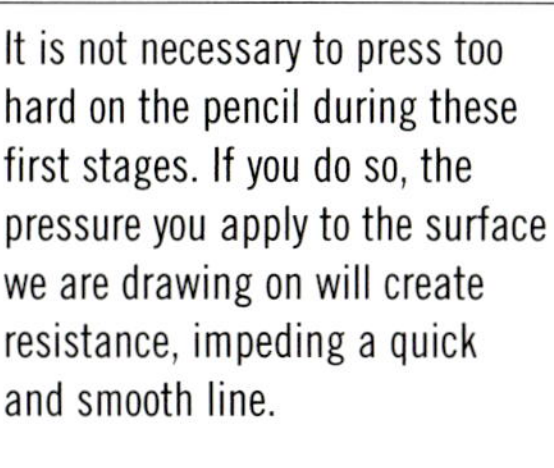

It is a good idea to draw the perspective lines freehand. If you do not have a steady hand you can use the edge of a book or a pamphlet or a ruler as a guide.

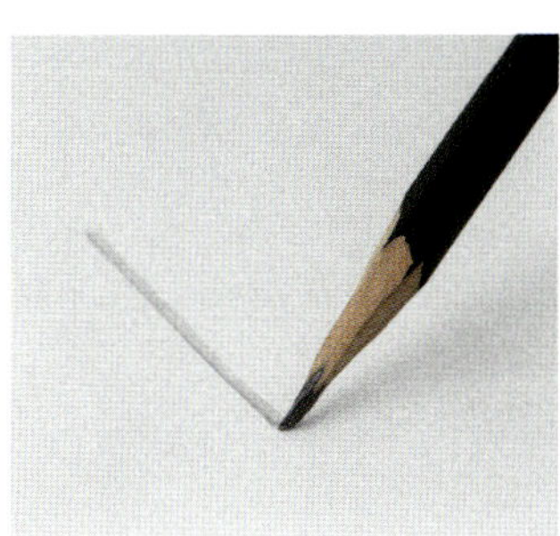

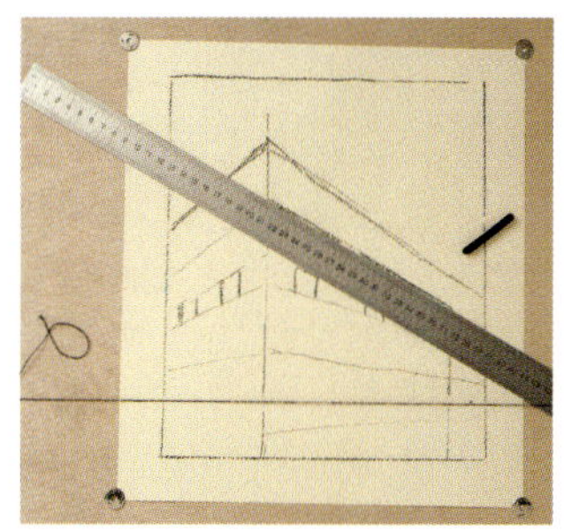

REFINING THE DRAWING AND SHADING. The play of light and shadow on a building is what makes it appear real and solid. When you apply shading, you must always look for the silhouette—the contrast between the walls and the background. Color large areas of gray on the buildings using the side of the pencil, applying only a little pressure.

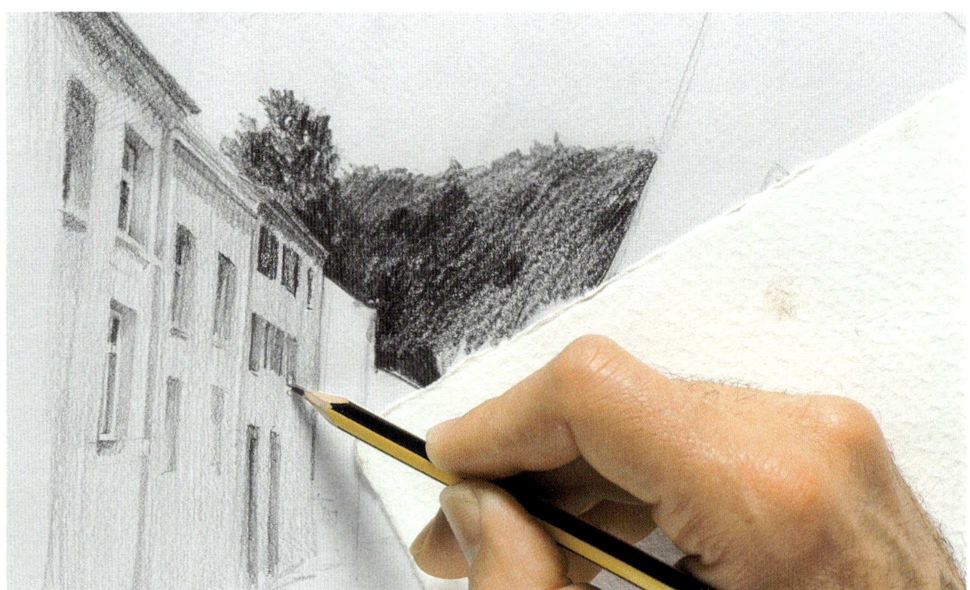

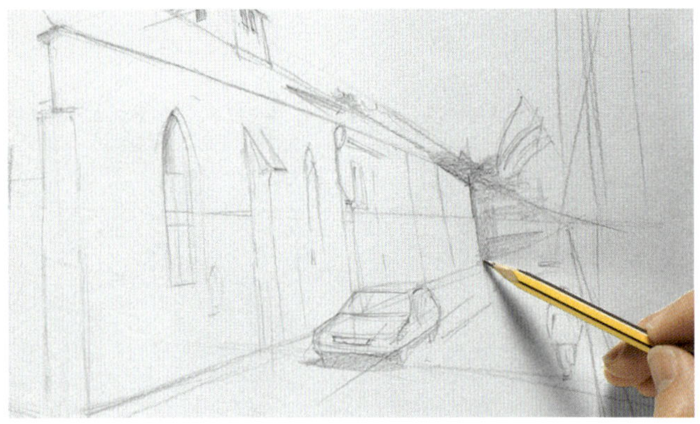

Define the previously sketched architectural details with more accurate and definitive strokes. Including figures and automobiles will add a sense of scale to the drawing. Shade the background using a medium-hard pencil, allowing the first grays to outline the walls even more.

Once you have established the principal lines and planes on the paper, approach the drawing with gray tones. Begin with the buildings in the background; apply light, even lines on the façades of the houses and darker lines in different directions on areas of vegetation. As in previous cases, use a piece of paper to avoid smearing the drawing with your hand.

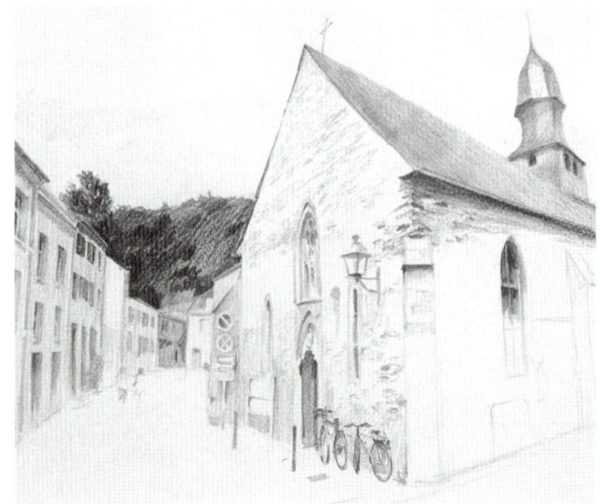

Add more details over the structural lines of the church: windows, a lantern, the parked bicycles and the stonework. Then shade the drawing with light applications of graphite to create a sense of three-dimensional form and space. Resolve the effect of the roof with gray gradations, somewhat blended with the fingertips.

To achieve a dark value it is enough to use a soft lead such as a 3B pencil. No matter how hard you press a hard lead pencil to the paper, you will never achieve a dark line. The paper will tear first.

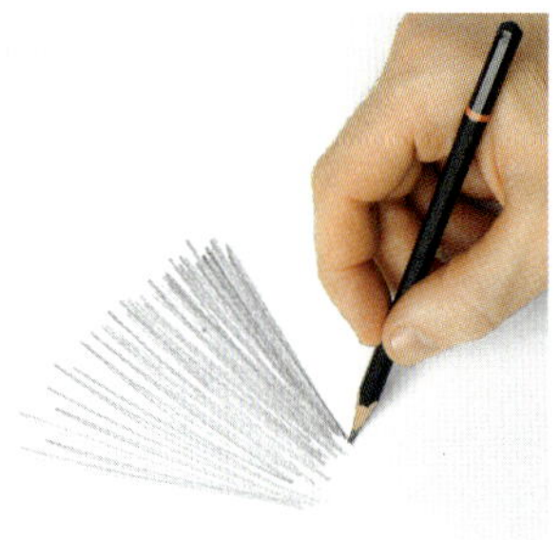

To an artist who is fascinated by details and textures, the small forms contained in general structures such as a façade offer a quantity of accessory material.

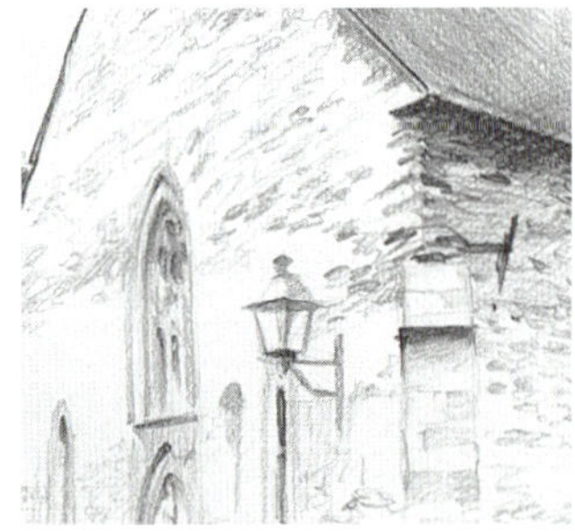

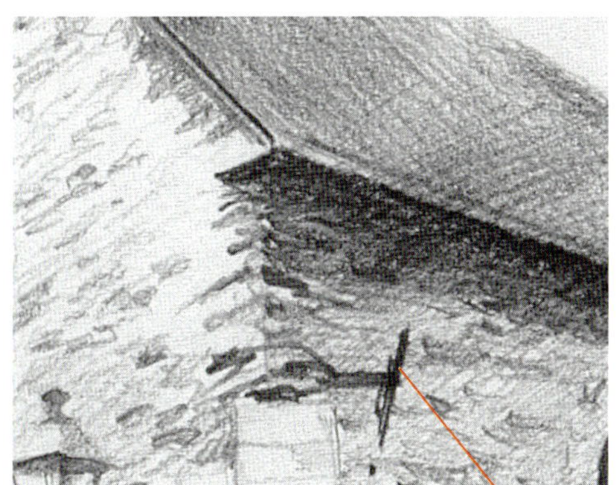

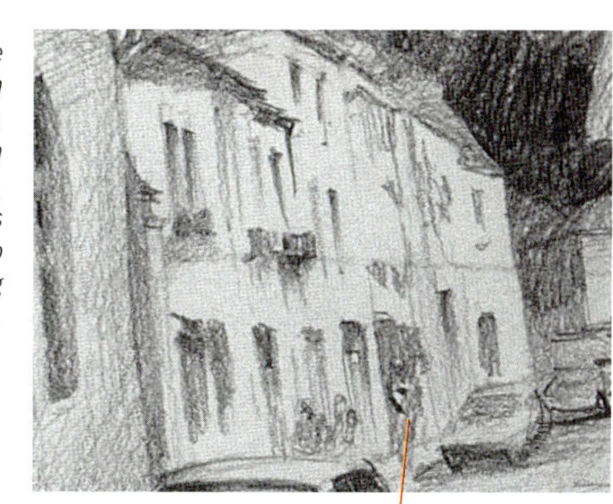

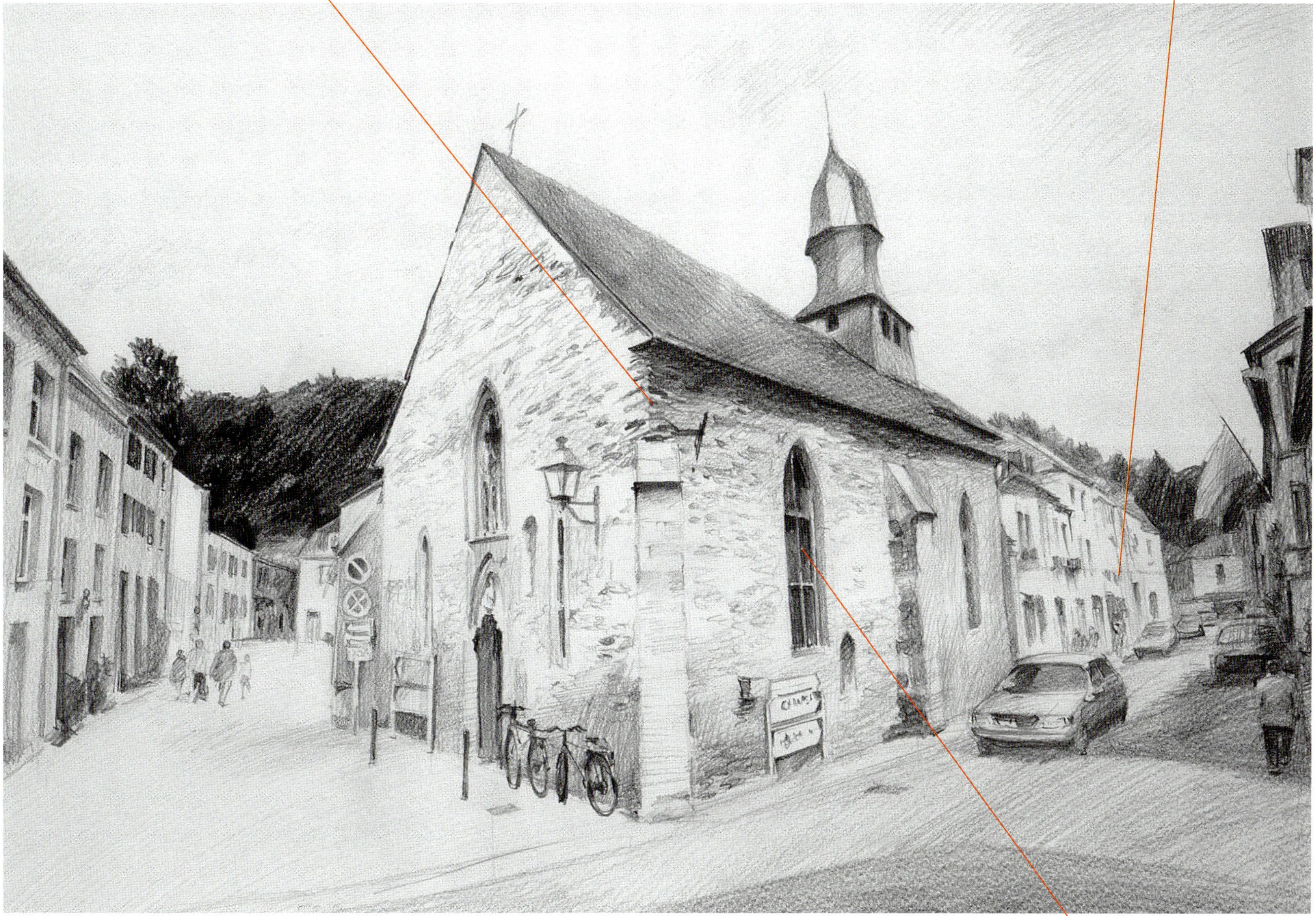

If you squint at this drawing you will see that it is made up of large areas of different tones. In reality, there are four basic values: the dark gray of the vegetation in the background and the church window; the medium gray of the rooftops, the asphalt, and the shaded façades; a light gray on the sunlit façades; and, finally, the white of the paper. Drawn by Óscar Sanchís.

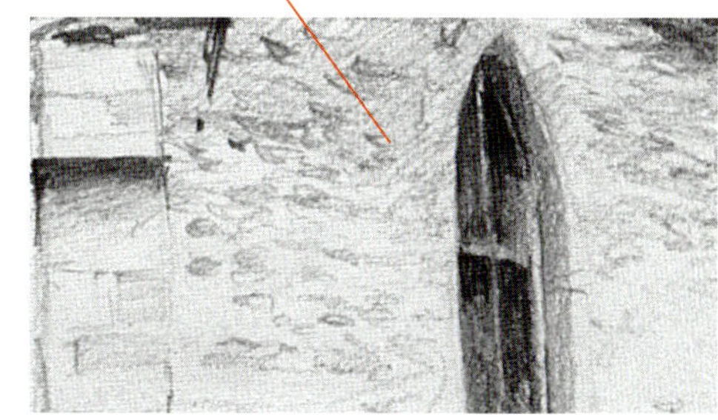

It is not necessary to indicate each block when drawing the texture of a stone wall. Instead, establish general tone with a bit of texture here and there. Often, the suggestion of texture is enough to communicate the effect.

GEOMETRIC STRUCTURE. In drawings, the illusion of depth is created by using linear and graphic approaches and following rules concerning the making of perspective drawings that help describe the geometric structure.

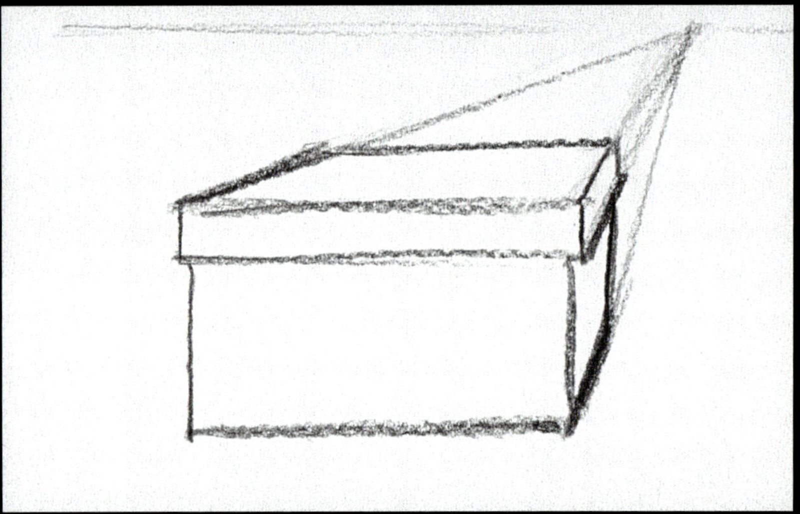

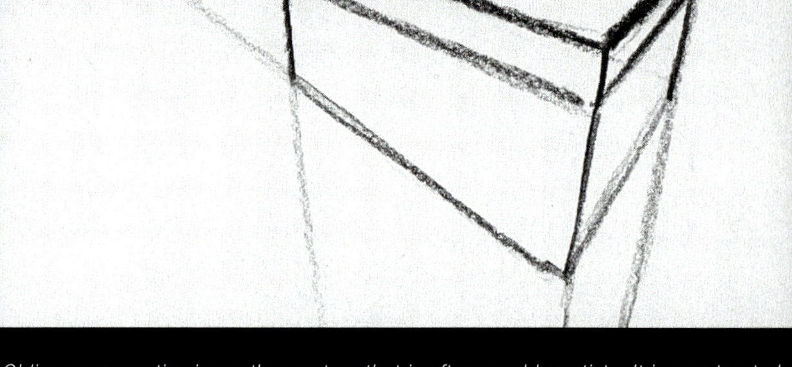

The simplest perspective system is based on one vanishing point located on the horizon line. Diagonal lines that move toward the background tend to converge at that point, while lines that look like they are vertical stay vertical.

Oblique perspective is another system that is often used by artists. It is constructed using two equidistant vanishing points located on the horizon line. This perspective system is the best way to represent corners or two walls of the same building.

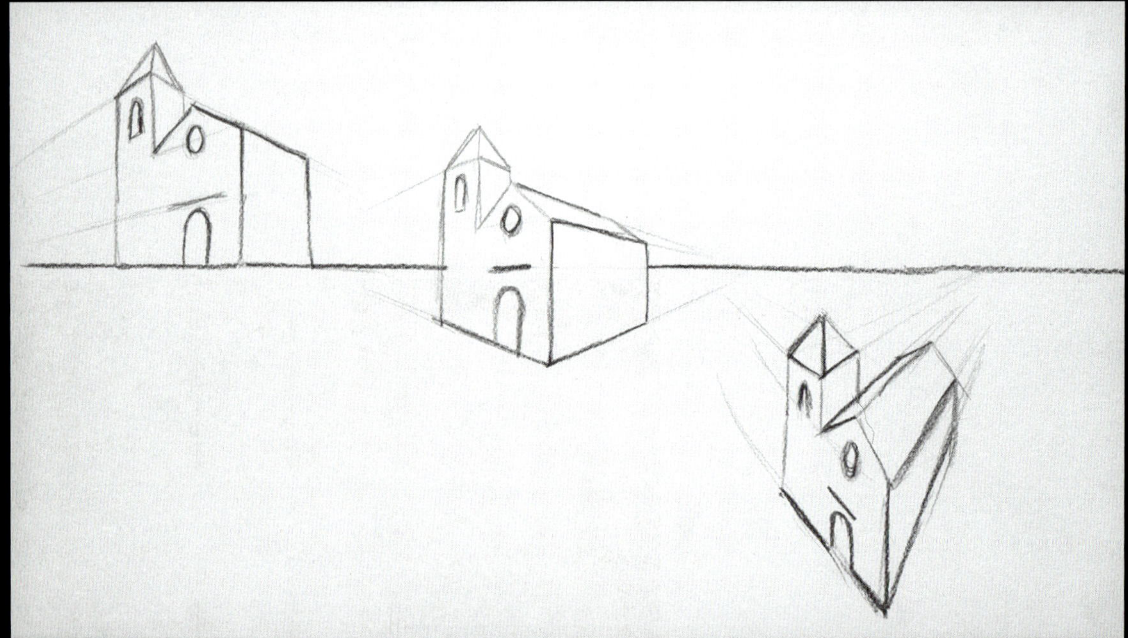

CHANGES IN THE POINT OF VIEW. The position the viewer adopts in relation to the model is important to choosing one perspective or another.

Changing the point of view in relation to the object also changes the perspective, and what would be an oblique perspective if the model were located closer to the horizon line becomes an aerial perspective in the last representation on the right.

PERSPECTIVE TRICKS. When a model is difficult to draw and you wish to create a more realistic representation of it, you should note in the layout all the lines that help show the space effectively. In this sense, the principles of perspective are very useful for correctly drawing these lines.

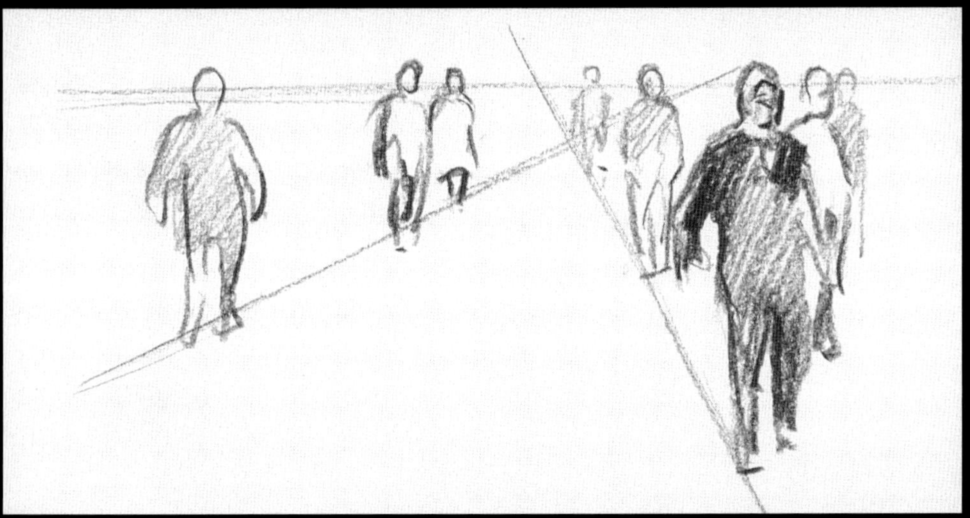

The relative sizes of the figures located in different positions are resolved by projecting two diagonal lines from a vanishing point on the horizon. If you draw a straight line perpendicular to the figures, you will have the height of each figure according to its distance. The figures here are drawn from an elevated point of view to facilitate understanding of the exercise.

Here we see the relation in size among the figures located on different planes, although unlike those in the previous example, these are located at the height of the viewer. The perspective lines determine the height of each figure in its particular location.

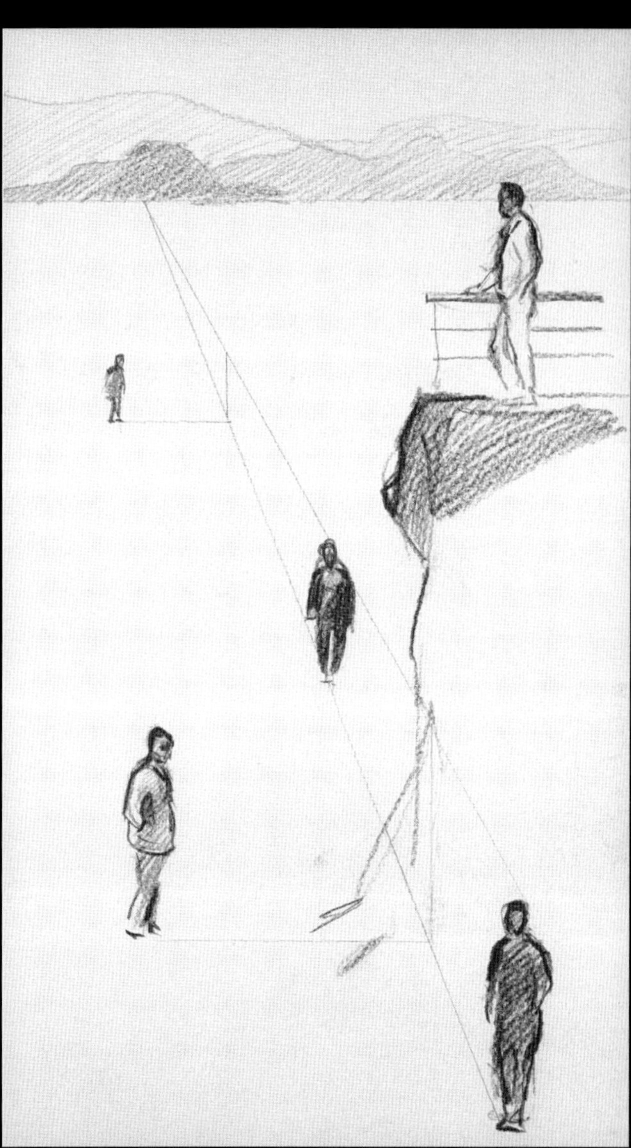

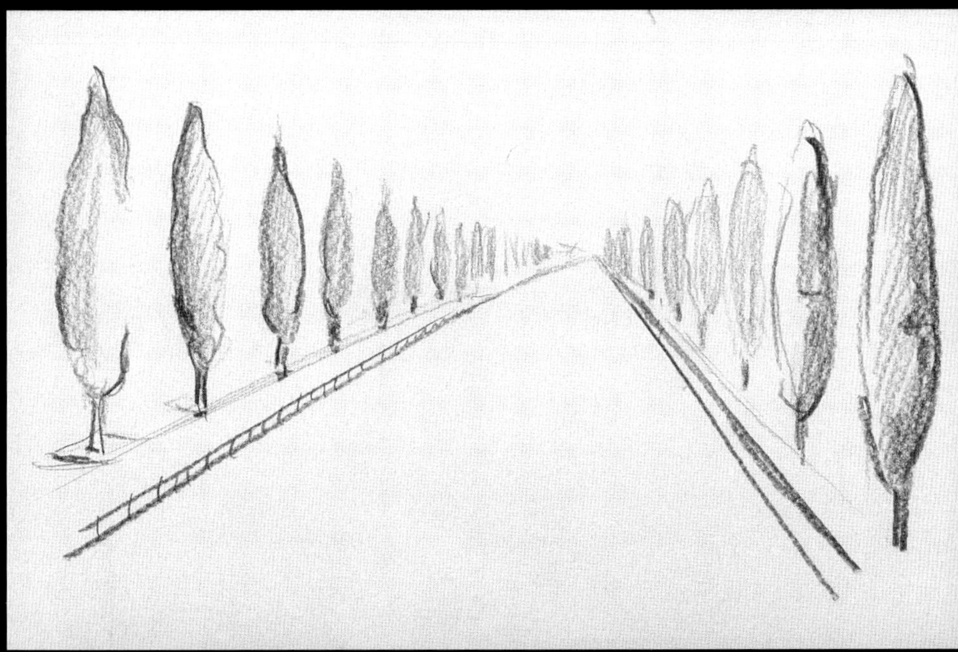

If you place several objects of equal size next to each other in perspective, they decrease in size, and the distance between them decreases as well, as they recede into the distance. One way to illustrate this effect is to draw an avenue with trees planted along both sides.

If you wish to learn to draw landscapes, you should become familiar with one of the most often used techniques for simulating the effect of distance: drawing atmospheric perspective. This is represented as a light haze that removes the color of the most distant areas.

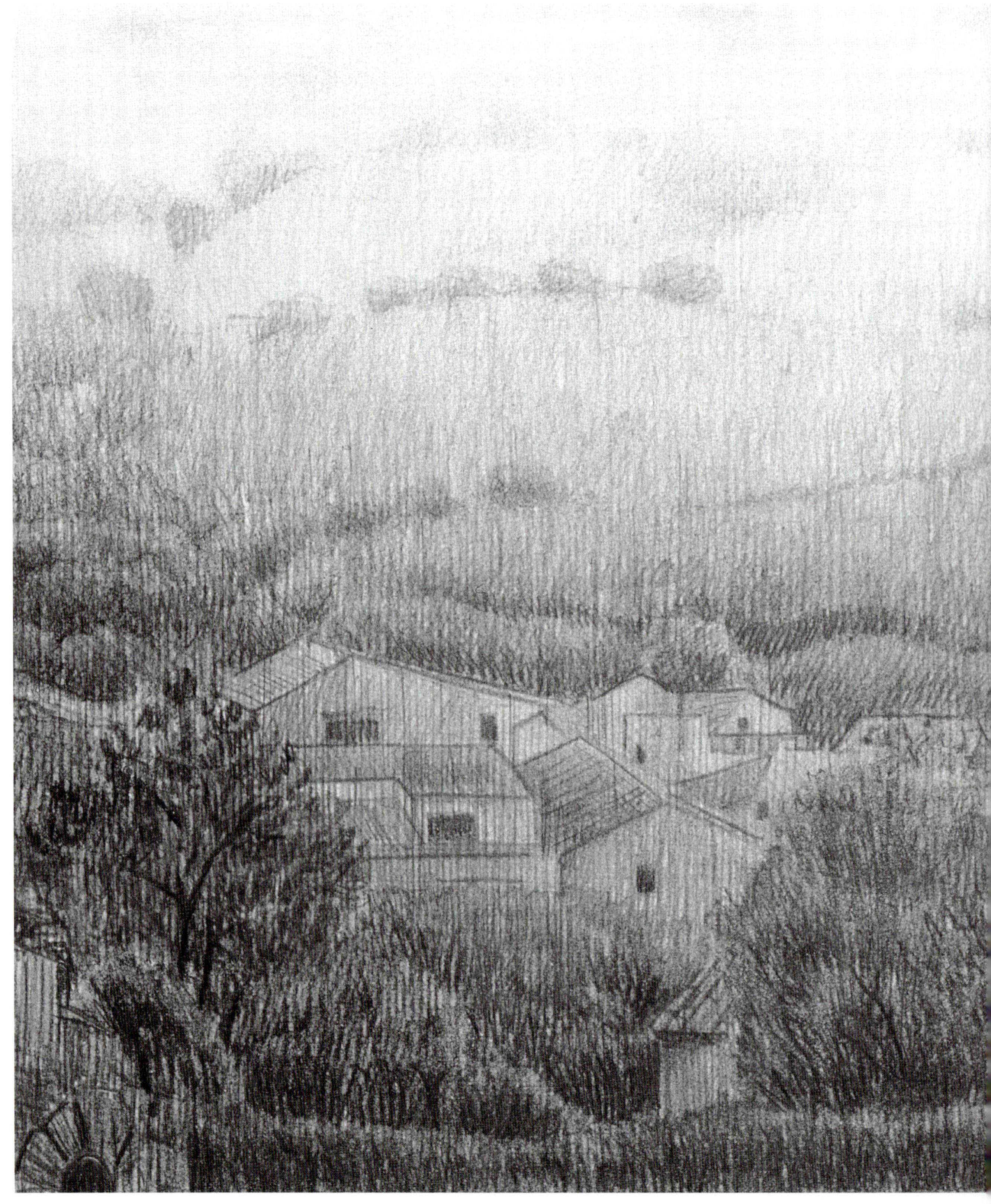

ATMOSPHERE: GRADATION AND BLENDING. The visual phenomenon known as *atmospheric perspective* is a function of tone. The colors in distant planes seem less clear and take on a grayed and more intermediate tone compared with the more diverse and brighter tones in the nearer planes.

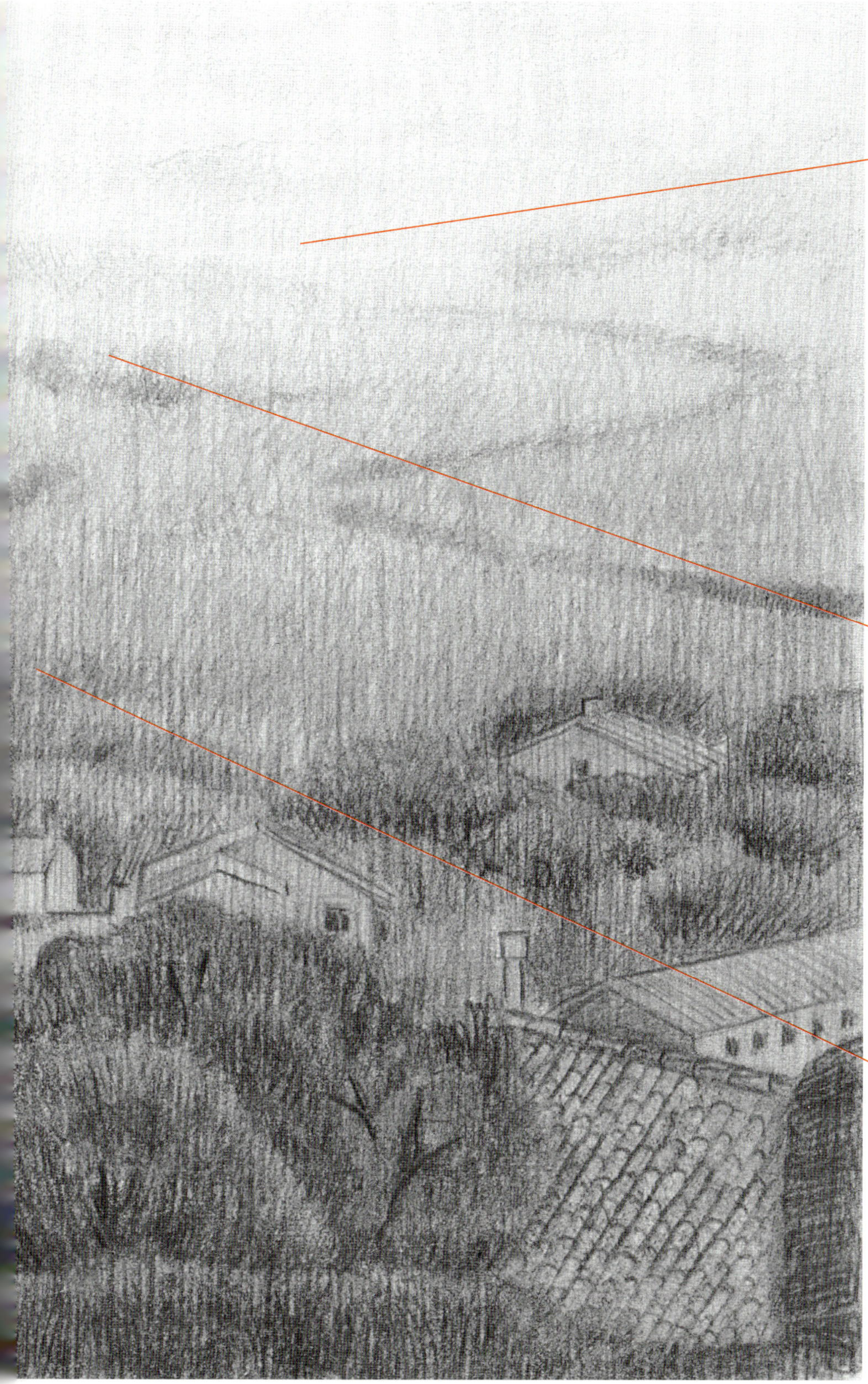

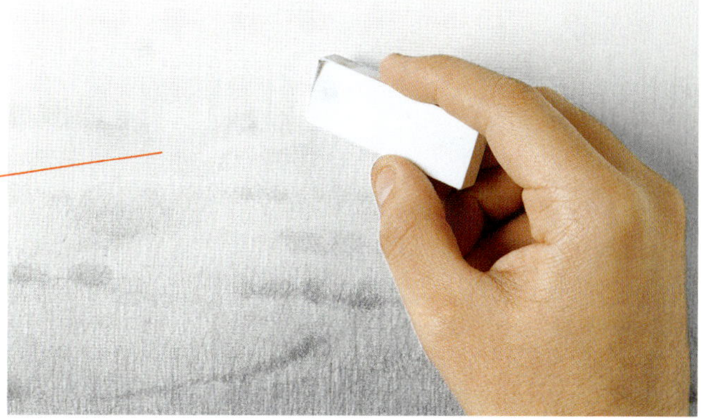

Lighten and remove detail from the farthest areas with a rubber eraser, barely applying pressure to the paper.

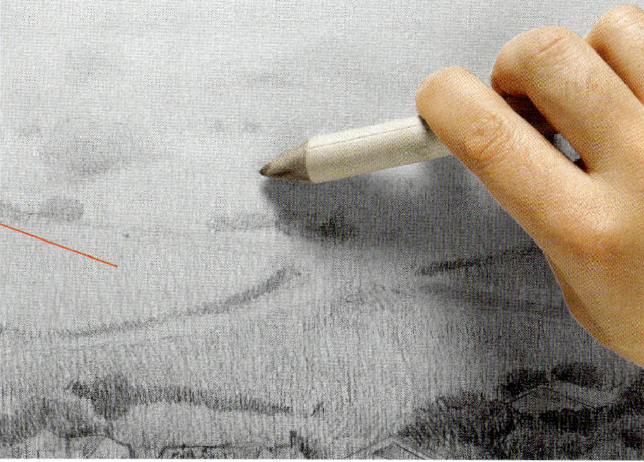

After applying graphite, it is a good idea to blend the drawing to eliminate any traces of lines in the most distant planes.

The shading should be very light and the tonal transitions very gradual; this way, the buildings and the trees blend into the terrain and the horizon disappears.

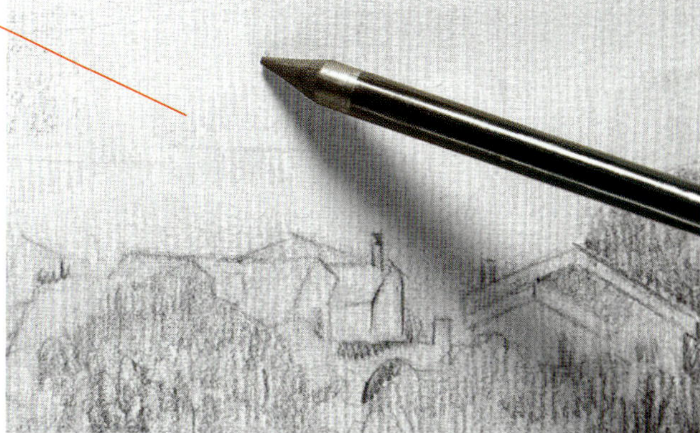

CLARITY OF TEXTURE. An object with texture will be clear in the foreground, while at a distance the surfaces will lose definition and show a lighter and less defined texture.

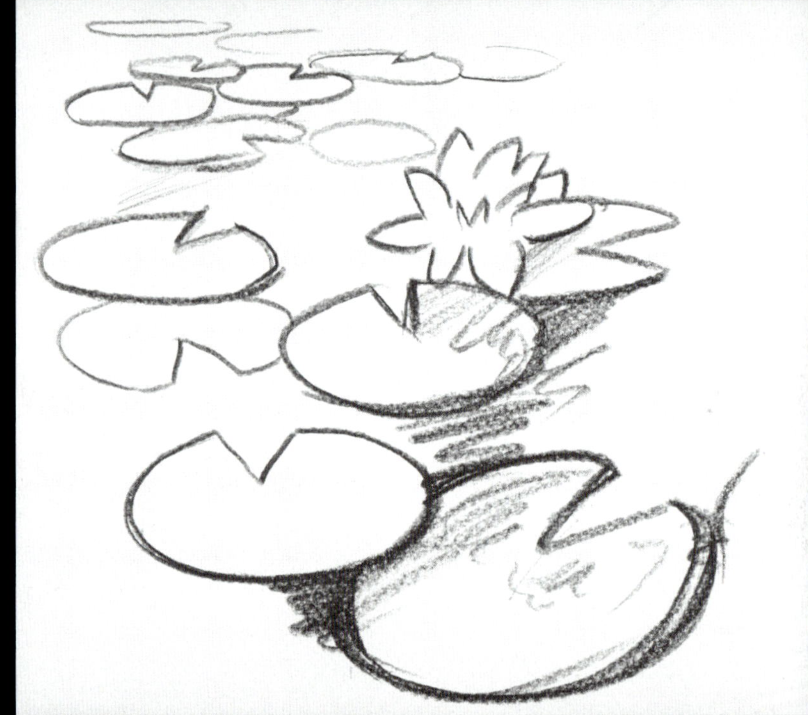

When an object is in the foreground, near the viewer, its outlines are very clear and contrasting. However, as the object moves away, the drawing's line becomes lighter until it becomes a simple, unfinished stroke in the background.

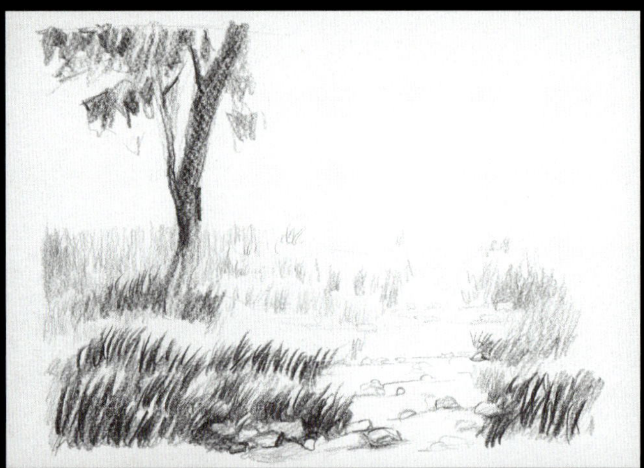

To draw the texture of the vegetation, represent the grass in the foreground with strong, differentiated lines. Resolve the middle ground with lighter drawing and greater intervals of white. In the background, all definition is lost and only a tone is applied.

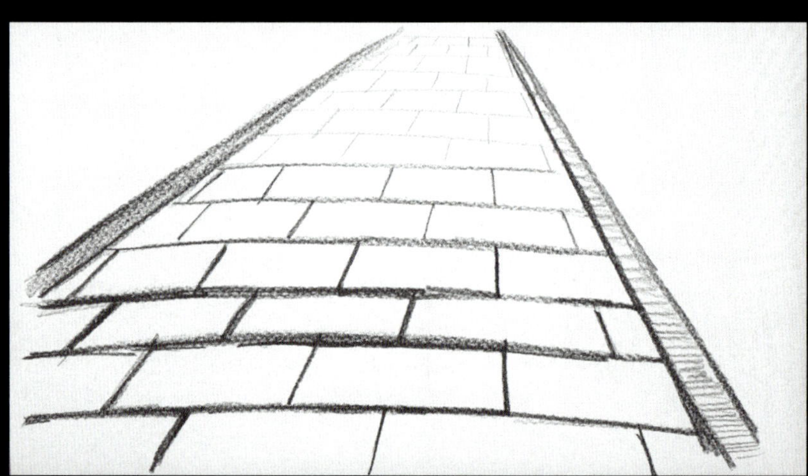

To represent the texture of these bricks in perspective, progressively reduce the dimensions of each row as they move away from you. At the same time, lessen the pressure applied with the pencil until the lines disappear in the distance.

TEXTURES IN PERSPECTIVE. Careful observation of the landscape will help confirm that forms in the distance lose their detail as well as the outlines that separate different elements from each other. Something similar happens to surfaces that have a pronounced texture. The graphic equivalent of atmospheric perspective, used in a purely linear drawing, causes the breakdown or dissipation of the edges or outlines of far objects, which can be drawn with weak, broken, or dotted lines.

VALUE AND HATCH LINES. When working with hatch lines, you should make the width and intensity of the lines different based on the plane they occupy. This way, nearer planes will be indicated with more precise and closer lines than distant ones, which are indicated with lighter lines that have more space between them.

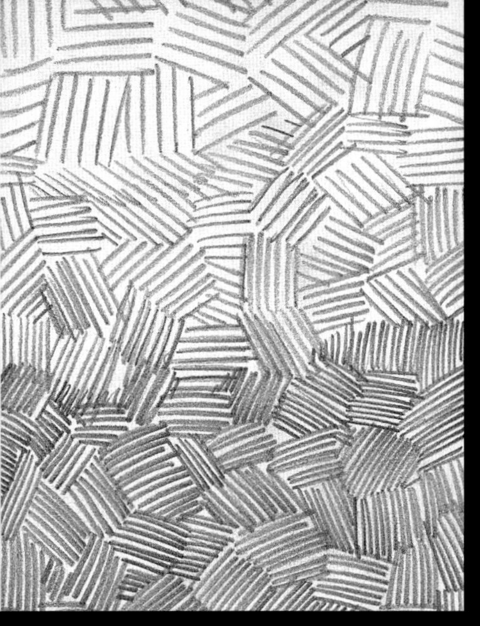

The distance between different sets of hatch lines also contributes to the creation of depth. In the foreground the lines are more tightly spaced, while in the distance they open up to leave more white area between the lines.

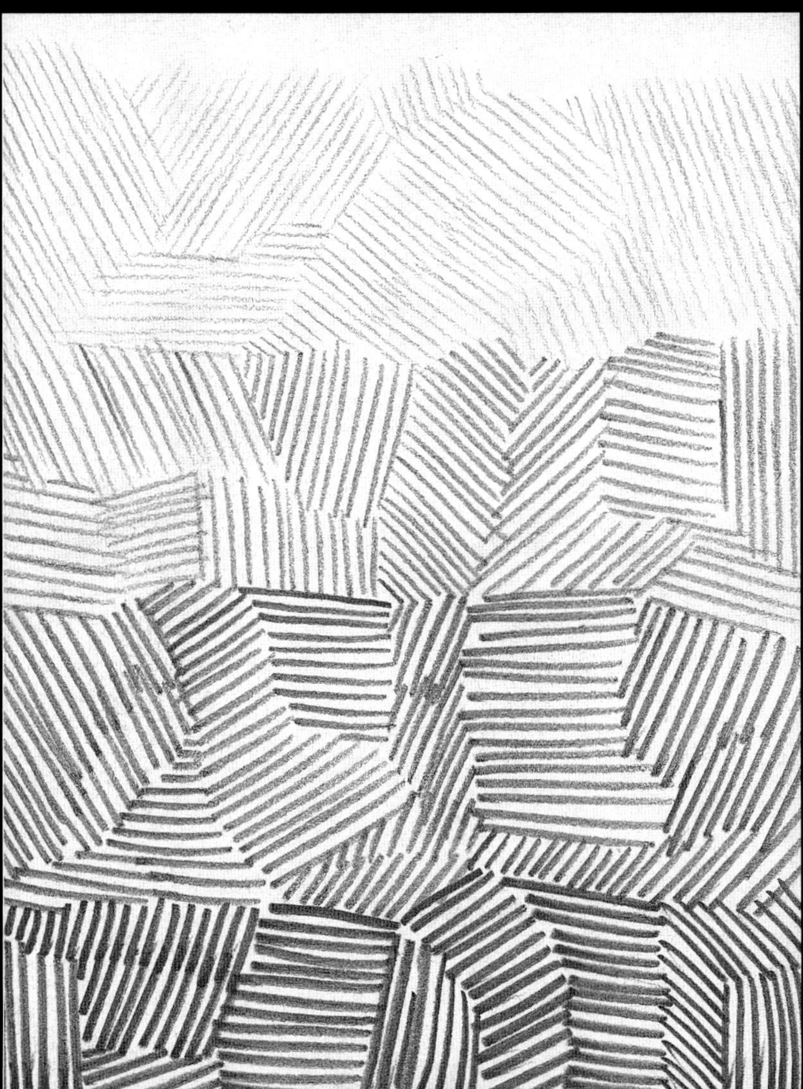

The hatching in the foreground should be constructed with thicker, darker lines. As the planes recede, the intensity of the lines should decrease.

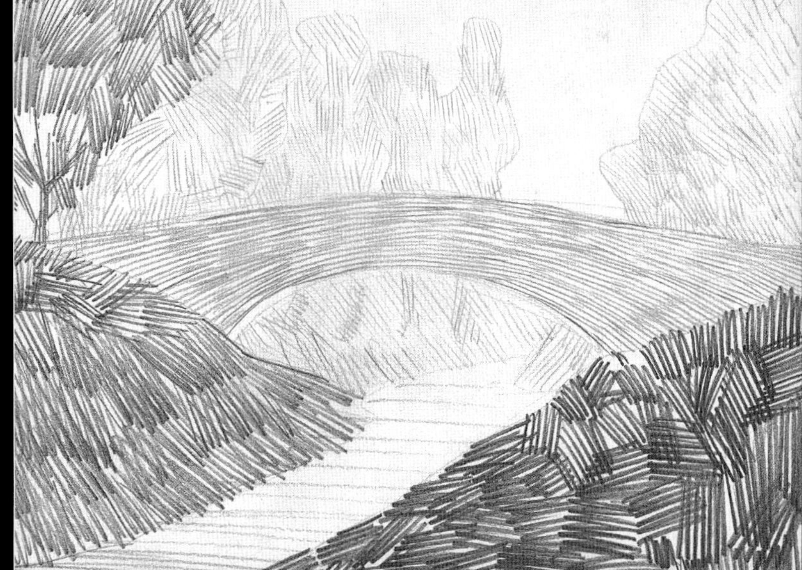

Here is a practical application of this technique. This landscape was created like a series of theatrical backdrops, with four planes clearly differentiated by variations in hatch lines.